American History

ISBN 0-75258-222-4 (Hardback)

This is a Parragon Publishing Book
This edition published in 2003

Parragon Publishing
Queen Street House
4 Queen Street
Bath BA1 1HE, UK

Copyright © 1999 Parragon

Printed in Indonesia
Created and produced by
Foundry Design & Production

Cover design by Blackjacks

American History

GENERAL EDITOR:
Rana K. Williamson, PhD

Contents

Contents

Introduction

Animals moving on the horizon drew the man and his companions forward onto the land bridge that had slowly opened up in the lapping waves of the Pacific Ocean. No historian recorded his name—if he had one—and only in imagination can we see what he saw 25,000 years ago, when he left his Siberian home to follow the animal herds that defined his existence. He didn't know he was bound for North America, or that the land bridge would just as slowly disappear behind him. But with a single footstep that Paleo-Indian began American history. It did not start with Christopher Columbus in 1492 or with the settlers of Jamestown, Virginia in 1607. It began with a hungry, primitive human answering the growling in his belly.

But then, all explorers answer a growling—if not a hunger for food, then one for wealth or for fame, like the Spanish Conquistadors who came after

Christopher Columbus; men like Hernando Cortés who discovered and destroyed the magnificent South American empire of the Aztecs in 1519. Until the last 50 years, American history textbooks suffered from Anglophilia. For those writers, little happened in this country until the first Englishman arrived. Now the Native Americans, the Spanish, the French, the African-Americans, and other groups like the Dutch or the Swedes get their due as well. But even with the recognition of the cultural diversity that has made America, the core of American culture

and political belief undeniably resides in the English origins of the settlers of the original 13 colonies, in particular with the religious dissenters known as Puritans.

In 1630, John Winthrop gave a sermon aboard the *Arabella*, a vessel carrying the first Puritans to the Massachusetts Bay Colony. He told them their settlement was part of a divine mission, that it would be a "city upon a hill." He meant specifically that they would show the Church of England the error of its ways and lead it to a purging of the final remnants of Catholicism. But the sense of mission he communicated became part of a larger American character. As Massachusetts Bay and the other New England colonies grew and matured in isolation from the Mother Country, developing their own political institutions and traditions, Americans came to see themselves as something special and apart from their European origins.

By 1776, when Thomas Jefferson penned the Declaration of Independence, Winthrop's religious mission had become a political one. America became the democracy on the hill, showing the world's monarchies and dictatorships what a self-governing people could achieve. Thus was born the dream that would draw the peoples of the world to the shores of the United States for the next 223 years, searching for their own piece of that freedom.

With only two centuries of history under its belt, America rates as a rank newcomer among the nations of the world; but it is a newcomer that has experienced civil war, industrial growth, racial strife, runaway prosperity, and crushing economic depression. Two world wars vaulted the United States into a position of global leadership, accompanied by the tragic development of weaponry capable of devastating the planet.

On the brink of the 21st century, Americans live in a world made smaller by electronic mail, the Internet, and cyberspace. Futurists Alvin and Heidi Toffler in *The Third Wave* (1991) described the transitional phases of human culture in terms of waves—agricultural, industrial, and informational. The Third Wave began after World War II, most likely in November 1945 when J. Presper Eckert and John Mauchly finished ENIAC, the machine credited with beginning the computer age. It had 17,468 vacuum tubes, 70,000 resistors, 10,000 capacitors, 1,500 relays, and 6,000 manual switches. Compared to today's handheld computers ENIAC was a hulking dinosaur with a pea for a brain.

The very complexity of life on the brink of the third millennium, demands an even greater understanding of the past. The future is less well-defined, more subject to radical change and sweeping innovation than at any other point in our existence. History, if written well and taught well, can tell us where we have been and help us to make judgements about where we are going. It should not be an exercise in trivial pursuit. It should not be regarded as a formulaic science. It is a story—our story—and herein lies its broad strokes, a tale of restless growth and relentless experimentation. Like our ancestor the Paleo-Indian, we stand and look out over a bridge, but not one linking two continents. Ours will carry us from one century to the next, and the cultural luggage that will accompany us on our journey is that thing we call our history.

KEY TO THEMES

🌏 Exploration and Empires

👤 Power and Politics

✡ Religion and Belief

☢ Science and Technology

🏛 Society and Culture

🏭 Trade and Industry

🔫 War and Peace

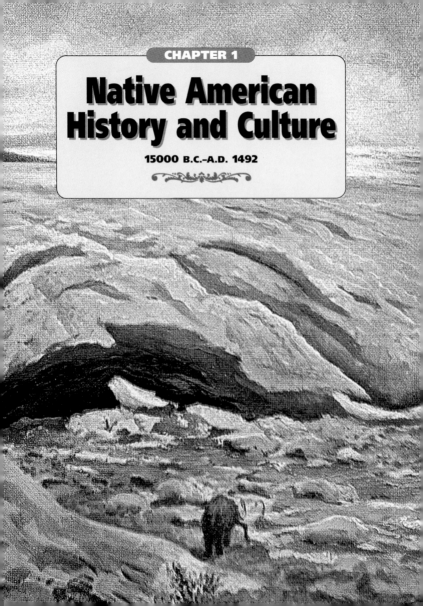

CHAPTER 1

Native American History and Culture

15000 B.C.–A.D. 1492

15000 B.C. PEOPLING THE AMERICAS

AT the height of the last Ice Age, about 17,000 years ago, as the ice sheets advanced and sea levels fell, men first migrated from the Eurasian landmass to the Americas. These nomadic hunters were following game herds from Siberia, across what is today the Bering Strait into Alaska, and then gradually spread southward. Based on linguistic research, some 10,000 years ago a movement of tribes occurred along the Rocky Mountain foothills and eastward across the Great Plains to the Atlantic seaboard.

▲ *The advancing Ice Age allowed man to migrate to the Americas*

8000 B.C. A DEVELOPING CULTURE

EARLY nomadic hunters forged stone weapons from around 10,000 years ago; as the age of metallurgy dawned, new technologies were used and more efficient weapons produced. Prior to contact with Europeans, most tribes used similar weaponry. The most common implements were the bow and arrow, the war club, and the spear. Quality, material, and design varied widely.

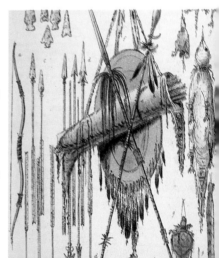

Large mammals such as the mammoth were largely extinct by around 8000 B.C., and the Native Americans were hunting their descendants, such as bison or buffalo. The Great Plains tribes were still hunting the buffalo when they first encountered the Europeans. The acquisition of the horse and horsemanship from the Spanish in the 17th century greatly altered the natives' culture, changing the way in which these large creatures were hunted and making them a central feature of their lives.

1500 B.C. SETTLING DOWN 🏛

BY 1500 B.C., many tribes had settled into small indigenous communities. These began as temporary settlements built by the hunter-gatherers, and over the centuries they grew into small villages, mostly established in the river valleys of North America, where crops could be raised. While exhibiting widely divergent social, cultural, and artistic expressions, all Native American groups worked with the materials available to them and employed social arrangements that augmented their means of subsistence and survival. Gradually these communities became more sophisticated; examples of more complex societies included the tribes of the southern United States from the Atlantic Coast to the Mississippi. These groups were the most highly developed Indian civilizations north of Mexico. They constructed large and complex earthworks, and were particularly skilled at small stone sculptures and engravings on shell and copper.

The large *pueblos* or villages, built on top of the rocky *talleland* or *mesas* of the Southwest around A.D. 700, were a complicated aggregate of family apartments. Towns were one large complex of buildings, with multistoried houses arranged around courtyards or plazas. Wooden ladders provided access to upper levels. Under the courtyards, subterranean *kivas*, or ceremonial structures, served as meeting rooms for religious societies.

◀ *Weapons such as the bow and arrow and spears were used by early Native Americans*

1500 B.C.–A.D. 1492
NATIVE AMERICAN SOCIETY 🏛

THE Iroquois tribes, living around the Great Lakes and extending east and north, used strings or belts called *wampum* that served a dual function: the knots and beaded designs mnemonically chronicled tribal stories and legends, and further served as a medium of exchange and a unit of measure. The keepers of these articles were seen as tribal dignitaries.

Pueblo tribes crafted impressive items associated with their religious ceremonies. *Kachina* dancers wore elaborately painted and decorated masks as they ritually impersonated various ancestral spirits. Sculpture was not highly developed, but carved stone and wood fetishes were made for religious use. Superior weaving, embroidered decorations, and rich dyes characterized the textile arts. Both turquoise and shell jewelry were created, as were high-quality pottery and formalized pictorial arts.

Navajo religion focused on the maintenance of a harmonious relationship with the spirit world, often achieved by ceremonial acts usually incorporating sand paintings. The colors—made from sand, charcoal, cornmeal, and pollen—depicted specific spirits. These vivid, intricate, and colorful sand creations were erased at the end of the ceremony.

▼ *Buffalo provided the Plains Indians with food as well as hides for clothing and shelter*

1500 B.C.–A.D. 1492
NATIVE AMERICAN ECONOMIES 🏛

SURVIVAL in the environments in which they lived defined the "work" of native groups. The Inuit, or Eskimo, prepared and buried stocks of dried meat and fish. Pacific Northwest tribes crafted seafaring dugouts 40–50 feet long for fishing. Farmers in the Eastern Woodlands tended fields of maize with hoes and digging sticks, while their neighbors in the Southeast grew tobacco as well as food crops. On the Plains, tribes engaged in agriculture but also planned buffalo hunts in which herds were efficiently driven over bluffs. Dwellers of the Southwest deserts hunted small animals, and gathered acorns to grind into a flour with which they baked wafer-thin bread on top of heated stones. Their more advanced neighbors on the region's mesas developed irrigation techniques, and filled storehouses with grain as protection against the area's frequent droughts.

As these native peoples encountered European explorers and settlers and engaged in trade, they exchanged food, crafts, and furs for trinkets, blankets, iron and steel implements, horses, firearms, and intoxicating liquors.

1500 B.C.–A.D. 1492
NATIVE AMERICAN SHAMAN ✡

IN native groups, only the *shaman* had the power to commune with the gods or spirits, to mediate between them and ordinary mortals, to talk with the souls of the dead on behalf of the living. The shaman—man or

An Indian soothsayer ▶

woman—was often an extraordinary character, both in physical appearance and in acting talents. He would be a mystic, poet, sage, healer of the sick, guardian of the tribe, and repository of stories. Those who did not possess the full range of shamanistic attributes became simply "medicine men," and functioned as respected healers.

To become a shaman, a person had to "receive the call"—to suffer a religious experience—and would then be initiated into the mysteries of the art. By symbolic death and resurrection, he acquired a new mode of being; his physical and mental frame underwent a thorough change. During this period of initiation, the novice would see the spirits of the universe and leave his body like a spirit, soaring through the heavens and the underworld. There he would be introduced to the different spirits and taught which to address in future trances.

Since sickness was thought to be caused by an evil spirit entering the victim's body, the shaman would call it out in order to affect a cure. He would do so by a special ritual, beating a rhythm on his drum, swaying and chanting, steadily increasing the sound and interspersing it with long drawn out sighs, groans, and hysterical laughter.

1500 B.C.–A.D. 1492
BELIEFS IN THE AMERICAN NORTHWEST

THE totem-venerating fishermen of the American Northwest told adventure tales of hunts on land and sea in which the salmon and bear played a central role. Military victories and their accounts were especially important. During the winters, totemic societies—which believed in a mystical relationship between their clan and a special emblem or symbol—played out their groups' legends dressed in animal masks, or the elders gathered an audience and retold the tribe's myths. Although there was no central godhead, the Sky Being, Sun, Moon, and the Trickster Creator (Raven) were all venerated. These tribesmen held no regular ceremonies and erected no temples, and they believed their dead went on to an underworld where they could be reached occasionally.

1500 B.C.–A.D. 1492
CREE BELIEFS ☒

THE tribes of the Cree Nation, living in the Canadian forests and U.S. Plains, venerated the spirits of the hunt. The Earth Spirit was the mother of all animals, and there was also an ill-defined Sky Being. Religion emphasized a close relationship with the tribes' ancestors, or "old people," believed to be always near at hand. Tribal shamans frequently entered trances to visit the land of the dead. Nature was seen as an integrated whole, so that animals spoke and told tales, while legends of the winds and of the four directions were common. Close contact with European traders and white settlers, coupled with the adoption of agriculture, greatly altered the mythology of these tribes.

▲ *A Cree squaw with her papoose*

1500 B.C.–A.D. 1492
INUIT BELIEFS ☒

THE Eskimo, or Inuit, people inhabit the land stretching from southeast Alaska to Greenland, an environment that heavily influenced a mythology filled with adventure tales of whale and walrus hunts. Long winter months of waiting for caribou herds or sitting near blowholes hunting fish and seals gave birth to stories of the mysterious and sudden appearance of ghosts and fantastic creatures. The Inuit looked into the *aurora borealis*, or

The Inuit believed that the spirits of their ancestors could be seen in the northern lights ▶

northern lights, to find images of their family and friends dancing in the next life, and they relied upon the shaman to cure the sick, control the weather, and foretell the future. Their only religious observances were séances called by the shaman, while the nearest thing to a central deity was the Old Woman, who lived beneath the sea. The waters, a central food source, were believed to contain great spirits.

1500 B.C.–A.D. 1492
GREAT PLAINS BELIEFS

GREAT Plains legends featured Buffalo Spirits and the Earth Mother. Men belonged to ritual societies that offered camaraderie, a focus for public duties, and a forum to organize war and hunting parties. Most tribes had a concept of a vaguely-defined but omnipresent supernatural power that manifested itself in all aspects of the world. Powerful beings communicated through dreams and visions, and the individual vision quest was an important part of life. This involved seeking a spirit guide or seeing an intended purpose to the future and required the performance of certain rituals, such as fasting, or the construction of a sacred space. In some tribes, from northern Mexico, the vision quest was achieved with the use of certain narcotic

◀ *A warrior of the Iroquois nation*

or psychedelic drugs. Medicine bundles provided portable shrines of venerated items or relics for personal interaction with the spirits.

1500 B.C.–A.D. 1492
IROQUOIS BELIEFS

THESE tribes, mostly members of the Iroquois nation, lived in the Northeastern territories of the U.S. and Canada, from the St. Lawrence River down to the Delaware Bay and inland to the Great Lakes. Their close contact with Europeans makes investigation of their original mythology and religion extremely difficult, but core beliefs included a conception of life as a struggle between the forces of good and evil. The "All-Father," an all-embracing deity, had no form and little contact with humans. Spirits animated all of nature and controlled the changing of the seasons. Key festivals coincided with the major events of the agricultural calendar.

1500 B.C.–A.D. 1492
PUEBLO BELIEFS

THE most highly developed Indian communities of the Southwest built large villages or pueblos at the top of the mesas, or rocky tableland typical to the region. Their archetypal deities appear as visionary beings who bring blessings and receive love. A vast collection of myths define the relationships between man and nature and plants and animals. Man depended on the blessings of the gods, who in turn depended on prayers and ceremonies.

1500 B.C.–A.D. 1492
SOUTHEASTERN FARMING BELIEFS

SOUTHEASTERN farming cultures from the Atlantic coastline to the Mississippi River included the advanced prehistoric mound builders who had disappeared by the point of European contact. The Natchez tribes still retained some traits of these earlier groups, including the veneration of a sacred king. Because the tribes of this region—including the Creeks, Choctaws, Chickasaws,

Seminoles, and Cherokee—became highly receptive to the white men's ways, their original myths are obscure. However, they told tales of a Trickster spirit, personified in the form of a rabbit, and had myths about the origins of tobacco and maize.

1500 B.C.–A.D. 1492
SOUTHWESTERN HUNTERS' BELIEFS

SOUTHWESTERN hunters lived in semidesert conditions and told typical hunting and ancestor tales. Shamans stayed in close contact with gods, ancestors, and the spirits of Maize, the Rainbow, the Sun, Thunder, and all natural powers. Shamans were expected to act as advisors on future events, to cure illness, and to protect crops. The individual vision quest for boys of 11 or 12 years was an important milestone.

▲ *A maize god, one of the many spirits with which the Native American shamans were in contact*

1500 B.C.–A.D. 1492
NATIVE AMERICAN LACK OF RESISTANCE

AT the point of contact with Europeans in 1492, the tribes of North America were loosely organized and given to regional conflicts over hunting or fishing grounds. Amazingly, these groups displayed an unexpected capacity for adaptation when threatened by the white man. They resisted for centuries by incorporating European technology and weaponry with their own, forging new alliances, and changing their community structures—all actions of an embattled people facing a foreign invader.

Native American Peoples

ALEUT

THE Aleut of southwestern Alaska lived in sod houses and were hunters and fishermen. The Aleut's skill in hunting sea mammals led Russian fur traders to exploit the tribe; the women employed a unique, two-strand twining technique in their weaving.

tobacco and derived their name from their black-dyed moccasins.

A medicine man from the Blackfoot tribe ▲

APACHE

THE southwestern Apache were hunters and fierce fighters who warred with the Comanche and readily adapted to the acquisition of horses from Europeans.

CHEROKEE

THE Cherokee lived in the southern Allegheny Mountains of Alabama, the Carolinas, Georgia, and Tennessee, and possessed an advanced agricultural culture.

ARAPAHO

THE Plains-dwelling Arapaho based their society on age distinction. Divided into northern and southern groups, they were known to other tribes as "dog eaters."

CHEYENNE

THE Cheyenne lived a sedentary life in the Great Lakes region of Minnesota, with a culture befitting the area's marshy woodlands, until they were forced onto the Plains by the arrival of the Europeans.

BLACKFOOT

THE hostile and nomadic Blackfoot of the Plains based their culture on the horse and buffalo. They grew

CHICKASAW

THE Chickasaw lived in northern Mississippi. Males wore panther, deer, bear, beaver, and otter skins in winter. Warriors shaved both sides of their head, leaving a central crest.

CHOCTAW

THE Choctaw were excellent farmers, and lived in central and southern Mississippi and some portions of Alabama.

COMANCHE

THE Comanche were a loosely unified tribe of eight to 12 subnations, who lived near the upper reaches of the Platte River in eastern Wyoming. Their culture was centered around the Great Plains horse and buffalo.

CREE

THE Cree occupied lands in the Canadian forests and U.S. Plains and, although warlike, worked closely with fur traders. In feuds with rival tribes, the Cree saw horses, captives, and scalps as symbols of glory and social achievement.

A family from the Cree tribe inside their tent ▶

CREEK

A confederacy of 50 bands made up the Creek, who settled mainly in Georgia and Alabama. They held land in common, and governed themselves democratically.

CROW

THE Crow were a hunting tribe of the Plains who also cultivated tobacco. Their highly complex social system stressed care of children.

DELAWARE

THE Delaware tribe of the Eastern Woodlands lived in rectangular, bark-covered houses instead of the more usual domed wigwams.

FLATHEAD

HISTORICALLY, the Flathead occupied land in western Montana, but they ranged eastward through the

Rocky Mountains and onto the plains to hunt buffalo. The Flathead were so named by neighboring tribes who shaped the front of their own heads to a point with bindings at an early age.

HOPI

THE Hopi lived on mesas at the edge of Arizona's Painted Desert. Tribespeople were divided into maternal clans, with property ownership passed from mother to daughter.

HURON

THE Huron, a name derived from a French epithet meaning "bristle-head," were a confederation of four groups who lived in palisaded, or fended-in, villages in the Ontario area of Canada. Clans were grouped for ceremonial and social purposes. The four clan divisions were designated Bear, Cord, Deer, and Rock.

INUIT

THE Inuit, or Eskimo, one of the world's most widely distributed people, have never exceeded a population of 60,000. They live from southeast Alaska to Greenland. The

Eskimo build their social organization around whale, seal, and caribou hunting. Their arctic environment has caused inventive measures such as ice igloos for shelter, the kayak, and special footwear for snow.

▲ *Inuit people from Greenland*

IROQUOIS

THE five tribes of the Iroquois confederacy (Mohawk, Oneida, Onondaga, Cayuga, Seneca) lived in the Northeast, specifically in New York, Ontario, and Quebec.

KICKAPOO

THE Kickapoo of southwestern Wisconsin had a society which was patrilineal. When pushed westward they acquired more characteristics of Plains buffalo culture. The Kickapoo often pitted their best horses against those of the Comanche in races.

KIOWA
THE Kiowa of Oklahoma believed in a number of gods, the chief one being the Sun, although they believed all natural elements had supernatural powers. They raided far enough into South America to become acquainted with parrots and monkeys.

MIAMI
ALTHOUGH Eastern Woodlands Indians, the Miami hunted buffalo. They fished, were gatherers and farmers, and used fire to clear fields and to control underbrush.

NARRAGANSETT
THE Narragansett occupied Rhode Island and, like other New England tribes, were horticultural, but they supplemented their diet with hunting and fishing. They lived in *wigwams*, domed houses with sapling frames covered with bark and deerskin.

NAVAHO
THE matrilineal Navaho of Arizona, New Mexico, and Utah are famous

▲ *A chief of the Navaho tribe*

for outstanding metalwork, especially in silver, and for their exquisite weaving.

NEZ PERCE
THE Nez Perce lived in western Idaho, northeastern Oregon, and southeastern Washington.

OJIBWA
THE Ojibwa lived on the shores of Lake Superior. They pictorially conveyed mythical tales via inscribed birch-bark scrolls.

OSAGE
THE Osage lived in the Ohio Valley. More than half of the tribe were vegetarians.

OTTAWA

FROM their home north of the Great Lakes, the Ottawa migrated to Georgian Bay, an inlet of Lake Huron in southeastern Ontario. They were seasonal wanderers, and frequently sailed the Great Lakes in superior birch-bark canoes.

PAWNEE

THE Pawnee lived south of the Great Plains but moved gradually north, planting and hunting, until the white men encountered them in the region of the Platte River.

SEMINOLE

BY the time the Spaniards "discovered" Florida in 1513, it held approximately 200,000 Seminole. Their society was divided into eight clans.

SHAWNEE

THE Shawnee were woodlands Indians living in Ohio, and were pushed from their hunting grounds into Kentucky and West Virginia.

SIOUX

THE Sioux exercised dominance and control of the northern plains, and practised a nomadic hunting and gathering culture before their acquisition of the horse.

UTES

SEVEN bands of Utes lived in Colorado and New Mexico, where family units hunted deer, elk, antelope, and other animals. They gathered seeds of grasses, wild berries and fruits, and occasionally planted corn, beans, and squash in mountain meadows.

YAQUI

FROM prehistoric times, the Yaqui inhabited northern Mexico and were a significant deterrent to the Spanish in the 16th and 17th centuries. For more than 300 years, the Yaquis were the most feared warriors in northwest Mexico.

◀ *Seminole chief Osceola*

CHAPTER 2

European Arrival in America

1492–1630

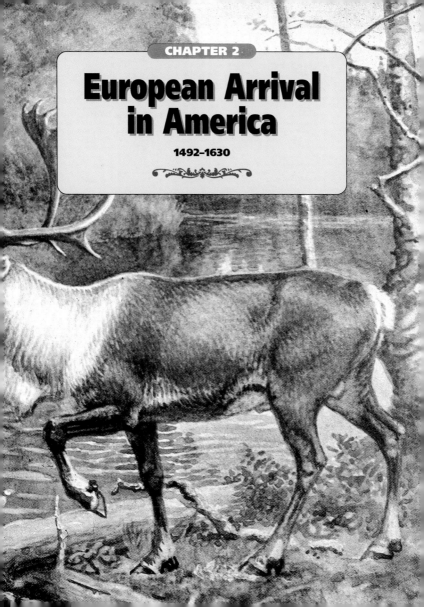

1492　　FOUR KEY INVENTIONS ☢

TECHNOLOGICALLY, four inventions played a pivotal role in making New
World exploration a reality. The magnetic compass made possible the great feats
of navigation necessary for the task. Gunpowder helped crumple the Medieval
feudal order and bring about centralization of power. The clock, with its
intricate inner workings heralded signficant improvements in tool making,
earning it the name "mother of inventions." Improvements in printing,
particularly movable type (1456), made more widely available the ancient classic
and modern works of navigation and travel such as Marco Polo's account of his
travels in Asia in the late 13th and early 14th centuries.

1492　　DISCOVERY OF AMERICA 🗺

CHRISTOPHER Columbus
(*c.* 1451–1506), a native of Genoa, Italy,
sought support in the royal houses of
Europe for a westward voyage to reach
the Far East. Unsuccessful until he
appealed to Ferdinand and Isabella of
Spain, Columbus departed in August
1492. His small fleet—made up of the
Nina, *Pinta*, and *Santa Maria*—sailed for
10 weeks before reaching land in the
Bahamas. He went on to Cuba and
Haiti. Spain based its claim to an
empire in the "new" world on
Columbus' voyage, although in reality
Columbus had engineered the collision
of two old-established worlds.

*Christopher Columbus greeting the natives on
his arrival in the "New World"* ▶

1497   ENGLISH  NEW WORLD EXPLORATION

ENGLISH exploration of the New World began in 1497 with the voyages of John Cabot, which reached Newfoundland. However, England's religious problems brought on by Henry VIII's break with the Catholic Church in 1534 interrupted further excursions until the reign of Elizabeth I (1558–1603). In the 1560s, Martin Frobisher searched unsuccessfully for a northern route around the newly discovered Americas—the "Northwest Passage." Both Sir Humphrey Gilbert and Sir Walter Raleigh received crown permission to colonize America. Raleigh explored territory he named "Virginia" in 1585 in honor of Elizabeth, who was known as the "Virgin Queen."

▲ *The English explorer John Cabot, whose exploration reached Newfoundland*

On the foundations of these activities, the British took the lead in North American colonization by the 17th century, with settlements along the Atlantic coast and in the West Indies. Overall, the British did not clash militarily with the natives until it became obvious that so-called "Puritan land-hunger" along the Atlantic seaboard would displace the natives from their homes.

1500s   NATIVE AMERICAN BELIEFS

THE Native Americans practised a widely diverse mythology when they came into contact with Europeans. Beliefs corresponded with the environment in which the group lived and with their method of survival. For instance, fishing tribes venerated the Old Woman who lived beneath the sea; Eskimos, or Inuit, looked into the northern lights for signs of their ancestors; hunting tribes venerated the animals who gave their lives so that the people might eat; and agricultural tribes practised ceremonies that corresponded with the major events of the agricultural calendar.

All tribes had at least a vague notion of a central spirit or god who looked over the world. They were animists, believing the world and everything it contained was infused with life and spirits, and thus seeing nature and natural phenomena as "on loan" to the people in a kind of communal relationship into which ideas of individual ownership had no place. This philosophy, as much as any other, put the tribes on a collision course with European ambitions.

1500s   NATIVE PEOPLES AT CONTACT 🏛

WHEN European explorers encountered the Native Americans in the 15th and 16th centuries, the tribes were in various stages of development and complexity which reflected the climate and available resources of the regions in which they

lived. The Inuit or Eskimo of Alaska survived in harsh conditions following the migrating caribou. The forest tribes north of the Great Lakes, mostly Cree, also depended on caribou as well as deer, beaver, and smaller animals. In the northeastern United States and southeastern Canada,

The Inuit peoples followed herds of caribou—the main source of their survival ▶

many tribes lived in semi-permanent villages of a thousand or more inhabitants whose homes were bark-covered longhouses. These peoples had adapted basic farming cultures, planting maize, apples, and vegetables, including beans and pumpkins. They traveled on inland waterways via birchbark canoes.

Farther south, the Cherokee lived in confederated villages of as many as 2,000 under a chief or chieftainess. They were an advanced agricultural people with well-developed trading networks and a complex ceremonial life attuned to the agricultural calendar. In the lower Mississippi area, tribes such as the Natchez built impressive ceremonial mounds, had a high level of craftsmanship, and divided their society into castes of aristocrats, priests, and commoners.

On the central plains south of the Great Lakes, tribes practiced a mixed economy. Their earthen homes were winter dwellings, while portable skin shelters, called *tipis*, were employed during hunts. Migrating buffalo herds provided ample food and supplies to these hunters, who used stone-tipped spears and arrows. Before the introduction of the horse by Europeans, these people drove the buffalo herds off cliffs onto prepared rows of sharpened upright posts.

On the Rocky Mountain borders of the Pacific, seafaring tribes availed themselves of bountiful fish, seal, and sea lion. These peoples lived in considerable comfort and plenty, allowing them to achieve sophisticated cultures which produced beautiful adzes, chisels, hammers, daggers, and spears with blades of flaked stone and shell. To the south, in the main Rocky Mountain—Pacific Coast areas, poorer hunting tribes gathered acorns, roots, and berries to augment the

▲ *The Rocky Mountains, which border the Pacific, where seafaring tribes survived on fish and seals*

meager game diet provided by this arid and harsh region.

The most advanced North American native cultures existed in the southwestern areas of Utah and Colorado, where agricultural life centered around large mud villages erected in desert river valleys. These Indians, especially the Hohokam, used irrigation to overcome periods of drought. The Pueblo Indians built fortified multistory towns on the top of isolated mesas. These tribespeople had a well-defined and ordered mythology, and a carefully organized social system in which aspirants to power moved up through layers of public office.

◀ *The Indians eventually began to establish more permanent settlements*

1500s   EUROPEAN DISEASE   🏛

THE most significant early effect of European contact for Native Americans was the introduction of diseases to which they had no immunity, such as smallpox, measles, typhus, and syphilis. Within a generation of contact, the Carib Indians, for whom the Caribbean was named, became extinct. Other tribes suffered a 90–95 percent population loss within the first century of European contact.

1500s   RENAISSANCE HUMANISM   🏛

THE Europeans who came to the Americas in the 16th and 17th centuries had all been affected by the Renaissance, a movement with a profound effect not only on art and architecture, but on views of life. In medieval thinking, humanity had been seen as inherently sinful and subject to the incontrovertible will of God. The Renaissance, by contrast, encouraged individualism, early concepts of human rights, and above all, the power of men and women to govern their own future. With such concepts gaining ground, people no longer needed to feel that poverty, destitution, and even disease and early death were inevitable burdens to be borne powerlessly. Politicians, physicians, scientists, and philosophers set out to prove that human fate was, after all, in human hands.

1500s   NEW WORLD—NEW START   🏛

THE "humanist" concept of life created a new self-sufficiency. In Britain, for instance, the dissolution of the monasteries by Henry VIII meant that, after 1539, people could no longer rely on the ministrations of monks and nuns as they had done for centuries. Merchants had grown wealthy, and the British Parliament more powerful, giving both a certain ascendancy over the kings and nobles who at one time possessed a monopoly of riches and power. The opening up of the New World after Columbus's discovery in 1492 offered escape from harsh conditions in Europe and the chance of a new start in a land of opportunity. Unfortunately, the humanist concepts did not extend to the native peoples the Europeans met in that new land.

◀ *Many people saw moving to the New World as a means of escaping harsh social and religious conditions under Henry VIII in England*

1500s   EXPLORATION MYTHS ✡

A VARIETY of tales picturing the "West" as a mysterious paradise, maybe even the lost Garden of Eden, fueled the imaginations of European explorers. These stories, coupled with the Christian desire to convert pagans, added the elements of belief and imagination to New World exploration. This religious desire for conversion was especially intense

Protestant reformer Martin Luther (far left) ▶

after the Catholic Church was beseiged by Protestant reformers following the lead of Martin Luther, who sparked the crisis in the early years of the 16th century which was to lead to the Protestant Reformation. Spain took the lead in the Counter Reformation funding the church's counterattack with gold and silver from the New World, and making the religious compound, or "mission," a central component in Spanish colonies.

1511 SPANISH CONTACT WITH INDIANS

THE most concerted destruction of native peoples in the New World during the period of exploration occurred in Spanish-held regions. Many historians describe the Spanish goal in the New World as the search for "gold, glory, and God." For instance, by 1511 Spaniards were already settled in Cuba and Hispaniola in the Caribbean, and were anxious to probe the mainland for mythical sites, such as the golden city of El Dorado or the more realistic empire of the Aztecs deep in the mountains of Mexico. A venture into the Yucatán in 1517 led to bloody encounters with the Maya, but yielded none of the desired treasures.

◄ *Peru fell to Francisco Pizarro*

1513 SPANISH NEW WORLD EXPLORATION

SPANISH explorers who followed Columbus (whose voyage took place in 1492) included Ponce de Leon (1513) on the Florida coasts; Vasco Nuas, searching for the golden city of El Dorado or the more realistic empire of the Aztecs deep in the mountains of Mexico; a venture into the Pacific, around Africa, and back to Europe; Hernando Cortés (1519) against the Aztecs of Mexico; and Francisco Pizarro (1531) into Peru against the Inca. Both Cabeza de Vaca (1535) and Francisco Vasquez de Coronado (1539–42) investigated the American Southwest, while Hernando de Soto (1541) trekked the distance from Florida to the Mississippi River.

The Spanish established a thriving New World empire 100 years before the establishment of the first permanent British settlement at Jamestown, Virginia in 1607. Spain used the wealth it gained from the New World to help finance the Counter Reformation, the church's campaign to reassert its authority and control after the Protestant Reformation began in 1517. Between 1500 and 1650, an estimated 200 tons of gold and 16,000 tons of silver were exported from the Americas.

1519 THE FALL OF TENOCHTITLÁN

HERNANDO Cortés (1485–1547) took up the Spanish quest in 1519. He set out from Cuba with a small force of 508 men, landed at Tabasco in southeastern Mexico, and worked his way across the mountains. On November 8, 1519, Cortés and his *conquistadors* entered Tenochtitlán, the Aztecs' capital city, on an island in Lake Texcoco and connected to the shore by causeways. The city included a massive palace, sacrificial towers,

The wall and gate of the great Aztec capital, Tenochtitlán ▶

statues decorated in metals, a thriving market place, and abundant gold. After a ferocious struggle, that reduced Tenochtitlán to ruins, the city fell on August 13, 1521. What followed was the destruction of Aztec society, a story replayed in varying degrees thoughout the history of Spanish contact with native groups.

▼ *Protestant reformer John Calvin*

1524   FRENCH NEW WORLD EXPLORATION

FRENCH explorers in the New World included Jacques Cartier (1534) on the St. Lawrence River; Jean Ribault (1562) in Florida; and Samuel de Champlain (1608) at Quebec and other northern areas. France's empire in the New World depended on the highly profitable fur trade with inland Indian tribes, and sparsely populated New France was marked by trading posts and forts. The French government attempted to encourage settlement by granting charters for the formation of fur-trading companies. Because this trade depended on a close and peaceful relation with the natives, the French proved the most successful of all European groups in the area of Indian relations.

1534   RELIGIOUS UPHEAVAL FUELS SETTLEMENT

ENGLAND experienced religious and political turmoil when Henry VIII broke with the Catholic Church in 1534 after the pope's refusal grant him a divorce from his first wife, Catherine of Aragon. These events set the stage for the popular discontent that helped to fuel a migration of English settlers to the eastern coast of North America. Through the reigns of Henry's children—Edward VI (1547–53), Mary (1553–58), and Elizabeth I (1558–1603)—religious groups argued about the degree of Catholic ritual and trappings that should or should not be allowed in the Church of England (the Anglican Church). Influenced by Protestant reformers from the Continent such as John Calvin (1509–64), two basic groups formed: Puritans, who believed the church could be purified of its Catholic elements; and Separatists, who advocated a complete break. As these groups increasingly clashed with the crown and government authorities, elements organized New World settlement ventures to establish communities in which they could worship as they saw fit.

1541   INTRODUCTION OF THE HORSE

AT least initially, the horse proved more valuable than firearms to the Native Americans. The tribes north of the Mesa Central of Mexico, especially those of the Great Plains of Texas and the North American Midwest, became the world's finest light cavalry astride descendants of Spanish horses. Indian herds of wild mustang probably originated with animals lost or abandoned by the Hernando de Soto expedition in 1541. It is also possible that horses and horsemanship were introduced in the 17th century by captive Indians who escaped Spanish ranches in the provinces of New Mexico, Sonora, Chihuahua, Nueva Vizcaya, and Coahuila. Whatever their origins, the dispersion of horses over the Great Plains was complete by 1784.

1558   ENGLAND'S COLONIES

AS Europe emerged from the Middle Ages and entered the Renaissance after 1500, centralization of power under the newly powerful monarchs allowed those individuals to direct and finance overseas exploration in the hopes of increasing their royal coffers. In England, Henry VII won the Wars of the Roses defeating the Lancastrian claimant. Although England's New World efforts would be delayed by religious turmoil, it was under the reign of a Tudor, Elizabeth I (1558–1603), that England's first American colonies were established. Most prominent among these European monarchs, Ferdinand of Aragon and Isabella of Castille, the consolidators of Spain, financed the voyage of Christopher Columbus in 1492, which resulted in the "discovery" of the Americas.

1630   PURITAN SENSE OF MISSION

ENGLISH settlements in the northeastern region known as New England were infused with a particular sense of mission courtesy of Puritan leaders like John Winthrop, who led a group of settlers to the Massachusetts Bay Colony in 1630. Aboard the *Arabella*, the ship which brought them to America, Winthrop delivered a sermon entitled "A Modell of Christian Charity" in which he said of their endeavor, "We shall be as a city upon a hill, the eyes of all people are upon us." Winthrop's sense of mission and divine guidance infused the New England settlements, and would become transformed into a political sense of mission after the American Revolution 150 years later.

▲ *The first English colonies in America were established during the reign of Elizabeth I*

CHAPTER 3

Colonial Foundation and Settlement

1600–1763

1600s THE COLONIAL ECONOMY

THE New England settlers tended cattle, pigs, and sheep, and—on rocky soils during a short growing season—were able to produce enough wheat, barley, and oats so that, by the end of the 17th century, there was enough surplus for export. The abundant forests provided lumber for shipbuilding materials, and thriving colonial shipyards were established at Boston, Salem, Dorchester, Gloucester, and Portsmouth. Rich fishing grounds stretched north to Newfoundland, yielding cod, mackerel, halibut, and other types of seafood, both for domestic consumption and for export to Europe. Whaling was an important industry, supplying oils for lighting, lubrication, and perfume production.

The southern colonies had the advantage of a more benign climate, enabling colonists to cultivate staple crops impossible to grow farther north. Virginia, for instance, was producing more than 20,000 pounds of tobacco a year by 1619; by 1688, this had increased to 18 million. Lumber and naval stores were key products of the southern woods and there was also a thriving cattle industry.

▲ *The manufacture of tobacco became a major industry in the 17th century, particularly in Virginia*

1600s   PURITAN DOCTRINE ✡

AMERICAN Puritans organized congregational churches whose members
entered into a covenant, or voluntary union, for the common worship of God.
As Calvinists, they believed in predestination, and also that an Elect had been
chosen for the salvation denied the Unregenerate; an individual could never
know to which group they belonged, nor change their status. The strictness of
this doctrine became weakened by second and third generations who introduced
theology like the Covenant of Works, based on the idea that God would not
allow a sinner to prosper. For an American Puritan, therefore, hard work and
commercial success were equated with salvation.

1600s   TRIANGULAR TRADE 🏛

BY the end of the 17th century, the colonies had established a regular trade
with the British Isles, the British West Indies, Spain, France, Portugal, Holland,
and Africa. The American colonists imported manufactured goods from
Britain and Europe, including hardware, machinery, paint, and navigation
instruments, as well as household items, thus serving as an important market
for English manufacturers.

To maintain a favorable balance of trade, the northern colonies developed
the "Triangular Trade,"—rum was shipped to the west coast of Africa, where it
was bartered for slaves,
who were taken to the
West Indies and exchanged
for commodities including
molasses, from which the
colonists manufactured yet
more rum.

*African slaves proved to be
important bartering commodity
for the American colonists* ▶

1607   TYPES OF COLONIES

AFTER the first permanent English settlement was founded at Jamestown, Virginia, in 1607, England's colonies were classed as either corporate, royal, or proprietary. In corporate colonies, decisions originated with the founding company, usually a joint stock arrangement in which investors bought shares in an entity that existed to settle or trade for profit. Royal colonies belonged to the monarch, and were overseen by an appointed governor or council. Proprietary colonies were given to an individual or group to do with as they pleased, providing there was no conflict with English law or title.

1607   JAMESTOWN, VIRGINIA

THE London Company founded England's first permanent American colony in Virginia. Three ships carrying 100 men arrived at Chesapeake Bay on May 6, 1607, where they settled approximately 40 miles inland along a river they christened the James, after England's King James I; the colonists named their settlement Jamestown, and erected a fort, thatched huts, a storehouse, and a church. The men had come in search of gold, and when this proved elusive, made miserable farmers instead. With no woodland skills to exploit, the area's abundant game and fish were of little help to the struggling community. The colonists would have surely starved had they depended on the irregular arrival of supplies from England. Instead, they traded with the local Powhatan Indians, who taught them to grow maize.

Captain John Smith, whose peaceful trading with the local Indians allowed the survival of the Jamestown community ▶

Captain John Smith, a member of the resident ruling council, imposed strict discipline and declared "he that will not work shall not eat." Smith explored and mapped the Chesapeake area, and is largely credited with Jamestown's survival. Virginia's true success would come with the cultivation of tobacco.

1619   BICAMERALISM

IN 1619, the Virginia settlers established a representative assembly, the Virginia House of Burgesses, open to all free men. It was to be the lower house of a bicameral governing body, one that consisted of two legislative bodies. The Company council served as the upper. The evolution of the two-house colonial legislature established a tradition of bicameralism assumed by the end of the colonial period, as was the concept of representative self-government. The latter was buttressed by the self-governing congregational churches established by New England Puritans. These ideas, coupled with an emphasis on covenants or contracts, marked the development of distinct political ideas in England's colonies, laying a foundation for their future political independence.

1620   PILGRIMS

IN 1620, a group of religious Separatists, or Puritans, who wished to sever all ties with the Church of England journeyed to the New World from England, via Holland, aboard the *Mayflower*. Blown off course from their Virginia destination, the group,

▲ *The Pilgrim Fathers celebrating the first Thanksgiving*

known as the Pilgrims, instead made landfall at Cape Cod. Outside of any formal government jurisdiction, 41 men made a formal agreement on

November 21, 1620 to abide by laws made by their chosen leaders, an agreement known as the Mayflower Compact. During their first winter at Plymouth Harbor, more than half the colonists died of exposure and disease. Their salvation came from the local Wampanoag Indians (later known as Narragansett), in particular an Indian known as Squanto, who instructed them in growing maize. By the autumn of 1621, the settlers boasted an abundant corn crop, a profitable fur trade, and a supply of lumber for trade.

◀ *The arrival of the Pilgrim Fathers in the New World*

1633   OTHER NEW ENGLAND COLONIES

OTHER New England colonies had diverse beginnings. Connecticut was settled in 1633 by a group from the English town of Plymouth under the leadership of Thomas Hooker; these and other settlers organized the self-governing colony of Connecticut in 1637. Tracts of land comprizing what is now New Hampshire and Maine were granted to Sir Ferdinando Gorges and Captain John Mason in 1622. They divided the land in 1629, with Mason taking the southern part, which he named New Hampshire. Disputes with Massachusetts over ownership of the area proved difficult, however. In 1679, New Hampshire became a royal colony, but Maine was incorporated into Massachusetts in 1691. In 1664, the English seized an area settled by Dutch colonists, and known as New Amsterdam; this would later become New York. New Jersey was granted to Sir George Carteret and Lord John Berkeley in 1664, and passed to a number of proprietors before becoming a royal colony in 1702.

1630   MASSACHUSETTS BAY

IN March 1630, a group of six ships carrying settlers of the Massachusetts Bay Colony, led by Governor John Winthrop, departed for America; these were followed by an additional 17 vessels before the end of the year. These Puritans wanted to be "as a city upon a hill," a phrase coined by Winthrop in a sermon delivered aboard the *Arabella* en route to New England. As Puritans they hoped to cleanse the Church of England of its remaining vestiges of Catholicism and believed they were part of a divine mission. Once settled, they established a theocracy: a government led by divine guidance.

1635   RHODE ISLAND

MASSACHUSETTS became a staging area for the settlement of the remainder of New England. Though often associated with the phrase "religious freedom," Puritans established their own orthodoxy and were not tolerant of differing beliefs. When a young minister, Roger Williams, questioned the validity of the Massachusetts colony, whose land had not been purchased from the natives and also suggested its government had no right to enforce religious conformity, he was invited to leave in 1635. He did so, establishing Providence at the head of Narragansett Bay, the initial settlement in what was to become Rhode Island, the first colony to actually legislate true religious freedom.

1669   THE CAROLINAS

DURING the English Civil War (1642–45), the colonies in the New World were left much to their own devices, though in 1643 Massachusetts Bay, Plymouth, Connecticut, and New Haven formed the New England Confederation for their own protection. After the restoration of the English monarchy, Charles II granted the Carolinas to eight Lord Proprietors. In 1669, three ships left London with 100 settlers to populate an area in South Carolina. They settled on a site several miles up the Ashley River, which became first Charles Town and later Charleston. The community remained at the initial site from 1670–80, before being moved downstream to Oyster Point overlooking Charleston Harbor. The proprietors surrendered their governing rights to North Carolina back to the Crown in 1719.

1681 PENNSYLVANIA

PENNSYLVANIA was given as a proprietary grant to the Quaker William Penn, a claim which his son, William, inherited in 1681. When the younger Penn assumed control, the land held a scattering of Dutch, Swedish, and English settlers. By the end of 1681 Penn's advertisements had attracted more than 1,000 settlers, most of whom were Quakers, and at the end of the year Penn himself arrived with an additional 100 colonists. The central town at the junction of the Schuylkill and Delaware rivers Penn called Philadelphia, the "City of Brotherly Love." The region known as Delaware was granted to Penn in 1682 and remained part of Pennsylvania until 1701, when it was given the right to choose its own assembly.

▼ *A meeting of Quakers, many of whom settled in Pennsylvania after William Penn colonized the area*

1681   QUAKERS

THE colonizing efforts of William Penn in Pennsylvania in 1681 drew Quakers in large numbers. The sect, founded by George Fox in 1647, emphasized individual inspiration and interpretation. Quakers discarded the sacraments, the ministry, and references to rank. They took no oaths, were pacifists, and extended religious freedom to all groups, as well as equality to the genders.

1689   KING WILLIAM'S WAR

KING William's War (also known as the War of the League of Augsburg, 1689–97), the first of the French and Indian wars between the French—supported by the Huron Indians—and the English settlers, saw scattered fighting around Hudson Bay posts. These outposts fell to the French, as did the formerly held Newfoundland. The French aroused their Indian allies on the frontier for an attack on New York which destroyed Schenectady in 1690. Various planned expeditions against French Canada failed to materialize, and the war then degenerated into scattered frontier raiding. The Treaty of Ryswick (1697) returned the colonies to their prewar status.

1692   COLONIAL SOCIETY

THE colonies were deeply patriarchal, with fathers subdividing their land among male offspring. In seaboard towns, the concentration of wealth enabled a social and economic elite to emerge. Civil consciousness, deference to sources of authority, and church membership were important. Religious commitment, however,

▲ *People flocked to the colonized areas of America, traveling in covered wagons*

struggled against the worldliness of a growing trading nation, and occasionally exploded in fundamentalist incidents like the Salem witch hunts. Frontier regions bred a rough democracy as survival demanded equal social status. Stubborn individualism became a hallmark of the American colonist.

The middle and southern colonies were a combination of more nationalities and races than the predominately Puritan, British New England colonies. Elements of Dutch, German, Scot, Irish, Welsh, Swiss, French, Danish, Portuguese, Spanish, Italian, Bohemian, and Polish settlers provided a rich social mix. Largely agricultural, these colonies were also the site of the greatest concentrations of African slaves.

1701   QUEEN ANNE'S WAR

THE brunt of Queen Anne's War (1701–13) in the colonies fell to New England and South Carolina. Charlestonians raised a force in 1702 that destroyed Spanish St. Augustine in Florida, earning a counter attack on Charleston in 1706. For seven years a ragged border war continued between English-held South Carolina and Spanish Florida. The Yemassee and Creek Indians fought with the English. In New England, the

Fighting aboard the Breda *during Queen Anne's War* ▶

frontier from Maine to Massachusetts suffered repeated raids from French and Indian forces, which sacked several Massachusetts villages in 1704. There were minor British attempts to move toward Quebec with greater successes in the Caribbean and in Europe. The war was settled by the Peace of Utrecht in 1713, in which British claims to the Hudson Bay, Newfoundland, Acadia (later Nova Scotia), and St. Christopher were recognized, as was their claim to sovereignty over the Iroquois.

▲ *The signing of the Treaty of Utrecht in 1713, in which the British laid claim to many lands in America*

1706 THE ENLIGHTENMENT ☢

AMERICANS proved receptive to Newtonian science and the Enlightenment: much of their success had come from observation and experimentation. John Winthrop, Jr. (1606–1676) was a member of the London-based scientific group known as the Royal Society, and brought the first telescope to the colonies. His cousin, John Winthrop IV (1714–79), brought the study of calculus to America, and worked in astronomy, geology, chemistry, and electricity. John Bartram of Philadelphia gathered a botanical garden in Philadelphia that remains a part of the city's park system to this day.

The premier figure of the American Enlightenment, Benjamin Franklin, was born in Boston in 1706. He made his career in Philadelphia as a printer, publishing the *Pennsylvania Gazette* and *Poor Richard's Almanac*. Before his retirement at the age of 42, he founded a library, set up a local fire company, founded the University of Pennsylvania, and began a debating club that evolved into the American Philosophical Society. In his "retirement" he conducted his famous experiments with electricity (1751), and was a leading statesman of the Revolutionary period.

1730s   THE GREAT AWAKENING

AS later generations lost the zeal of the first Puritan settlers, religious revivalism began in the 1730s with ministers like Jonathan Edwards of Massachusetts conducting extended meetings and delivering fiery sermons. This movement, the "Great Awakening," fractured churches and was responsible for the evolution of sects like the Baptists, Presbyterians, and Methodists.

1733   GEORGIA

GEORGIA, the last British colony established, was given to 21 proprietors. Set up as a philanthropic experiment and a military buffer against Spanish-held Spain, Georgia was carefully planned by General James E. Oglethorpe, the resident trustee who accompanied the first settlers in 1733. Oglethorpe organized defenses and populated the colony with the poor, the persecuted, and even with convicts. In 1733 he arrived with 120 colonists and founded Savannah, near the mouth of the Savannah River.

1744   KING GEORGE'S WAR

KING George's War (1744–48) saw border raids flare up along the northern frontier. Massachusetts' Governor, William Pepperell, mounted an expedition

against French Canada on behalf of the British Crown, and conquered Fort Louisbourg on Cape Breton. The war ended in a stalemate. In the Treaty of Aix-la-Chapelle (1748), the British exchanged the port of Louisbourg for Madras, which the French had taken in India.

1755   FRENCH AND INDIAN WAR

IN 1755, the French and Indian War—also known as the Seven Years' War—broke out between France and England over rival claims to the Ohio Valley. The bulk of the fighting in this conflict occurred in the New World. At first the war went badly for the colonists and the French captured Forts Oswego, George and Ticonderoga, but, in 1758, the tide began to turn. Louisburg, Fort Frontenac, and Fort Duquesne were captured by the British, and in 1759 General James Wolfe attacked Quebec, the center of French Canada. At the battle of the Plains of Abraham in September 1759, the British forces destroyed the army of General Louis Joseph de Montcalm and then captured Quebec five days later. French power in North America was ended under the Treaty of Paris (1763), under the terms of which the French were effectively driven from America and India. For the colonists, the war led to increasing opposition to British rule due to raised taxes in order to help pay for the fighting.

▼ *Statue of General James Wolfe, the British leader during the French and Indian War*

◀ *Sea attack during King George's War*

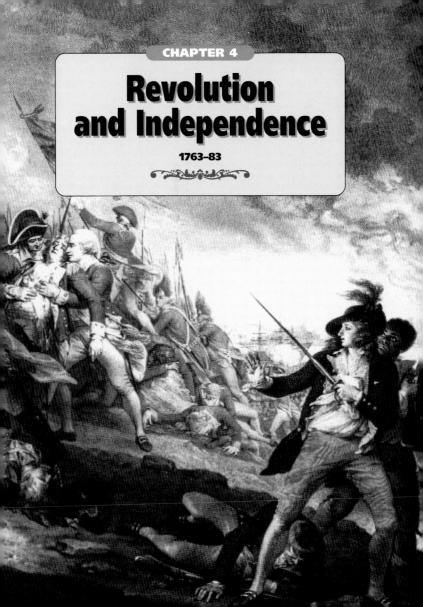

CHAPTER 4

Revolution and Independence

1763–83

1763   COLONIAL LEGISLATURES

BY the 1760s, the colonial legislatures in America had become a safeguard against the commonly held fear that all royal officials were corrupt. With the barrier of the Atlantic Ocean effectively protecting these officials from close scrutiny, the colonists' belief that fees, taxes, and fines collected in the name of the monarch would go no farther than the officials' own pockets seemed wholly reasonable. The colonists, by insisting that their local legislatures had the right to pass laws, raise taxes, authorize military actions, and examine accounts were, in their minds, protecting their own liberty. Although always seen as obstinate, the emphasis placed on the role of the colonial legislatures by the colonists did not come into concerted conflict with the Crown until King George III assumed the throne in 1760 and the French and Indian War ended in 1763.

1763   AFTERMATH OF THE FRENCH AND INDIAN WAR

INCREASED taxes levied on the American colonists after 1763 had a dual purpose. The British national debt had almost doubled during the French and Indian War (1755–63), and the government wanted to reduce that figure. The additional funds were also needed to finance George III's military policy; the British army did not demobilize after the war, but remained at near wartime strength (85 regiments) in the event of renewed hostilities with France. This army was to be maintained by being stationed in America and Ireland, where the local population was expected to support the troops.

▲ *King George III became the target of animosity from the British colonists*

Five pieces of legislation affecting life in the colonies began the road toward the American Revolution. The Proclamation of 1763 forbade colonists to settle West of the Appalachian Mountains. The Revenue Act of 1764 redefined the colonies' purpose as revenue generating. The Currency Act of 1764 outlawed the printing of paper money in the colonies. The Quartering Act of 1765 required settlers to house and feed the British troops stationed in America. Finally, the Stamp Act of 1765 placed a tax on all printed goods.

1763   CHURCH AND STATE ✡

MANY American Revolutionary leaders, including Thomas Jefferson and Benjamin Franklin, were Deists. Popular in 18th-century Europe, Deism portrayed God as the Master Clockmaker, who had planned and built the universe, set it in motion, and left it to its own fate. People could use their reason to grasp natural laws, and to improve their lot in life and that of others. Established colonial churches that taught passive obedience and subservience to the government in exchange for state-enforced tithes ran counter to the Enlightenment belief that the will to resist tyranny originated in the minds of the citizen. From this situation came the American concept of the separation of church and state.

▲ *The Deist Thomas Jefferson, third president of the United States*

▲ *The English philosopher John Locke, whose theories formed the basis of the American Enlightenment*

1763 THE ENLIGHTENMENT

THE most important political theories in the American Enlightenment were derived from English philosopher John Locke's *Two Treatises on Civil Government* (1690) and from English radical republicans known as the "commonwealthmen." American political thought was a conglomerate of Enlightenment ideas, Scot common sense, English common law, Puritan theology, and the experience of colonial life itself. John Locke's ideas heavily shaped those of the colonists when they argued that the British government, in taking away their liberties, had effectively dissolved the political bonds between the colonies and the Mother Country.

Like the English radicals, the Americans believed in representation, contractual government, and natural rights. The commonwealthmen advocated the abolition of the monarchy in favor of a republic governed by a representative government, and regarded the English Parliament as hopelessly corrupt. This group also opposed parliamentary taxation and the existence of standing armies.

1765 STAMP ACT

THE Stamp Act of 1765 generated a wave of protest in the colonies. The law attempted to derive internal revenue by levying consumer taxes primarily on printed materials, such as newspapers, pamphlets, legal documents, and even dice and playing cards. The legislation affected the most powerful elements of colonial society, those who handled paper on a daily basis—lawyers, publishers, merchants, shopkeepers, real estate holders, speculators, and tavern-keepers, among others. The fact that the taxes were to be paid in either gold or silver, and that violators were to be tried in vice-admiralty courts without benefit of juries made the law especially hated.

1765   ECONOMIC BOYCOTTS

THROUGHOUT the revolutionary period, American colonists employed economic boycotts against the British. In the wake of the 1765 Stamp Act and Sugar Act, for instance, colonists adopted nonimportation agreements. Because the colonies served as an important market for British products, such agreements gave the Americans real leverage. British tea was forsaken in favor of sage and sassafras brews, and homespun garments became a patriotic fashion statement. Boycotts were again employed in 1767 after the passing of the Townshend Acts, remaining in place until all the laws but one were repealed in 1770, that being the tax on tea. Economic pressure was again a weapon when the First Continental Congress formed the Continental Association in 1774, which recommended that every county, town, and city form committees to enforce boycotts on all British goods.

1765   STAMP ACT CONGRESS

COLONIAL delegates met in New York in October 1765, and generated a document called the Resolutions of the Stamp Act Congress. This demonstrated a deep loyalty to the British Crown and to English institutions and constitutional values, but also attempted to inform the monarch of the manner in which this legislation adversely affected the

▲ *The Virginia Assembly on the British Stamp Tax question*

colonies. The delegates further denied the right of a body in which they were not directly represented to tax them. Taken with the Declaration of Independence

(1776), the two documents bracket the germination and culmination of the colonists' expression of revolutionary ideas. Although the Stamp Act was repealed in March 1766, at the same time, Parliament passed the Declaratory Act affirming its absolute supremacy over all colonial matters, and thereby setting itself up as the archvillain in the colonists' eyes.

1767 THE TOWNSHEND ACTS

THE Townshend Acts, passed by the British Parliament in May and June 1767, reawakened the taxation issue with the colonies. These laws suspended the activities of the New York assembly until the colony fully complied with the Quartering Act. The Revenue Act of 1767 placed taxes on glass, lead, paint, paper, and tea, the money generated being used to pay colonial governors and officers, thereby removing their dependence on the colonists for their livelihood and safeguarding their loyalty to the Crown. A Board of Customs Commissioners was established at Boston to clamp down on smuggling, and the hated vice-admiralty courts were increased by four. Colonial protests and boycotts followed including John Dickinson's *Letters of a Pennsylvania Farmer* (1767), in which he affirmed Parliament's right to regulate commerce but not to levy taxes on the colonies for revenue.

1768 RESISTANCE IN BOSTON

BOSTON, Massachusetts served as the center of American resistance to British rule in the 1760s and 1770s. Because they relied on trade, Bostonians were far more affected by British restrictions than other, more agricultural colonies to the south. In May 1768, when a crowd attempted to prevent customs agents from seizing the cargo of John Hancock's ship the *Liberty*, the agents requested troops be sent from England for their protection. In September that same year, two regiments of Redcoats and some foreign mercenaries arrived in Boston and camped on Boston Common. The atmosphere in the city was tense and hostile.

1770 BOSTON MASSACRE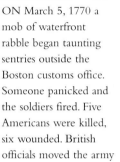

ON March 5, 1770 a mob of waterfront rabble began taunting sentries outside the Boston customs office. Someone panicked and the soldiers fired. Five Americans were killed, six wounded. British officials moved the army to an island in Boston Harbor to prevent further hostilities, but the colonists saw the incident as an example of British tyranny, and promptly dubbed it the "Boston Massacre."

▲ *The British troops opening fire on the mob in what became known as the "Boston Massacre"*

1770   DEPENDENCE ON IMPORTS

ALTHOUGH no clear statistics were kept in the colonial period, population increases alone suggest significant economic growth. From 1607 to 1770, the colonial population grew from just 105 settlers to more than two million. Unquestionably, the colonial economy depended on the export of raw materials and the importation of finished products, but increasingly restrictive trade laws passed by the British narrowed and ultimately confined the source of these items to the British Empire, eliminating free trade and freedom of economic choice for the colonists. Limitations on their economic activities and the domestic effect of increased taxes were key causes in the outbreak of the American Revolution.

1773   THE BOSTON TEA PARTY

IN December 1773, when tea from the East India Company arrived in Boston, it was dumped into the sea by Bostonians disguised as Indians, in an act of rebellion dubbed the "Boston Tea Party." In June 1774, England responded

▲ *The "Boston Tea Party"—the reaction of Bostonians to British trade restrictions*

by closing the port of Boston, and Massachusetts lost many of its rights of self-government and justice in legislation colonists referred to as the "Intolerable Acts." Representatives of all of the colonies, except Georgia, met at Philadelphia in September 1774 in the First Continental Congress, when an agreement was reached to boycott British goods after December 1774.

1774   FIRST CONTINENTAL CONGRESS

IN the wake of the Boston Tea Party (1773) and the attempted British isolation of Massachusets as reprisal, a meeting of 55 delegates from 12 colonies convened in Philadelphia on September 5, 1774. This First Continental Congress called for the elimination of all oppressive legislation passed by Parliament since 1763; protested the punishment of Massachusets; planned the collection of, but not the transmission of, tax funds until such time as the oppressive legislation was repealed; and took the precaution of suggesting that arms be collected for colonial defense. In keeping with the literate tradition of the Revolution, the delegates drafted a Declaration of American Rights, once again affirming Parliament's authority to regulate commerce but denying to that body the right to tax the colonists. From the convening of the Continental Congress in 1774, the English king, George III, held the colonies to be in a state of rebellion.

1775   LEXINGTON AND CONCORD

WAR broke out between the colonists and the British in April 1775. British authorities recognized the need to seize arms available to the Americans in the highly charged area around Boston. General Thomas Gage, the military governor of Massachusets, sent a force of 700 men under the command of Lieutenant Colonel Francis Smyth and Major John Pitcairn to Concord, Massachusets to destroy a weapons stockpile belonging to the Massachusets Committee of Public Safety.

The British met a ragged line of some 70 American militiamen at Lexington, under the leadership of Captain John Parker. The British told

The opening shots of the American Revolution at Lexington ▶

the colonists to disband. A few insults were bandied about, Smyth ordered a volley fired into the stragglers, and, in the proverbial "Shot Heard Round the World," 10 Americans were killed and eight wounded. The British troops hastily left the scene and continued to Concord, where they discovered that most of the arms had been removed. As the British returned to Boston, the Americans followed and flanked the troops with great success. As the soldiers straggled back through colonial fire originating from both sides of the road, 250 were killed. The Americans lost only 93 in the fighting.

1776 REVOLUTIONARY BATTLE

MUCH of the early fighting centered on Boston, which the British were forced to evacuate in March 1776. After the "battles" of Lexington and Concord and the early successes around Boston including the Battle of Bunker Hill (June 17, 1775), the colonists were optimistic of their eventual victory. In truth, the Americans won only two decisive victories during the Revolutionary War: the

▲ *The Battle of Bunker Hill, during the Revolution*

Battle of Saratoga (October 17, 1777), which solidified the invaluable alliance with the French the following year; and the Battle of Yorktown (August 30–October 19, 1781), which brought about the capitulation of the English under General Charles Cornwallis, thereby ending the war.

1776   BREAKING TIES TO THE MONARCHY

AFTER the battles of Lexington and Concord (April 1775); the convening of the Second Continental Congress (May 1775); the Battle of Bunker Hill (June 1775); and two last efforts at compromise in the Olive Branch Petition (July 1775) and The Declaration of the Causes and Necessity of Taking Up Arms (July 1775), the colonists were still not prepared to declare independence. It was not until the publication of Thomas Paine's pamphlet, *Common Sense*, in January 1776, that the colonists were able to divorce themselves from an inherent sense of loyalty to the British monarch. Selling 150,000 copies in just three months, Paine's pamphlet stripped kingship of historical and theological justifications, arguing for the correctness of breaking from an hereditary monarch who denied his subjects individual rights. The colonists had seen Parliament as their enemy since the end of the French and Indian War in 1763; the enemy now became King George III.

◀ *Thomas Paine, whose writings encouraged British colonists to sever their loyalty to the Crown*

1776   DECLARATION OF INDEPENDENCE

THOMAS Jefferson drew up the Declaration of Independence, which was approved by the Continental Congress on July 4, 1776. A two-part document clearly reflecting the influence of the Enlightenment, it restated John Locke's compact theory of government, and outlined the British actions that brought the colonists to the point of rebellion. The document marked a new precedent in power and politics, with the colonists asserting the right of a people to throw off their allegiance to their king and establish for themselves a new and different form of government. The composition of the Articles of Confederation and Perpetual Union, signed in November 1777, completed the next organizational step by providing for a governmental framework and rules of operation. The United States of America came into being in 1781 when the British forces in America surrendered.

1776   BUSHNELL'S SUBMARINE

DAVID Bushnell, a colonial inventor, built a one-man submarine powered by a hand crank in 1776. A soldier took the *Turtle*, as it was called, under the British

◄ Bushnell's *Turtle, the first submersible craft to be used in action, in New York, 1776*

ship *Eagle* planning to deploy an explosive, but, once onsite, the soldier could not attach the charge to the copper hull of the vessel. The charge harmlessly exploded in open water, but the potential of such weaponry was clear. The *Turtle*'s voyage was the first known use of the submarine in warfare. Within a year, Bushnell was at work on floating mines to use against British ships at Philadelphia.

1776   PATRIOTS AND LOYALISTS   🏛

THE Revolution was also a civil war, dividing families between Patriot and Loyalist sentiment. For instance, Benjamin Franklin's son, William, refused to join the rebellion. During and after the conflict, 100,000 Loyalists, almost three percent of the population, left America. American Loyalists were usually concentrated in seaport cities, but came from all walks of life. Governors, judges, and royal officials were almost totally loyal. Colonial merchants went both ways, depending on how much they had been affected by the prewar taxes and trade restrictions. Large planters were torn between their dependence on Britain on the one hand, and their debts to the Mother Country on the other. In the back country the more humble colonists rallied to the Crown. Still, in this mix of conflicting allegiances, Patriot sentiment prevailed.

1776   THE REVOLUTION IN ART   🏛

THE Revolution provided America's first generation of artists with plentiful inspiration and high hopes for full freedom to express their creative energies. Charles Willson Peale, who fought at Trenton and Princeton, New Jersey, and survived the brutal winter at Valley Forge, produced a gallery of Revolutionary War figures. His portrait of George Washington, painted in 1779, is believed to be the most faithful representation of the general at that phase of his life. Ironically, the best American painters, John Singleton Copley and Benjamin West, spent the duration of the war in London.

1778   WORLD WAR

DURING the American Revolution, England was occupied in other areas of the globe as well. After the French allied themselves with the Americans in 1778 after the Battle of Saratoga, the conflict assumed the proportions of a world war. Spain declared war on Great Britain in 1779, when the Spanish allied themselves to the French. In 1780, the Dutch joined in when Holland went to war with Britain over naval rights.

1780s   THE AMERICAN REVOLUTION AND SCIENCE

AFTER the 1720s, the rapid growth of towns in the colonies gave rise to the founding of more libraries, colleges, and newspapers. Amateur scientists, chiefly physicians and inventors like Benjamin Franklin, depended on Europe as a source of their equipment and theoretical guidance. The Revolution was beneficial to the American scientific community in that it weakened ties to British scientists, challenging the Americans to prove that the political freedom for which they had fought nurtured intellectualism and discovery. In the years just after the Revolution museums opened, journals and societies were founded, and new colleges opened their doors. The government patent system for inventions, the postwar economic expansion, and abundant natural resources encouraged advances in transportation and in the development of labor-saving devices that continued to escalate in the years before the Civil War.

1783   TREATY OF PARIS

IN the Treaty of Paris of September 3, 1783, the British formally recognized American independence. The boundaries of the new country were set in the south at the 31st parallel, the Mississippi River on the west, and at the 45th parallel in the north. All debts and contracts between Americans and Englishmen were to be honored, and the American Congress agreed to recommend that the rights and properties of all Loyalists be returned. British forces were to evacuate "with all convenient speed." The last British soldiers left New York City in the fall of 1783.

◄ *The inventor Benjamin Franklin*

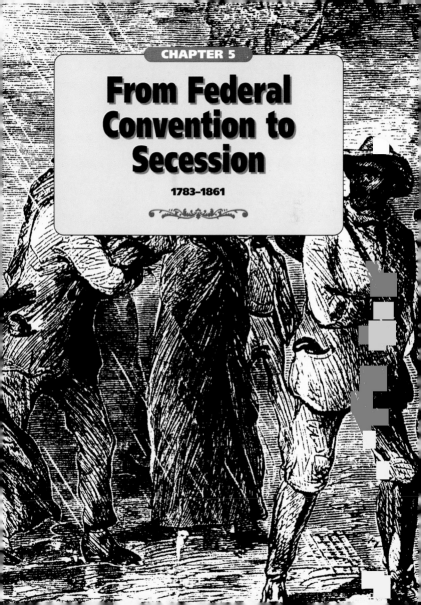

CHAPTER 5

From Federal Convention to Secession

1783–1861

1783　　　TEXTILES AND TELECOMMUNICATIONS ☢

BETWEEN 1783 and 1861, technological change became a dominant feature in American life. Samuel Slater, a British mechanic, established Slater's Mill in 1791 for the production of textiles, hailed as the country's first efficient, productive manufacturing plant. In 1794, Eli Whitney developed his famous "gin" for separating cotton fiber and seeds. In 1836, Samuel Colt patented the revolver. William Morton developed the anesthetic ether in 1846. Cyrus McCormick developed a successful machine to reap grain in 1831. In 1851, Isaac Singer patented an improved mechanical sewing machine.

Samuel Morse, (1791–1872), the inventor of the Morse Code, built the first electric telegraph (1835), which was the first form of telecommunication. Some 40 years later, in 1876, Alexander Graham Bell (1847–1922) put together an assemblage of components devised in part by other electrical scientists, thus inventing the telephone.

▲ *Samuel Morse, who built the first electric telegraph*

◄ *Alexander Graham Bell demonstrates the first telephone*

1786 ARTICLES OF CONFEDERATION

IN 1775, the Second Continental Congress appointed a committee headed by John Dickinson to compose the Articles of Confederation. In debate, his original plan, calling for a strong central government with control over all aspects of foreign and domestic policy, was emasculated. The approved version (1781) created a "firm league of friendship" in which "each state retains its sovereignty, freedom, and independence." The unicameral (one body) legislature controlled foreign policy and the mechanics of domestic policy, but could not tax the people or regulate interstate or foreign commerce. The government had no visible means of support except voluntary state contributions. The executive branch consisted of an Executive Committee whose members elected a chairman.

Alexander Hamilton led a movement in the 1780s to revise the Articles. Delegates from five states met in Annapolis, Maryland in September 1786 to discuss creating a unified system of commercial regulation. The group recommended a larger convention to overhaul the Articles and make them more useful for the task of governing. Congress readily agreed, and scheduled the second meeting for May 1787.

1787 CONSTITUTIONAL CONVENTION

THE delegates to the Constitutional Convention in Philadelphia (May–September 1787) abandoned their stated purpose of revision, and instead crafted a new instrument of government. Meeting in secret, with George Washington (1732–99) serving as the convention president, the delegates sought a compromise between letting the people rule and avoiding the rule of the "mob." The greatest areas of debate were on population determination, appropriation of taxes, and representation. The final document provided for a government with executive, legislative, and judicial branches, each having powers to "check" and "balance" the others. Ratified by the states in 1787, the Constitution provides guidelines for governmental power, stability in trade and commerce, and reflects the lessons learned under the weaker Articles. By achieving the goals laid out in the Declaration of Independence (1776), it fully completed the American Revolution.

▲ *Alexander Hamilton, first Secretary of the Treasury, who introduced financial reforms in the 1790s*

1790   HAMILTON'S FINANCIAL PROGRAM

THE first Secretary of the Treasury, Alexander Hamilton (1757–1804) outlined a national financial program in three reports to Congress between January 1790 and December 1791. First, he called for the funding of the $54 million federal debt and the assumption of the $21 million state debt. Second, he proposed an excise tax on distilled spirits to set a precedent for such revenue generating taxes in the future, and further proposed the creation of a national bank to serve as a centerpiece of government finance. Finally, he called for a protective tariff on imports to foster developing American industries and to reduce their European competition.

1791   BILL OF RIGHTS

IN 1791, the first 10 amendments to the Constitution, the Bill of Rights, went into effect. Amendments one through nine deal with specific rights. For instance, the first protects freedom of speech, press, and religion; the fourth

The Bill of Rights, which was adopted in 1791 ▶

guards against unreasonable search and seizure; the fifth against self-incrimination; and the sixth guarantees the right of counsel, trial by jury, and speedy and public trials. The tenth came almost exclusively from the Articles of Confederation: "The powers not delegated to the United States by the Constitution, nor prohibited by it to the States, are reserved to the States respectively, or to the people."

1800s   A GROWING ECONOMY

FROM 1770 to 1800, the ratio of the value of items exported by the United States to that of the gross national product fell from a fifth to a tenth. From the 1830s to the eve of the Civil War, it amounted to only six percent. These figures point to a domestic economy whose importance outstripped that of international commerce. On the home market, the growth of cities and the specialization of farms contributed significantly to this change. The growth of foreign trade was explosive, however. In the early 1790s, the annual figure hovered around $22 million, while in 1800 the numbers reached $81 million. Merchandise imports grew from $30 million annually in the 1790s to $360 million by 1860. Foreign commerce financed much of American development, except for a period of depression from 1837 to 1844. In the 1850s, however, a renewed economic boom in America encouraged new foreign investment totaling $190 million.

1800   JUDICIAL REVIEW

IN 1800, John Marshall (1755–1835) became Chief Justice of the Supreme Court. Under his leadership, a number of decisions strengthened the power of the central government over that of the states. In *Marbury v. Madison* (1803), the court established its powers of judicial review to judge the constitutionality of national and state laws and of decisions made by lower courts. In *McCulloch v. Maryland* (1819) it denied the power of a state to tax a federal entity, and in *Gibbons v. Ogden* (1824) affirmed the power of Congress to regulate interstate commerce.

1803   LOUISIANA PURCHASE

IN the Louisiana Purchase of 1803, the United States doubled its territories, acquiring the lands west of the Mississippi River from France for $11 ⅓ million. President Thomas Jefferson (1743–1826) dispatched an expedition led by Meriwether Lewis and William Clark to explore and map the new region, an undertaking that took place in 1804–06. A Shoshone woman, Sackajawea, served as a valuable interpreter and guide as they moved through present-day North Dakota, Montana, Idaho, Washington, and Oregon.

1812   TECUMSEH

PROBLEMS with Native American resistance continued in varying intensity as the United States' boundary continued to move westward. The Shawnee chief Tecumseh (1768–1813) attempted to unite tribes from Canada to Florida before and during the War of 1812. Osceola (*c.* 1804–38) led an uprising of Florida Seminoles following the passage of the 1830 Indian Removal Act. Cochise (*c.* 1812–74), a Chiricahua Apache born in Arizona, raided outposts and settlements from the 1850s until his capture in 1871.

The Shawnee chief, Tecumseh, who attempted to unite the Canadian tribes against the colonists ▶

1812   WAR OF 1812

FROM the earliest days of its independenence, America experienced problems with Britain and France failing to recognize American rights as a neutral carrier. Caught up in the series of wars following the French Revolution (1789) and culminating in the Napoleonic Wars (1803–15), the Europeans tried to bring the United States into the fighting. This situation led President James Madison (the fourth president) to declare war on the British on June 1, 1812. The War of 1812, opposed in New England, and fostered by the designs of many Americans to gain land in Canada and Florida, was ended by the Treaty of Ghent in 1814. The war created a sense of national unity and accomplishment for the United States, mainly based on the victory of General Andrew Jackson against British forces at New Orleans.

▲ *George Washington, first president of the United States*

1816   KING COTTON

FARM products dominated early American exports, with cotton quickly becoming the dominant crop. Between 1816–20 cotton accounted for two-fifths of exported items; after 1820, half to two-thirds. English and New York capitalists loaned money to southern plantation owners to expand their fields and to buy more slaves. This further encouraged Southerners to specialize in cotton, to the detriment of the economic diversification of their region.

Finished manufactured goods comprised more than half of all imported materials into America in the period 1820–60. Factories developed in New England and the mid-Atlantic States, supplanting the small cottage shops in textile and shoe production. Most of these goods were traded domestically in the South, Midwest, and West. Exported finished goods slowly increased, reaching a 20th of the total figure by 1820 and an eighth by 1850.

1817   FURTHER DEFINING U.S. BOUNDARIES

THE boundaries of the United States were further defined and expanded in three agreements. The 1817 Rush–Bagot Agreement demilitarized the border with Canada and set limits on the number of naval vessels on the Great Lakes. The Convention of 1818 defined the portion of the U.S./Canada border between the Lake of the Woods in Minnesota to the Rocky Mountains, as the 49th Parallel. The Adams–Onis Treaty (1819) secured the purchase of Florida from the Spanish, and defined the boundaries of the Louisiana Purchase.

1817   ABOLITION OF SLAVERY

VARYING degrees of thought characterized the American movement to secure the abolition of slavery. Some favored gradual emancipation and colonization, with monetary compensation for the former owners; the American Colonization Society was created in 1817 in support of this position. Moderate abolitionists appealed to the conscience of slave owners, and formed the Liberty Party in the mid-1840s. "True" or "radical" abolitionists advocated slave flight, rebellion, or any other means necessary to achieve immediate emancipation. Their leader was William Lloyd Garrison, publisher of the Boston journal *The Liberator* and founder of the American Anti-Slavery Society (1833).

▲ *Slaves working on the sugar plantations*

1820   MISSOURI COMPROMISE 🐾🗺️

MISSOURI'S petition for statehood generated the first nationwide debate over the extension of slavery. The issue was settled by the 1820 Missouri Compromise, in which Missouri gained admittance as a slave state, the Maine district of Massachusetts came into the Union as a free state (preserving an equal balance in Congress), and the southern boundary of Missouri (the 36–30 Line) became the dividing mark for the westward extension of slavery. Slavery north of the line was forbidden except in Missouri itself.

1827   MORMONS ☥

THE Church of Jesus Christ of the Latter Day Saints—whose followers are known as Mormons—was founded by Joseph Smith (1805–84), following a vision in which he was shown the *Book of Mormon* in 1827. The original book was supposedly written in an American Indian language on golden plates buried under his parents' farm. He published a translation in 1830, and declared himself the priest of the new church. The *Book of Mormon* was not intended to supplement the Bible.

Smith was killed by opponents in 1844, and eventually Smith's supporters were driven out of several states. They were led by Brigham Young (1805–77) to Utah, where they founded a community at Salt Lake City.

The Mormon temple at Salt Lake City, Utah ▶

1829 NEW DEMOCRACY

AFTER 1829, a new sense of democracy began to permeate American political thought. Known as the New Democracy, the movement believed that for a country to have true self-government, wide citizen participation was necessary. Social divisions began to melt away under the influence of the movement, and it became possible for self-made men, like Andrew Jackson (1767–1845), to rise to positions of power. As new states entered the Union their constitutions contained fewer and fewer restrictions on the franchise so that more adult, free males could vote, regardless of their economic status. The political process began to be tailored to have greater appeal to the masses, with candidates staging barbecues and parties and using campaign paraphernalia such as buttons and ribbons.

1830 INDIAN REMOVAL

IN 1830, Congress approved the Indian Removal Act and by 1835, 94 removal treaties had been negotiated. The Cherokee fought removal in two Supreme Court cases. *Cherokee Nation v. Georgia* (1831) ruled the court had no jurisdiction over a "domestic dependent nation." In *Worcester v. Georgia* (1832), the court declared the Cherokee "a distinct political community" within which state law had no force. Both state authorities and President Andrew Jackson, however, showed no signs of honoring the decisions, leading the Cherokee to capitulate and sign a treaty in 1835. They departed for the Indian Territory in 1838, followed by the Choctaws, Chickasaws, Creeks, and Seminoles. So many of them died on this harsh journey that it became known as the Trail of Tears.

1840s TRANSCENDENTALISM

RALPH Waldo Emerson (1803–82), with his colleague Henry David Thoreau (1817–62), initiated a philosophical and literary movement, known as American Transcendentalism, which drew upon the teachings of the *Bhagavad Gita* and other Eastern texts to provide a basis for experiencing the divine in the natural world. The basis of their belief was the oneness of life in all its forms. Despite its

◄ Seminole chief Osceola refused to sign the treaty confining his people to certain territories

somewhat exotic origins, the movement's values, such as self-reliance and simple living, fitted well with American society. Unitarianism, a religious movement in New England in the 1840s, laid the groundwork for American Transcendentalism. Unitarians believed religion functioned to free individuals to use their reason to discover saving truth beyond the confines of organized worship.

1845   MEXICAN CESSION

IN 1845, the United States government annexed Texas. Because the border between Texas and Mexico had never been defined, conflicting claims led to war between the United States and Mexico (1846–48), which resulted in the United States acquiring California and the lands in between. The Mexican Cession covered half a million square miles, including the present states of California and Utah, and parts of New Mexico, Arizona, Colorado and Wyoming. In 1853 the Gadsden Purchase, settled a dispute over the southern boundary of the Mexican cession and gained for the United States the southern portions of Arizona and New Mexico, thus completing the continental boundaries of the United States with the exception of Alaska.

1845   MONROE DOCTRINE

LATE in 1845, President James Polk (1795–1849) offered the British a compromise to end the joint occupation of the Oregon Territory. Polk offered to divide the holdings at the 49th parallel. When the British refused, Polk used the 1823 Monroe Doctrine, stating America's opposition to any further interference of the Old World in the New, to declare Oregon under the control of the United States. This arrangement was formalized in the 1846 Oregon Treaty.

1845   MANIFEST DESTINY

IN 1845, John Louis O'Sullivan, editor of *United States Magazine and Democratic Review*, coined the phrase "manifest destiny" to describe the tremendous movement westward then occurring in America. The expansion was a matter of national fate, seen as part of a divine process because of the superiority of the United States.

1848 CALIFORNIA GOLD RUSH

JAMES Marshall discovered gold while building a mill on the banks of the Sacramento River in California, in 1848. Within a year, thousands of people, gripped by gold fever, were rushing to California from as far afield as Europe, in the hope of making their fortunes.

▲ *Gold prospectors became known as "forty-niners", after the year in which the gold rush started*

1854 KANSAS AND NEBRASKA

IN 1854, Stephen A. Douglas, a Congressman from Illinois, proposed an act to create Kansas and Nebraska as territories, with government and constitutions arrived at by popular sovereignty, allowing the voters of each region to decide if it would be free or slave. The resulting controversy aided the emergence of the new Republican party and led to open fighting in Kansas where slave and free elements resorted to violence as they attempted to arrive at a constitution.

1857 DRED SCOTT CASE

THE growing sectional crisis in America over the question of the extension of slavery into the western territories was worsened in 1857 with the Supreme Court ruling in *Dred Scott v. Sanford*. Speaking for the majority, Chief Justice Roger Taney argued that no black, slave or free, was a citizen of the United States, and therefore was not entitled to any protections or liberties granted by the constitution and could "be reduced to slavery for their benefit."

▲ *Roger Taney, the judge in the Dred Scott case*

The decision also denied to Congress the right to prohibit the extension of slavery into the western territories.

1860 SOUTHERN SECESSION

WHEN Republican Abraham Lincoln (1809–65), an opponent of the extension of slavery into the western territories, was elected president, seven southern states seceded from the Union, beginning with South Carolina in December 1860 and ending with Texas in February 1861. The other five states were Alabama, Mississippi, Florida, Georgia, and Louisiana. In 1861, in Montgomery, Alabama, they formed the Confederate States of America, with Jefferson Davis as president.

Republican president Abraham Lincoln, whose election led to the Civil War ▶

1861 UNDERGROUND RAILROAD 🏛

HARRIET Tubman (1820–1913), a former slave who had escaped along a secret route of hiding places known as the "underground railroad," resolved to help others and returned countless times to the South, becoming the railroad's most famous "conductor." Between 1850 and 1861, she rescued more than 300 slaves. During the Civil War (1861–65), she served as a nurse, laundress, and spy for the Union army.

▲ *Fugitive slaves fleeing from Maryland by means of the "underground railroad"*

Not all slaves were sold to brutal masters who extracted maximum labor through threats, punishments, deprivation, and torture. But even in households where they were well treated, the lowly position of slaves was never in doubt. They lived in rough huts, ate plain, cheap food and worked long hours. The cruel master, however, was far too common. Slaves were flogged, starved, and grossly overworked, and could be killed by their masters—even, most sadistically, by being blown up with sticks of gunpowder. On recapture, escaped slaves could have their toes chopped off so they could not escape again.

1861 FORT SUMTER 🗡

ON April 12, 1861 Confederate General P. G. T. Beauregard fired on federal ships attempting to supply Fort Sumter in Charleston, South Carolina. The next day President Abraham Lincoln called out the troops. On April 17, Virginia left the Union followed in the next five weeks by Arkansas, Tennessee, and North Carolina.

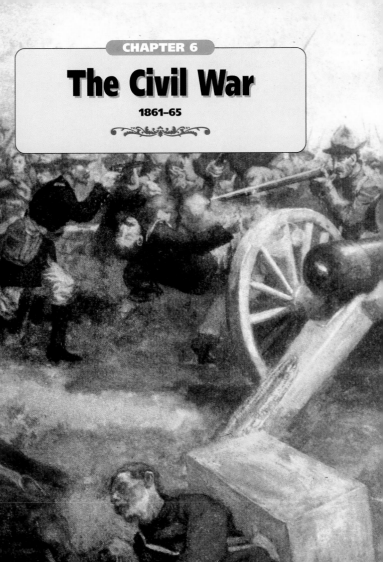

1861   THE TWO PRESIDENTS

ABRAHAM Lincoln and Jefferson Davis faced unique problems as the leaders of their respective nations. Lincoln was in the position of preserving the United States, Davis of creating the Confederate States. Although Lincoln faced problems with increasingly Radical Republicans in Congress, Davis discovered first hand how a states' rights emphasis could cripple a national government. Although there were no Southern political parties, pro- and anti-Davis factions existed. The Confederate president did not have a strong relationship with his Congress; during the war he vetoed 39 bills to Lincoln's three. Maintaining social unity was also a problem, as the bulk of Southerners, who were yeoman farmers rather than wealthy planters, perceived the conflict as "a rich man's war and a poor man's fight."

▲ *Jefferson Davis, leader of the Confederacy during the Civil War*

1861   UNION STRATEGIC GOALS

PRESIDENT Abraham Lincoln refused to use the term "Confederacy," or to acknowledge that the Southern states had left the Union. His major war goal was to preserve the governmental and territorial integrity of the United States while restoring the Union of 1861 by suppressing the Southern insurrection. Military force kept the border states of Maryland, Missouri, and Kentucky in the Union, but it soon became obvious that nothing short of military conquest would bring the remainder of the Confederacy back into the national fold. In the spring of 1862, Northern troops occupied 50,000 square miles in Tennessee and the lower Mississippi Valley. When these victories, however, brought Southerners no closer to capitulation, the Union (Federal) generals realized the Confederate armies would have to be destroyed. In 1863, Ulysses S. Grant captured one army at Vicksburg, Mississippi, and crippled another at Chattanooga, Tennessee. In Pennsylvania, the Confederate general Robert E. Lee suffered a terrible defeat at the July 4, 1863 Battle of Gettysburg. The final phase of the Union assault on the Confederacy was to take the war to the homefront, a tactic best employed by the hated Northern general William T. Sherman, who marched through Georgia and South Carolina in 1864 and 1865, destroying everything in his path.

◀ *Confederate general Robert E. Lee, who was defeated at Gettysburg*

1861　　FINANCING THE WAR IN THE NORTH

THE Union government financed its war effort through taxes, loans, and the printing of paper money. In 1861, the Internal Revenue Act placed a three percent tax on incomes of more than $800, a law which remained in force until 1872. In addition, $450 million in "greenbacks" were printed and circulated. Nothing more than the success of the federal government backed these bills, intended as a temporary wartime measure. At the end of the war, the greenbacks were worth 67 cents on the dollar. When Americans refused to turn the inflated bills in to the government, it laid the foundations of the currency controversies that would mark American political debate for the remainder of the 19th century.

Efficiency became the by-word of the wartime manufacturers in the North. By 1863, Northern factories and farms produced adequate goods to support and feed the army without working any hardships on the civilian population. The Republicans encouraged and promoted industrial growth and increased the role

of the federal government in the economy. Industry benefited from higher tariffs in 1862 and 1864, and the government granted land and money subsidies to railroad companies in the Pacific Railroad Acts of 1862 and 1864.

◀ *The railroad joins the east and west coasts of the country*

1861 CONFEDERATE STRATEGIC GOALS

THE Confederacy's goal in the Civil War was to defend both its political existence and its 6,000-mile border. Initially, contingents of troops were scattered at as many points as possible to defend against invasion from any angle. In part, this dispersal was a military by-product of the states' rights emphasis of the entire Confederate experiment. Regiments recruited locally, though incorporated into the Confederate army, were still controlled by the governors of the states in which they originated. Some governors, like those in South Carolina and Arkansas, did not want to send their troops away, leaving their home states defenseless in the event of an invasion. Although unwise for a country with limited resources, President Jefferson Davis and his generals could never completely abandon such a dispersed defensive war.

1861 FINANCING THE WAR IN THE SOUTH

THE Confederate government worked with extremely limited financial resources during its brief existence. Only some $27 million in hard currency was available in the southern states, with the bulk of Confederate wealth tied up in land and cotton. The Union blockade of southern ports gradually eliminated foreign trade and drained away the meager monetary reserve. Attempts at bond drives and other public loan measures proved unsatisfactory, as did efforts to collect income and profit taxes. When the government gave in to the temptation to print paper money, high inflation followed. By 1864, the Confederacy had printed $1 billion in bills with no backing in precious metal. In 1863, the Confederate dollar was worth eight cents in gold. Prices skyrocketed accordingly, with cigars selling for $10, a yard of cloth at $125, a pound of beef at $5, and a barrel of flour at $300. Appropriation of private produce, machinery, and livestock provided only minor relief for the armies in the field. Southern soldiers often marched barefoot, went hungry, and wore captured Union uniforms dyed brown.

1861   CONFEDERATE TROOP MOVEMENTS

DESPITE the characteristic dispersal of Confederate troops, generals made superior use of interior lines of communication to move men and material to spots where they could accomplish the maximum good. In July 1861, for instance, Joseph Johnston brought his force from Winchester, Virginia to Manassas Junction where they joined P. G. T. Beauregard's men in victory at the Battle of Manassas. Likewise Robert E. Lee summoned Thomas J. (Stonewall) Jackson from the Shenandoah Valley in June 1862. Jackson, fighting with Lee's Army of Northern Virginia, drove Union forces away from the Confederate capital at Richmond. Such rapid troop movements followed by an attack were known to Confederate strategists as the "offensive–defensive."

The Confederate naval battery at Manassas in Virginia ▶

1861   CLARA BARTON ☖

AT the outbreak of the Civil War, Clara Barton (1821–1912) of Massachusetts saw the need for an organization apart from the War Department and U.S. Sanitary Commission, to distribute food and medical supplies to the troops in the field. Her efforts at battlefields like Antietam and Fredericksburg in Virginia, won her the love and appreciation of the fighting men. The end of the war found her helping to sort out the identities of missing and captured persons, as well as those who lay in unmarked graves. She spent the next 17 years of her life lobbying for the creation of an American Branch of the Red Cross, which came about in 1882.

1861   THE SOUTHERN "CAUSE" ☖

SOUTHERNERS began the war with great optimism, fueled in part by the resignations of a number of high-ranking officers in the United States Army to accept Confederate commissions. The purpose of the war was euphemistically referred to as "The Cause," meaning the Southern assertion of its states' rights political philosophy. At the war's end that would become transmuted into the "Lost Cause," a near cult of regret and nostalgia that affected elements of Southern culture well into modern times.

1862   ESPIONAGE ☖

ESPIONAGE during the Civil War was more a matter of personal flamboyance than of organized activity. One well-known spy, Belle Boyd, was only 17 when Federal troops invaded her home; angered and traumatized by this experience, she became an active supporter of the Confederacy, for which she not only spied but committed murder. She was arrested several times between 1862 and 1864, but on one occasion received a pardon from President Abraham Lincoln and on another escaped retribution by marrying her jailer.

Abraham Lincoln adopted an
emancipation policy in 1862 ▶

1862 EMANCIPATION POLICY

PRESIDENT Abraham Lincoln's adoption of an emancipation policy in 1862, freeing slaves in regions occupied by Union forces, had a dual purpose. First, Lincoln was attempting to preserve his position in the Republican Party, which was increasingly coming to be dominated by radical elements, and to protect his chances for reelection in 1864. In addition, the policy aimed at uprooting the Southern labor force and transferring it into Union fighting units. By 1863, several hundred thousand slaves had been freed within Union lines, and ultimately 180,000 were recruited into the Union army.

1862 CONFEDERATE INTERNATIONAL RELATIONS

THE Confederacy worked throughout the war to gain diplomatic recognition and materials from European powers. The greatest prize would have been an alliance with England— one that never developed despite the fact that Southern plantations supplied 80 percent of the raw cotton used in Britain's mills. In the summer of 1862 when Confederate forces were on the offensive, Britain and France discussed a joint proposal to mediate a peace on the basis of Confederate independence, planning to recognize the Confederacy if the Lincoln administration rejected the offer. When the Union army turned the vastly outnumbered Southerners back at the indecisive battles of Antietam and Perryville, however, Britain dropped the offer. This was the closest the South would ever come to gaining the diplomatic recognition of a European nation.

1862   CONSCRIPTION

BOTH the North and the South resorted to conscription to maintain fighting numbers. The Southern draft began in 1862, and eventually applied to all males between 17 and 50. Of the one million Confederate soldiers, 21 percent had been drafted. In the North, Congress adopted the conscription of males between 20 and 45 in 1863. Those selected had the option of paying a replacement or paying a $300 commutation fee to the government (the latter option was eliminated in 1864). Four Northern drafts produced 46,000 conscripts and 118,000 substitutes for some 2–6 percent of the Union army's manpower total (2.1 million).

▼ *Soldiers from both sides were being conscripted into the armies by 1862*

1862 CHAPLAINS

AT the beginning of the war, neither side had a clearly defined policy regarding the appointment of and role of chaplains in the armies. Union regimental commanders had the authority to appoint a chaplain as long as he individual was an ordained minister in one of the Christian sects. Initially, most chaplains were Protestant or Catholic. The first Jewish chaplain was appointed in September 1862 after a year-long debate in Congress.

Union chaplains received $100 a month, and were required to report on the moral and religious state of the troops. In April 1864, the responsibility to hold regular church services was added to their duties. In actual fact, chaplains worked at those things where they seemed to be able to contribute the most to the welfare of their men. They foraged for goods and supplies, elicited donations from congregations on the home front, defended enlisted men at courts-martial, served as correspondents for hometown newspapers, escorted the wounded home, wrote to families, and delivered mail. Since most chaplains served with regiments raised from their own communities, they had close ties with the men and with their loved ones back at home. Records indicate that 2,300 chaplains served with the Union army. At least 66 died in service, and three were awarded the Medal of Honor.

1862 RELIGION IN THE SOUTH

IN general, it is fair to say Southern units were more religious than northern. Confederate commanders made greater efforts to recruit chaplains for their units, but there was a chronic shortage during the war, in part because their pay was so low. In May 1861, their salary was set at $85 a month, but was cut to $50 three weeks later. Another reason for the shortage was that Southern ministers preferred to serve in the ranks. Southern soldiers judged their chaplains by their vigorous and regular preaching. Home congregations supported chaplains who formed associations and worked together to make sure units had a minister. Jews were not excluded from serving, but there is no record of any having done so. About 600 chaplains served with the Confederate army; 25 died in service and 14 in battle.

1863   BRITISH OBSERVER

DESPITE England's failure to recognize the Confederate government, the British maintained an interest in the fortunes of the South. When General Robert E. Lee's Army of Northern Virginia moved into Pennsylvania, bound for its fateful confrontation with the Union army at Gettysburg (July 1863), a British observer, Lieutenant Colonel Arthur Fremantle, accompanied the troops.

Fremantle remained in the Confederacy for three months, and the diary he kept and the book he wrote after the war provide excellent first-hand insights into life in the Confederate army. At Gettysburg on July 2 he wrote in his diary, "When the Cannonade was at its height a Confederate band of music, between the cemetery and ourselves, began to play polkas and waltzes, which sounds curious accompanied by the hissing and bursting of the shells."

◀ *General Lee, who suffered a massive defeat at Gettysburg*

1863   CONFEDERATE NAVAL SUCCESSES

CONFEDERATE agents contracted with private British shipyards to build warships with which to oppose the Northern blockade although such arrangements were a violation of British neutrality laws. Two vessels constructed in this manner, the *C.S.S. Alabama* and the *C.S.S. Florida*, sank or captured nearly 100 American merchant vessels. In 1863, the Laird shipyards constructed two iron-clad ships outfitted with seven-foot iron ramming spikes that would have undoubtedly served the Confederacy well and constituted a serious breach of British neutrality had the British government not seized them just as they were to put to sea.

1863   RIFLED MUSKETS

THE development of rifled muskets in the 1850s gave an infantryman a firing range of 400–500 yards, with sharpshooters able to achieve accuracy at even

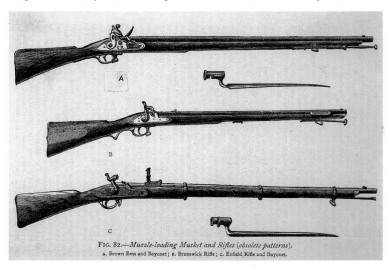

FIG. 82.—*Muzzle-loading Musket and Rifles (obsolete patterns).*
A. Brown Bess and Bayonet; B. Brunswick Rifle; C. Enfield Rifle and Bayonet.

▲ *Muzzle loading musket and rifles, an advance in weaponry used during the Civil War* greater distances. By 1863, Civil War soldiers were abandoning the Napoleonic Era tactics of close-order assaults for the greater protection offered by entrenched positions. In the face of enemy fire, the heroic cavalry assault became suicidal for man and horse. Other innovations included ironclad ships, observation balloons, and wire entanglements.

1864   GATLING GUN ☢

THE Civil War either drew scientists into military service, distracting them from their work or redirecting their efforts toward military applications. For instance, the Gatling Gun, a multiple-barrel, revolving machine gun, was first used by Union General Benjamin F. Butler at the siege of Petersburg, Virginia (1864–65). The weapon's inventor, Dr. Richard Jordan Gatling, sold machine guns to the Union army, but also belonged to the Order of American Knights, a secret society that supported the Confederacy.

◄ *The Gatling Gun, which was first used by the Federal army*

1864   SAND CREEK MASSACRE

THOUGH fully occupied with fighting the Civil War, President Lincoln still faced problems in relations with Native Americans. In 1864, the Cheyenne chief, Black Kettle, began moving a band of 500 natives through the Colorado Territory on the government's promise of safe conduct, only to be attacked at Sand Creek by Colonel J. M. Chivington's militia. The troops entered Black Kettle's camp where the American flag and a white flag of truce both flew, slaughtering 170 women and children. After the battle, Chivington, a former Methodist minister, displayed a personal collection of a hundred scalps.

1865   RAILROADS AND COMMUNICATION

THE Civil War was the first conflict in which railroads played a major role. In 1860, the national rail network stretched to 30,000 miles. As in other key areas, the South lagged behind seriously in equipment, track, and personnel; in addition, the intense fighting in the southern states put what railroads that did exist in a state of near complete destruction by 1865.

▲ *Fighting around the railroads in the South caused them extensive damage*

Journalists during the Civil War made use of telegraph lines to file their reports on battles more quickly than at any other time in the past. Newspapers and periodicals had wide readerships and millions of Americans followed the details of the fighting in the articles and woodblock prints contained in the pages of *Harper's Weekly* and *Frank Leslie's Illustrated Newspaper*.

1865   SURRENDER AT APPOMATTOX

BY March 1865, the Confederate army was stretched to a thin 1,000 men per mile. On April 2, General Robert E. Lee abandoned the capital of Richmond, Virginia and began a retreat south. He met with Union General Ulysses S. Grant on the morning of April 9 in the parlor of the McLean home at Appomattox, Virginia; his surrender came four years to the day after the decision had been made to shell Fort Sumter, the action which began the war. The Confederate President Jefferson Davis was captured in Georgia on May 10.

1865   CONSTITUTIONAL AMENDMENTS

TWO amendments were added to the Constitution as a result of the Civil War: the 13th Amendment (December 18, 1865) abolished slavery and the 14th (July 28, 1868) forbade any state to abridge the privileges and immunities of a citizen or to deprive them of life, liberty, property, or due process of law. The acceptance of both amendments became a condition for the readmittance of the former Confederate states to the Union.

1865   RAMIFICATIONS OF THE WAR

THOUGH a bloody conflict that killed more than 620,000 Americans, the Civil War proved that the republic could survive in a world of monarchs and dictators without collapsing under the weight of civil strife. The war came as a climax to a long series of quarrels between the North and South over constitutional interpretation. In general, the North favored a loose interpretation that would grant the federal government extended powers. The South wanted to reserve all undefined powers to the individual states. The war further settled the issue of slavery, which the Founding Fathers had not addressed in crafting the Constitution (1787). In abolishing the "peculiar institution," the war freed 4 million slaves. It did not, however, define the parameters of their freedom and citizenship, thus setting in motion bitter civil rights struggles that would plague the United States into modern times.

◀ *Military leader Ulysses S. Grant*

CHAPTER 7

Reconstruction, Invention, and Industry

1865–1914

1865   LINCOLN ASSASSINATION

PRESIDENT Abraham Lincoln and his wife Mary attended the play *Our American Cousin* at Ford's Theater in Washington, D.C. on April 14, 1865. During the third act, the actor John Wilkes Booth entered their box, put a pistol to Lincoln's head, and fired. Booth, a Confederate sympathizer, escaped. The mortally injured Lincoln was taken to a boarding house across the street, where he died the following morning—becoming the first American president to be assassinated. The former Tennessee governor, Andrew Johnson (1808–74) succeeded him in office.

▼ *President Lincoln was assassinated while attending a play with his wife at Ford's Theater*

1865   RECONSTRUCTION

RECONSTRUCTION, the controversial period following the Civil War, lasted from 1865 through 1877 and was to be, in part, a social transitional vehicle for the freed slaves. Lincoln had favored a moderate plan for reconstruction, but was assassinated before it could be set in motion. Radical Republicans in Congress wanted a more stringent program, requiring a loyalty oath before a constitutional convention could be called and a state could begin the readmission process. After Lincoln's assassination, the newly appointed Democrat president, Andrew Johnson worked to prevent the planter class from regaining power, but made no efforts to guarantee their civil rights. Congress refused to accept the Southern governments thus organized, opening the first round in a battle between Johnson and Congress that would end with his impeachment. In 1868, Johnson escaped removal from office by just one vote.

1865 WORLD TECHNOLOGICAL LEADER ☢

THE United States became a world technological leader after the Civil War. Thomas A. Edison (1847–1931) registered more than 1,000 patents for devices, including the quadruplex telegraph, carbon-button telephone transmitter, phonograph, electric light, and an electrical generation and distribution system. Alexander Graham Bell (1847–1922) patented the telephone in March 1876. The achievements of both Edison and Bell produced devices regarded as household necessities by the end of the 19th century.

▲ *Thomas Edison's inventions saw the rise of the U.S. as a world leader in technology*

1865 INSULAR EXPANSION

AMERICA engaged in strategic insular, or island, expansion in the second half of the nineteenth century. This was inspired by the "New Navy" crowd, the students of Alfred Thayer Mahan at the United States Naval Academy. Mahan developed Napoleonic tactics for sea battles and argued that in an industrial age, markets must be found abroad for surplus American products. Once these markets were found, the merchant marine fleet would require the protection of a capable navy. As a result of this, the expansion involved the construction of island stations for fuel and repair yards.

1867 CONGRESSIONAL RECONSTRUCTION

AFTER 1867, Congress passed a series of Reconstruction laws treating the former Confederate states as conquered provinces. The states were divided into military districts under military governors who called a constitutional convention when a majority of voters had taken the loyalty oath. All new state constitutions were required to ratify the 13th Amendment abolishing slavery, and the 14th forbidding any state to abridge the privileges and immunities of a citizen or to deprive them of life, liberty, property, or due process of law. Meanwhile

Southerners, hostile to military Reconstruction, applied the derogatory term "carpetbaggers" to all Northerners who entered the South after the Civil War. Southerners who worked with the Northerners after the war were referred to as "scalawags."

1867 CONFINING THE NATIVES

QUANAH Parker, the last Comanche chief, the son of a Comanche chief and a captured white girl, Cynthia Ann Parker, was born around 1845. Refusing to accept the 1867 Treaty of Medicine Lodge, which

◀ *The last Comanche chief, Quanah Parker*

▲ *The Battle of Little Bighorn*

confined the southern Plains Indians to a reservation, Quanah and his band raided in Texas and Mexico. The U.S. Army, however, was relentless in its Red River campaign of 1874–75 driving the Indian warriors to exhaustion and near starvation. Quanah surrendered at Fort Sill in Oklahoma on June 2, 1875.

Sitting Bull, a Hunkpapa Sioux, together with tribal chieftans Crazy Horse and Red Cloud, agreed to a Sioux resettlement in the Dakota Black Hills in 1868. Later, however, gold was discovered in the Hills, and the United States government broke the treaty, trying to clear the Sioux of these now-valuable lands. The chiefs led their tribes in an uprising that culminated in the massacre of Colonel George Armstrong Custer and his troops at the Battle of Little Bighorn (June 25, 1876). Custer and all 264 of his soldiers were killed. Crazy Horse was captured and killed the following year.

1869   TRANSCONTINENTAL RAILROAD

ON May 10, 1869, at Promontory, Utah, the Central Pacific and Union Pacific Railroads met, unifying the coasts of the United States by rail. Construction of the transcontinental line had begun six years earlier. The Central Pacific built eastward from Sacramento, California; the Union Pacific west from Omaha, Nebraska. When completed, the line stretched 1,770 miles.

1869   SOCIAL REFORM

THE women's movement in America fractured in 1869, when Susan B. Anthony and Elizabeth Cady Stanton founded the National Woman Suffrage Association which worked for a women's suffrage amendment to the constitution, but saw the issue as only one among many feminist causes. The American Woman Suffrage Association, founded that same year by Lucy Stone and Julia Ward Howe, focused completely on suffrage as the basic reform that would lead to all others.

By 1900, African-Americans caught the spirit of progressive reform. A black college professor, W. E. B. Du Bois, believed a "talented tenth" of the black population would instill a sense of confidence in their people and lead the way in tearing down restrictive barriers imposed by white society. In 1909, he founded the National Association for the Advancement of Colored People (NAACP).

◀ *Women's suffrage saw a rise at the end of the 19th century, and they eventually won the vote in 1920*

1870   FREE SILVER

DURING 1870–90, American silver production quadrupled with the opening of huge silver mines in Nevada. European nations turned to the more scarce, and thus more valuable, gold. In the United States, the official monetary position was bimetalism, but the use of silver was extremely limited. Silver advocates, many of them the owners of the Western mines, clamored for the free and unlimited coinage of silver at a ratio of 16 to 1 with gold, known as the "free silver" movement.

1875   HAWAII

THE greatest prize of America's insular expansion was Hawaii. In the 1820s New England missionaries moved into the islands and established a presence large enough that, when Britain showed an interest in 1842, the United States claimed Hawaii fell under the protection of the Monroe Doctrine. After 1875, an American plantation elite dominated the population and, in 1893, staged a bloodless revolution. The United States annexed the islands as a U.S. territory on July 7, 1898.

1877   COMPROMISE OF 1877

RECONSTRUCTION ended in all the southern states with the Compromise of 1877, which settled the disputed presidential election of 1876. During this election, conflicting sets of returns came in from the three states still under Reconstruction law. An electoral commission of eight Republicans and seven Democrats decided the election in favor of the Republican Rutherford B. Hayes, over Democrat Samuel Tillman, in exchange for the withdrawal of federal troops from the South.

1880s–90s INDUSTRIAL REVOLUTION

IN the 1880s and 1890s, the Industrial Revolution transformed American society. In 1859, the gross national product totaled $2 billion, a figure that rose to $9.1 billion in 1870, $13 billion in 1899, and $37 billion in 1900. The value of American exports rocketed from $858 million in 1870 to $1.4 billion in 1900.

In 1882, John D. Rockefeller formed one of the first and largest trusts in America, Standard Oil. Seventy-seven companies transferred the majority of their stock to a nine-member board of trustees solidly under Rockefeller's control. By the mid-1880s, Standard Oil controlled 90 percent of American oil production.

▲ *The Rockefeller dynasty; John D. Rockefeller was known as "the Oil King"*

1885   GERONIMO

GERONIMO (1829–1909), chief of the Chiricahua Apache, fought federal troops and settlers in southeast Arizona and New Mexico from 1875–85 when he surrendered and was incarcerated in Florida for two years. After a short stay in Alabama, he was moved to Fort Sill, Oklahoma in 1895, where he spent the last 14 years of his life. A popular attraction at the Exposition in Omaha in 1898, the Pan-American Exposition in Buffalo in 1901, the St. Louis World's Fair in 1904, and Theodore Roosevelt's inaugural parade in 1905, Geronimo was never allowed to return to Arizona. On a cold night in his 80th year, he fell from his horse in an alcoholic stupor, spent several hours on the ground, contracted pneumonia, and died on February 17, 1909.

◀ *Geronimo, chief of the Chiricahua Apache*

1886   AMERICAN FEDERATION OF LABOR

MARSHALL Field opened the world's first "modern" department store in Chicago in 1879, while the F. W. Woolworth Company store, a chain store, dates from the same year. The mail-order house appeared in the last quarter of the 19th century. All three types of enterprise developed rapidly, encouraged by increasing urbanization and efficient transport systems.

The American Federation of Labor, founded in 1886 by Samuel Gompers, represented the most successful labor union in 19th-century America. The AFL worked for higher wages, shorter hours, and better conditions with only limited use of the strike and the boycott. As long as the workers received just compensation for their labors, the A.F.L. did not oppose trusts or monopolies.

Between 1895 and 1904, America experienced an "Era of Mergers"—in 50 industries, a single holding company controlled 60 percent of the production. These included many names familiar today including DuPont, General Electric, General Foods, Nabisco, and Westinghouse.

1890   WOUNDED KNEE

ON December 29, 1890, at Wounded Knee, North Dakota, an accidental rifle shot caused nervous soldiers to fire into a group of Indians attempting to surrender to authorities. By the time the firing stopped, nearly 200 Indians and some 25 soldiers had been killed. Regarded as the last "battle" of the Indian wars, Wounded Knee offers a characteristic example of the brutality with which Native Americans were treated.

"Buffalo Bill" Cody at the Battle of Wounded Knee ▶

1892 POPULISM ✡

IN 1892, at Omaha, Nebraska, farmers founded the Populist Party. Its manifesto called for expanded government powers to combat oppression; public ownership of transportation and communication services; the free coinage of silver; the secret ballot in national elections; a graduated income tax, direct election of U.S. Senators; and labor reform. In 1892, the Populist candidate James Baird Weaver ran unsuccessfully for the presidency and, in 1896, William Jennings Bryan did the same. Populist influence dwindled after 1896, but modern politicians have often appropriated the term in an effort to describe themselves as candidates of the people. Classic Populism, however, was a retrogressive movement that sought to turn America back to the days of the Jeffersonian citizen farmer.

1893 TURNER'S FRONTIER THESIS ✡

AT the 1893 American Historical Association meeting, Frederick Jackson Turner read a paper based on the 1890 census, "The Significance of the Frontier in American History." He redefined the study of American history for the next 100 years, writing, "The existence of an area of free land, its continuous recession, and the advance of American settlement westward, explain American development."

1898   SPANISH–AMERICAN WAR

AMERICAN business interests in Spanish-held Cuba and Puerto Rico led the U.S. to declare war on Spain on April 19, 1898, a decision spurred on by the February 15 explosion of the *U.S.S. Maine* in Havana Harbor, killing 260 American sailors. The Spanish-American War lasted from April to August 1898. More than 5,000 men died, but only 379 of those in battle; the remainder succumbed to disease.

During the Spanish-American War, the United States gained the Philippine Islands and subsequently fought a three-year war with the Filipino people who wished to gain their independence. In this little-known war the Americans lost 4,300 people, the Filipinos 57,000. The Philippines became an American territory in 1902 and the islands' independence was recognized in 1946.

▲ *A gun-deck during the bombardment of Santiago*
◀ *The Spanish intercepting a merchant ship during the Spanish American War*

1900 SETTLEMENT HOUSES

DEDICATED social reformers combated urban problems by organizing so-called "settlement houses" in the industrial, immigrant neighborhoods, where childcare, health clinics, adult education, and cultural opportunities were provided. By 1900, more than 100 of these institutions existed. The best known were Hull House in Chicago (1889), founded by Jane Addams and Ellen Starr; South End House in Boston (1891), founded by Robert A. Woods; and Henry Street Settlement in New York (1895), founded by Lillian Wald. Most settlement house workers were idealistic middle-class young people, with college-trained women in the majority.

1900 SOCIAL DARWINISM

THE American social philosopher, Herbert Spencer, coined the phrase "survival of the fittest," and developed Social Darwinism, a corruption of the biological theories of Charles Darwin. Spencer believed the natural social process only failed when an external agent, such as the federal government, intervened. Social Darwinists promoted laissez-faire or non-interventionist economics, and opposed any regulatory or social legislation to better the lot of industrial workers, a class that numbered 3.2 million by 1900.

1901 IMPERIALISM AND THE CONSTITUTION

WHEN America acquired foreign holdings in the 19th century, constitutional questions surfaced and became the focus of an anti-imperialist movement. The controversy culminated in the "insular cases," which reached the Supreme Court between 1901 and 1904. In three cases—*De Lima v. Bidwell, Dooley v. U.S.*, and *Downes v. Bidwell*—the court ruled the constitution did not automatically apply to inhabitants of land acquired by the United States, and therefore they did not possess any privileges of citizenship unless formally conferred by the Congress.

▲ *Cigarette card showing the Panama Canal*

1901   PANAMA CANAL

ONE economically and strategically based foreign policy goal for the United States in the second half of the 19th century was the construction of a canal across the isthmus of Central America, which would allow ships to pass more easily between the Atlantic and Pacific Oceans for commercial and military purposes. Construction did not get underway until the administration of Theodore Roosevelt from 1901–08, though negotiations for the project began as early as 1850.

1903   FLYING MACHINES AND AUTOMOBILES

THE first manned powered flight happened in 1903, when Orville Wright (1871-1948) took to the air at Kittyhawk in North Carolina, in the "Flyer", built by Orville and his brother Wilbur (1867–1912). This earliest "airplane" was propelled by a 12 horse power gasoline engine, and the flight lasted just 12 seconds.

The industrialist Henry Ford (1863–1947) developed design concepts and production techniques that allowed the automobile to explode into American society in the early 20th century. By 1908, his company was producing 10,607 of its famous Model T's annually, at a price of $850 each. The advent of the moving

assembly line and truly interchangeable parts drove the
yearly output to 730,041 in 1916, at $360 each.
Americans registered just 8,000 automobiles in 1900,
but 1.2 million in 1913. Ford introduced a conveyor to
his assembly line for producing the Model T in 1913.
Conveyors subsequently became accepted as key to
achieving optimum efficiency in all kinds of industries.

1904   ROOSEVELT COROLLARY

▲ *Automobile king
Henry Ford*

IN 1904, President Theodore Roosevelt argued that the
United States could only hope to enforce the Monroe
Doctrine by assuming "international police power" to
prevent incidents that might warrant European intervention. This Roosevelt
Corollary to the Monroe Doctrine guided American policy toward South
America until the 1930s.

1907   THE PROGRESSIVE MOVEMENT

THE middle-class social response to post-Civil War industrialization was the
Progressive movement. Its members did not focus on any single issue, but rather
touched on all aspects of social reform and saw increased government regulation
as the greatest tool at their disposal. Progressives tended to be well-educated,
urban-dwelling, middle-class Americans. They were not radicals, but were infused
with a patriotic, nationalist belief in America's potential.

William James, a Harvard psychologist, authored *Pragmatism* (1907), a
book that praised tough-minded people who efficiently tackled problems by
concentrating on the methods which worked and abandoning those that
failed. The successful methods, solidly grounded in experience and common
sense, constituted the truth. *Pragmatism* was a favored book and philosophy
among Progressives, and encouraged their reliance on experts to study and
solve social problems.

▲ *President Theodore Roosevelt*

1908   CONSERVATION 🏛

PRESIDENT Theodore Roosevelt added millions of acres to the national forest system, aided by Gifford Pinchot, the head of the Bureau of the Forestry. Pinchot set up bureaus and commissions manned with geologists, hydrologists, foresters, and engineers. In 1908, a National Conservation Congress resulted in conservation commissions in most states.

1910   IMMIGRATION AND URBANIZATION 🏛

IMMIGRATION swelled the American population and changed its face dramatically during the second half of the 19th century. In 1869, the annual immigration figure was 352,569; this grew so markedly that in 1884 alone over 1.5 million immigrants flooded into the country. Until 1870, immigrants came from Northern and Northwestern Europe, though after 1879, new arrivals were from Southern, Central, and Eastern Europe as well as Asia. These "new" immigrants were considered somehow less acceptable, and faced hostility in the form of nativism and xenophobia.

Industrialization and urbanization went hand in hand in 19th-century America. The new urban society exhibited an unusually diverse cultural and racial mix due to high immigration figures. In 1880, approximately 28 percent of Americans lived in cities; by 1910 this figure had risen to 46 percent.

Immigrants traveling to the U.S. ▶

CHAPTER 8

World War I

1914–20

1914   AN ASSASSINATION IN SERBIA 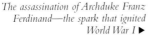

WORLD War I began in Serbia in June 1914, when the heir to the Austro-Hungarian throne, the Archduke Franz Ferdinand, was assassinated, thereby activating an interlocking series of European alliances. Americans reacted with horror at what they considered primitive behaviour by the Europeans. As a result, the government adopted an official position of neutrality.

The French stopped Germany's first land push at the September 1914 Battle of the Marne. Afterward fighting ground down to an agonizing deadlock of trench warfare, in lines that ran from the English Channel to the Swiss border. Any significant gains to be made by either side would be accomplished by their navies.

The assassination of Archduke Franz Ferdinand—the spark that ignited World War I ▶

1914   WARTIME XENOPHOBIA   🏛

THE 1910 census revealed that one in three Americans were foreign born or had foreign-born parents. Of 32 million Americans with strong foreign ties, 10 million came from Germany or Austria-Hungary. Not surprisingly, sentiments in America in regard to the war were mixed, and elements of American society were subject to nativism and xenophobia during the war years. For instance, a mob of 500 stripped a German-American in St. Louis, bound him with an

American flag, and lynched him. Many large universities stopped offering German as a language. Street names in communities with a Germanic heritage were Americanized. Children no longer contracted the German measles, they had the "liberty" measles, just as the family Dachshund became a "liberty" pup.

1914   ALLEGIANCE TO FRANCE   🏛

AMERICAN sentiments rested strongly with the Allied Powers (France, Great Britain, and Russia) during World War I. Germany had an international reputation for aggressive, militaristic, autocratic behavior. America had long since buried its animosities with Great Britain and had warm feelings of loyalty for the French, whose assistance had been invaluable during the American Revolution. In the period of U.S. neutrality before 1917, many young Americans formed private units, such as the Lafayette Escadrille, and volunteered for service in France.

1914   PRO-WAR PROPAGANDA   ✡

DURING World War I, the Committee on Public Information headed by George Creel had the task of mobilizing public opinion. Creel marshaled a massive pro-war propaganda movement. He produced a series of "Hang the Kaiser" films, printed hundreds of thousands of posters, and erected billboards. Over 75,000 pamphlets were printed in various languages and distributed. Finally, the Committee raised an army of 75,000 "Four Minute Men," who were paid to deliver pro-war speeches on street corners.

An allegorical illustration of German victories in Poland ▶

1915　　FREEDOM OF THE SEAS

IN February 1915, Germany designated a war zone around the British Isles and warned neutral vessels to steer clear. President Woodrow Wilson adopted a rigid stance, insisting on full neutral trading rights with all belligerent powers, and promising to hold Germany accountable for any loss of American life. On May 7, 1915, a German submarine sank the passenger liner *Lusitania* off the coast of Ireland; of the 1,198 killed, 128 were Americans. Wilson dispatched three diplomatic notes to the Germans, each demanding an end to submarine warfare.

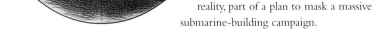

Following the sinking of the British liner *Arabic* with two Americans onboard, on August 19, 1915, Germany's Kaiser Wilhelm I publicly ordered his submarine commanders to halt attacks on passenger vessels. The pledge placated President Wilson, but the accidental sinking of the ferry *Sussex* in the English Channel elicited a threat by the United States to sever its diplomatic relations with Germany. The Kaiser responded with a promise not to sink merchant vessels without warning—a promise that was, in reality, part of a plan to mask a massive submarine-building campaign.

▲ *The German Kaiser Wilhelm I*

1915 MILITARY TECHNOLOGY ☢

WORLD War I saw significant advances in military technology, including the magazine rifle and the Maxim gun, the first truly automatic weapon, patented in 1884. By 1915, increased firepower and the widespread use of barbed wire removed the possibility of cavalry charges on the European battlefields. This situation led to an increased alliance on artillery. By 1914, all armies utilized field guns capable of firing 15lb shells at a rapid rate. Poison gas was developed in 1915, and the tank a year later. Dirigible airships and balloons were more advanced than the fragile airplanes of the era, but all were used for bombing and reconnaissance.

▲ *The Maxim machine gun—the first automatic weapon*

1915 MOTION PICTURE INDUSTRY 🏛

HOLLYWOOD, California, became the center of America's motion picture industry. D. W. Griffith (1875–1948) revolutionized film making with his innovative techniques. His 1915 *Birth of a Nation*, though controversial in racial terms, established the feature film as a legitimate art form. Mack Sennett made slapstick comedy the trademark of comedians like Charlie Chaplin. The actress Mary Pickford became "America's sweetheart," and William S. Hart dominated the popular Westerns. After 1916, powerful companies came to the fore of the film industry, and increasingly films came to reflect the changing social and moral values in America. During the war, news agencies sent motion picture photographers to the front lines allowing the homefront to see trench warfare first hand via newsreels. These newsreels did much to disabuse people of their romantic notions of warfare, and contributed to feelings of postwar disillusionment and isolation.

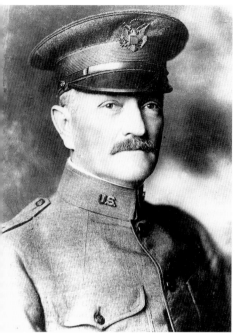

▲ *General John J. Pershing, known as "Black Jack"*

1916 "PANCHO" VILLA

IN March 1916, President Woodrow Wilson ordered General John J. "Black Jack" Pershing to enter Mexico in response to a series of border raids by the bandit leader Francisco "Pancho" Villa. Pershing chased Villa through the mountains of northern Mexico for six weeks, with no success, and was ordered home in January 1917, as events in Europe increasingly drew the United States into world affairs. The American Expeditionary Force—under Pershing's command—accomplished American participation in the European fighting after 1918. Although late and limited, the American presence provided a tremendous morale boost to troops that had been in the trenches for three years.

1916 WILSON'S RE-ELECTION

WOODROW Wilson portrayed himself as a peace candidate in the election of 1916. He advocated "preparedness" in the event that America was drawn into the European fighting, doubling the army's manpower, and instigating a shipbuilding program. His apparent success in halting submarine warfare, however, united the Democratic party behind Wilson's candidacy with the slogan, "He kept us out of war." Wilson defeated the Republican nominee Charles Evans Hughes.

1916   WARTIME ECONOMY

AMERICAN business profited from World War I. Although President Wilson insisted the United States be granted full trading rights with all the belligerents, the British unquestionably controlled the surface of the Atlantic. By 1916, American trade with Germany was just one percent of its 1914 value. War contracts poured into the United States, quadrupling trade with the Allied Powers; by the time America did enter the war, its banks had loaned almost $4 billion to the Allied war effort. The United States' war expenses totaled $26 billion, but taking into account the dispersal of veterans' benefits, eventually climbed to $112 billion.

1917   SEVERING DIPLOMATIC RELATIONS

IN the wake of his 1916 re-election to the presidency, Woodrow Wilson had launched a campaign to become the mediator for the warring European nations. In December 1916 he had asked both sides for a statement of war goals. The Central Powers, led by Germany, refused to answer, but the Allied Powers, led by Britain and France, made it clear that they intended to see Germany held accountable for the causes of and costs of the war. When Germany announced the resumption of unrestricted submarine warfare on January 21, 1917, Wilson severed diplomatic relations.

1917   ZIMMERMANN NOTE

IN February 1917, following the sinking of several American ships, British intelligence intercepted a message from the German foreign secretary, Alfred Zimmermann, to the German ambassador in Mexico. The telegram instructed him to offer Mexico an alliance with Germany in the event that the United States entered the war. In return, Germany promised to help Mexico regain its "lost" territories—New Mexico, Texas, and Arizona. In view of the strained relationship between America and Mexico at that time, the Zimmermann Note had to be taken as a serious threat, and was listed among Wilson's reasons for requesting a declaration of war.

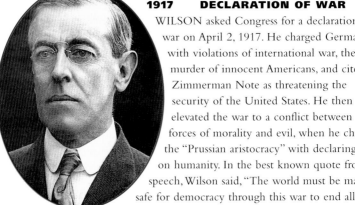

1917   DECLARATION OF WAR

WILSON asked Congress for a declaration of war on April 2, 1917. He charged Germany with violations of international war, the murder of innocent Americans, and cited the Zimmerman Note as threatening the security of the United States. He then elevated the war to a conflict between the forces of morality and evil, when he charged the "Prussian aristocracy" with declaring war on humanity. In the best known quote from his speech, Wilson said, "The world must be made safe for democracy through this war to end all wars." Such language could not fail to appeal to Americans imbued with the spirit of Progressivism and its belief in the perfectibility of society. The reality of war would, by 1918, drive the Progressive spirit underground in America, where it was not to resurface until the 1930s. In 1917, six senators and 50 representatives—including the first congresswoman, Jeanette Rankin of Montana—voted against the war resolution.

▲ President Woodrow Wilson, who brought the U.S. into the war in 1917

1917   INTERVENTION IN RUSSIA

FOLLOWING the Russian Revolution (1917) and the Treaty of Brest-Litovsk (1918), in which the new Bolshevik government removed Russia from involvement in World War I, 8,000 American troops landed in Russia's Arctic ports. This was just part of a 14-nation Allied effort to protect Allied supplies and to encourage anti-Bolshevik forces. The first Americans arrived on August 2, 1918, with a second contingent entering Siberia two weeks later. The intervention failed and generated long-standing suspicions on the part of the Soviets toward the Western Powers.

1917 WARTIME MOBILIZATION 🏛

AMERICA entered World War I on the Allied side, but as an independent nation. A massive mobilization of America's resources saw the creation of nearly 5,000 special government agencies. The Council on National Defense had the job of unifying the diverse elements of business, labor, and government behind the war effort. Americans were introduced to such things as daylight savings time and the rationing of coal and oil. A sense of voluntarism, which led the people to give up foodstuffs on designated days, prevented a need for food rationing.

▲ *Wilson addressing Congress, urging that war should be declared on Germany, April 2, 1917*

1917 ASSAULT ON FREE SPEECH

DURING World War I, the government suppressed the free speech of dissenting groups like the American Socialist party, the Industrial Workers of the World, and pacifists. Attorney General Thomas W. Gregory made the ironic statement, "Free expression of opinion is dangerous to American institutions." Three pieces of legislation addressed treasonous activity: the Espionage Act of 1917; the Trading-With-the-Enemy-Act of 1917; and the 1918 Sedition Act. In all, more than 1,500 individuals were prosecuted during the war under one of these laws.

1917 AFRICAN-AMERICANS IN WORLD WAR I

WARTIME labor shortages drew thousands of African Americans from the Southern states to the North, seeking jobs in industry, laying the basis for large black populations in Chicago and New York. This type of relocation led to race riots in St. Louis in July 1917 and in Chicago in July 1919. African Americans served in the armed forces in segregated units under white officers. For the most part, they were occupied with non-combat activities such as construction, although units of the 92nd and 93rd divisions saw combat in France.

1917 PERSECUTION OF GERMAN-AMERICANS

THE wartime emphasis on "100 percent Americanism" raised issues of cultural patriotism. In 1917, when Karl Muck, the German-born conductor of the Boston Symphony Orchestra refused to play the "Star Spangled Banner," he was arrested and deported. Songs of German origin were ripped out of songbooks and the works of German composers

The "Star Spangled Banner" ▶

were struck from the repertoires of symphonies and opera companies. The Boston Symphony hired its first American-born concertmaster in 1918 as a result of wartime restrictions on hiring foreigners.

1917   THE DRAFT 🏛

ALL males between the ages of 18 and 45 were required to register for the draft under the 1917 Selective Services Act. The army had 200,000 "doughboys" in 1917, and this number had risen to 4 million by 1919. For the first time, women were allowed in the armed services. The value of their contribution to the war effort made the passage of the 19th Amendment (1920)—granting women the vote—much easier and more acceptable. In addition to those in the armed services, one million American women entered the workforce during the war.

▼ *By necessity, women took on many jobs previously done by men—such as factory work—during the war*

1918   THE SPANISH FLU   🏛

IN the spring of 1918, a global epidemic of the Spanish Flu began. It was brought to America by returning servicemen. Before it ended a year later, 22 million had died around the world; 500,000 of those victims were American. The crisis was so severe that public facilities, including churches and saloons, were closed. Individuals could be arrested for spitting on the sidewalk or sneezing in public with no handkerchief. Millions wore surgical masks to work. Life insurance companies teetered on the brink of bankruptcy, hospitals were besieged, and cemetery space was at a premium.

1918   AMERICAN TROOPS IN FRANCE   🗺

AFTER the Russian Revolution, the Bolsheviks withdrew from the war, freeing the German army to make a major offensive in March 1918. By the end

▼ *The Battle of the Somme—one of the biggest offensives launched during World War I*

of May they had once again reached the Marne River. Advance units were only 50 miles from Paris. There, for the first time, the Germans met four divisions of Americans. In June, the American Expeditionary Force pushed the Germans behind the Marne and held Belleau Wood through a vicious three-week battle. By mid-July the Americans boasted a strength of one million men, and mounted an offensive against the Germans in the Meuse-Argonne. In November, a revolution ousted the German Kaiser from power, putting in place the Weimar Republic.

1918 DISSOLUTION OF EMPIRES

IN his plan for a non-punitive peace to end World War I—the Fourteen Points (1918)—President Woodrow Wilson specifically called for the dissolution of empires. It was a policy that put him at odds with two of the Allied nations: Britain and France. Although America had acquired foreign holdings in the latter half of the 19th century, including the Hawaiian and Philippine Islands, World War I plunged the nation into a period of isolationism throughout the 1920s and 1930s. Germany, encouraged by the goals outlined in Wilson's Fourteen Points, signed an armistice ending the fighting at 11 a.m. on November 11, 1918. Taking into account the combined losses of all nations participating, military casualties totaled 8,020,780, with civilian losses at 6,642,633.

1918 JAZZ

AMERICAN popular music was exported to France and the remainder of Europe during World War I. Composers and performers in the postwar years began to employ the muted brass of jazz and to incorporate blues notes in their work. In America after the war, the center of jazz music traveled northward and settled in places like Chicago, Kansas City, and New York while more mainstream composers such as George Gershwin, Jerome Kern, and Irving Berlin, contributed to the stage extravaganzas of the famous producer Florenz Ziegfeld.

1919   AMENDMENTS 🏛

THE 18th Amendment was added to the Constitution in 1919. It prohibited the manufacture, sale, transportation, import and export of intoxicating alcohol. The amendment's passage was largely the work of the Anti-Saloon League. The amendment remained in force until its repeal in 1933.

The 19th Amendment was added to the Constitution in 1920—partially in recognition of women's service in and aid to World War I. The "suffrage amendment" gave women the vote.

▼ *Celebrations at the end of Prohibition*

1919   TREATY OF VERSAILLES

THE Treaty of Versailles was signed in the Hall of Mirrors at the Palace of Versailles on June 28, 1919. It had been negotiated by the "Big Four"— Woodrow Wilson, British Prime Minister David Lloyd George, French Premier Georges Clemenceau, and Vittorio Orlando of Italy. Although Wilson had bargained away virtually all his Fourteen Point plan in the debates over the Treaty, the final document did contain his international association, the League of Nations.

1919   AMERICAN OPPOSITION TO THE TREATY

THE Treaty of Versailles met with considerable opposition in the United States, led by the Chairman of the Senate Foreign Relations Committee, Henry Cabot Lodge. The treaty required a two-thirds vote in the Senate for ratification. A point of particular opposition was the League of Nations. Article 10 of the League Covenant pledged all member nations to come to the aid of the others in the event of an attack. Americans, horrified at the carnage of World War I, did not want to be drawn into another European conflict. Neither Lodge nor Wilson bothered to explain that such an action would require a unanimous vote of the League council, of which the United States was to be a member. The Senate twice defeated the Treaty, leaving the United States to conclude a separate peace with Germany and the other central powers.

The signing of the Treaty of Versailles in 1919 ▶

1919 THE RED SCARE

IN 1919, following a series of mail bombs—including one that destroyed the front porch of Attorney General A. Mitchell Palmer's home—Palmer, a man with presidential ambitions, aided by a young member of the Justice Department, J. Edgar Hoover, began a Red Scare. This was a search for Communists, or "bolsheviks" as they were known in the vernacular of the day,

▲ *J. Edgar Hoover, who was responsible for the "Red Scare" in 1919*

and was characterized by "Palmer Raids." More than 5,000 suspicious individuals were arrested, and 249 were deported. Palmer predicted that widespread rioting would break out on May 1, 1920, but when this prediction came to nothing, the Red Scare evaporated.

1919 LABOR UNREST

A SHORT-LIVED post-war economic boom gave way to serious labor unrest in 1919, when thousands of strikes took four million American workers away from their jobs. The most famous strike—the Boston Police Strike—made Governor Calvin Coolidge a national figure. He mobilized the National Guard and told the press, "There is no right to strike against the public safety by anybody, anywhere, any time."

1920   WILSON SUFFERS A STROKE

IN his campaign to win acceptance for the Treaty of Versailles and the League of Nations in 1919, Woodrow Wilson destroyed his health. After an 8,000-mile trip over 22 days, during which he gave 36 speeches, the president collapsed in Colorado and a few days later suffered a massive stroke that paralyzed his left side. He served out his term with the help of his second wife, Edith, and that of his secretary Colonel House. In the 1920 election, American voters turned to the Republican Warren G. Harding, who promised a return to "normalcy."

1920   FUNDAMENTALISM

IN the opening years of the 20th century, religion took a fundamentalist turn, influenced by the belief that modernism threatened the nation's spiritual life. Intellectuals who suggested the Bible should be studied in terms of modern scholarship and Charles Darwin's theories of evolution were ridiculed and scorned by fundamentalists. The movement took its name from a series of pamphlets published in Los Angeles in 1910, *The Fundamentals*. Five points were identified as being fundamental to the Christian faith: an inerrant Bible; belief in the virgin birth of Jesus Christ; the vicarious experience of atonement, known as being "born again;" faith in the Resurrection; and in the return of Christ—the Second Coming. The fundamentalists were especially distinguished by their complete intolerance of and hostility toward any other belief.

Charles Darwin's theories on evolution shocked the U.S. establishment ▶

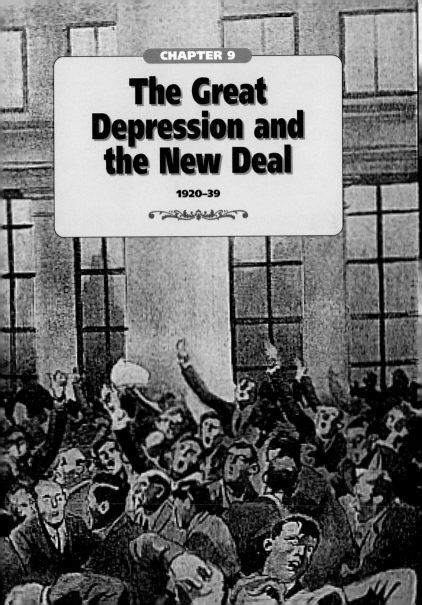

CHAPTER 9

The Great Depression and the New Deal

1920–39

1920s   KU KLUX KLAN

IN 1915, William J. Simmons revived the Civil War Era hate-organization, the Ku Klux Klan, at Stone Mountain, Georgia. By the peak of Klan popularity in the 1920s, membership reached from three to eight million. Simmons lost control of the organization in 1922 when a Dallas dentist, Hiram Wesley Evans, became Imperial Wizard. Unlike its 19th-century predecessor, the modern Klan advocated 100 percent Americanism, and accepted only native-born, white Protestants. It persecuted African-Americans, Roman Catholics, Jews, immigrants, and women who practiced the "new morality." Although the Klan's appeal was national, its adherents in the Southwest felt as if they were part of a moral crusade. The organization's political and social influence suffered irreparably when Indiana Grand Dragon, David C. Stevenson, was convicted of second-degree murder.

▼ *Members of the Ku Klux Klan, which saw a revival in the 1920s*

1920s AGRICULTURE IN THE TWENTIES

THE post-World War I agricultural boom lasted into 1920 when prices collapsed; wheat fell from $2.50 a bushel to less than a dollar in 18 months. Although farmers increasingly mechanized their operations and joined bodies such as the 1920 American Farm Bureau Federation to promote more businesslike operations, the heart of the problem lay in surplus production. A Congressional farm bloc was formed in the 1920s, comprised of western Republicans and southern Democrats, but legislation that actually helped farmers did not materialize until F. D. Roosevelt's New Deal in 1933.

1920s CONSUMER REVOLUTION

INCREASED efficiency and innovative developments fueled the consumer and technological revolution of the 1920s. In 1925, the Ford Motor Company assembly line produced an automobile every 10 seconds, while 20,200,000 telephones were in use by 1930. Factories churned out new products, such as cigarette lighters, oil furnaces, wristwatches, antifreeze fluids, reinforced concrete, paint sprayers, matchbooks, dry ice, Pyrex glass for cooking utensils, and panchromatic motion picture film. The use of rayon transformed the textile business and, in 1924 DuPont established a cellophane plant in Buffalo, New York.

Few businesses grew as rapidly as the electric light and power industry, however, the chief field for mergers in the 1920s. By 1929, electrical power output reached 117 billion kilowatt-hours. As local electrical companies were interconnected into vast regional grids, financiers merged small firms into utility empires. By 1930, 10 holding-company groups controlled 72 percent of the country's electrical power.

▲ *The Ford Motor Company introduced the moving assembly line in 1925*

1920s   URBAN–RURAL CONFLICT ☯▮

THE 1920s saw the rise of a social confrontation in America between cosmopolitan, urban areas and insular, rural communities. The banality of small-town life became a pervasive influence in the literature of the period, such as Sinclair Lewis' 1920 novel *Main Street*. The countryside looked at the cities as pools of vice, crime, corruption, and foreigners.

New social theories denied the existence of absolute values, thereby undermining concepts of personal responsibility and absolute standards. Anthropologists changed the meaning of the word "culture" from "refinement" to a whole system of ideas, folkways, and institutions within which any group lived. No culture was any more valid than another as shown in *Coming of Age in Samoa* (1928) by Margaret Mead and *Patterns of Culture* (1934) by Ruth Benedict.

1920s   MODERNISM ☯▮

THE Modernist Movement attempted to plumb the human psyche, and viewed the universe as turbulent and unpredictable. Conflict was held in a positive light, and reality was prized over gentility. Such ideas surfaced in the abstract paintings,

atonal music, free-verse poetry, stream of conscious narratives, and interior character monologues that appeared in the 1920s. The first artistic bohemian communities appeared on Chicago's South Side and in New York's Greenwich Village.

Led by the Viennese founder of psychoanalysis, Sigmund Freud (1856–1939), Americans began to

◀ *The founder of psychoanalysis, Sigmund Freud*

explore the interior of their own minds in the 1920s and '30s. Cocktail party conversations were littered with Freudian words and phrases—libido, inhibition, Oedipus complex, transference, sublimation, and repression—as Americans endlessly analyzed each other and themselves.

1920s PROHIBITION

THE greatest social experiment of the 1920s, Prohibition, resulted from the 1919 passage of the 18th Amendment forbidding the manufacture, sale, or transport of intoxicating beverages. The 1919 Volstead Act defined such beverages as containing more than 0.5% of alcohol. Pushed through by the Women's

Christian Temperance Union and the Anti-Saloon League, Prohibition made drinking a fashion fad and illegal distilling a highly profitable business. In Detroit, the production of "bootleg" liquor was second only to the automobile industry. Such endeavors gave gangsters such as "Scarface" Al Capone an enormous source of income, and contributed to the rise of organized crime. The law remained in effect until 1933.

◀ *The gangster Al Capone ran a bootleg campaign during Prohibition*

1920 HARDING ADMINISTRATION

PRESIDENT Warren G. Harding (1865–1923), elected in 1920, set about dismantling the social and economic programs of the Progressive Era. Supreme Court Justice (and former president) William Howard Taft (1857–1930) presided over decisions that struck down child-labor laws and a minimum wage for women. Injunctions were issued against striking unions and the power of federal regulatory agencies diminished. The pro-business Secretary of the Treasury, Andrew J. Mellon, supported high tariffs and lowered taxes for the upper classes. In 1921 the wartime excess-profits tax was repealed and the maximum rate on personal incomes lowered from 65 to 50 percent; it dropped further to 40 percent in 1924, and 20 percent in 1926. The Revenue Act of 1926 lowered estate taxes and repealed the gift tax. Government spending fell from $6.4 billion in 1920 to $3.4 billion in 1922, and then to $3 billion in 1927. The national debt went from $25.5 billion in 1919 to $16.9 billion a decade later.

1920   WOMEN GET WORKING AND GET THE VOTE

AMERICAN women went to work in increasing numbers after World War I. By 1910, women held 25 percent of the nation's nonagricultural jobs. In 1920, they were listed in all but 35 of the 572 job categories listed on the national census, which showed 8.2 million women in the work force; this number

▼ *The triumph of women's rights—women won the vote in 1920*

climbed to 10.4 million in 1930 and 13 million by 1940. For the most part their efforts were still directed in "traditional" jobs; domestics, office workers, teachers, clerks, salespeople, dressmakers, milliners, and seamstresses.

With the passage of the 19th Amendment in 1920, women gained the vote. While the League of Women Voters was formed in 1919, the broader feminist movement floundered through the 1920s. The Equal Rights Amendment, first introduced to Congress in 1923, did not gain passage until 1972, and then failed to be ratified by the states.

1920   MEDIA COMMUNICATION ☢▲

WHILE used for communication before 1920, radio only became a vehicle for information and entertainment when WWJ in Detroit began transmitting news bulletins in August 1920; KDKA Pittsburgh began regular programing in November of that same year. WEAF New York broadcast the first commercial in 1922. By the end of 1922, America boasted 508 stations and 3 million receivers. The National Broadcasting Company began linking stations into a network in 1926. By the following year, the Federal Radio Commission was established, becoming the Federal Communications Commission in 1934.

In 1926, inventor Philo Taylor Farnsworth produced the first all-electronic television image. His patents covered mechanisms dealing with television scanning, focusing, synchronizing, contrast, controls, and power. He also developed the black lights for night vision used during World War II. By the mid-1930s, movie theaters in large cities and most small towns made motion pictures America's chief mass entertainment. Warner Brothers produced *Don Juan* (1926), the first "talkie," followed by the widely popular *The Jazz Singer* (1927).

The first electronic television image was produced in 1926 ▶

1920 SACCO AND VANZETTI

PARTICULARLY vivid nativism in the 1920s surfaced in the case of the Italian immigrants Nicola Sacco and Bartolomeo Vanzetti, who were arrested in 1920 on suspicion of payroll robbery and murder. Both claimed to be anarchists. During the trial the judge referred to the defendants as "anarchist bastards." The men were found guilty and sentenced to execution. The case became an international cause with critics charging that the men had been convicted for their beliefs rather than on evidence of having committed the crimes. They were executed in 1927.

1921 PARTIAL ISOLATIONISM

IN the period between the two world wars, America assumed a position of partial isolationism, engaging in economically profitable foreign arrangements but avoiding those that could lead to war. In general, the United States retreated from its responsibility as a powerful member of the world community. Rather than become involved in the League of Nations, created by the Treaty of Versailles in 1919, the nation instead tied itself to a series of meaningless agreements, including the treaties arising from the 1921 Washington Disarmament Conference calling for naval arms reduction, and the Kellogg-Briand Pact of 1928 that optimistically outlawed war.

America's partial isolationism led the nation to ignore or respond weakly to disturbing events in the world community in the 1930s. In 1931, Japan overran the Chinese province of Manchuria. Militant nationalism infected Europe with Benito Mussolini's rise to power in Italy in 1922 and Adolf Hitler's in Germany in 1933.

1923 COOLIDGE BECOMES PRESIDENT

IN June 1923, President Warren G. Harding left Washington on a speaking tour of the western states and a trip through the Alaska Territory. He apparently had a heart attack in Seattle, from which he briefly recovered before dying in a San Francisco hotel. The new president, Calvin Coolidge (1872–1933), was an even

▲ *President Calvin Coolidge*

more avid proponent of business, saying, "The chief business of the American people is business. The man who builds a factory, builds a temple. The man who works there, worships there."

1923 FLAMING YOUTH 🏛

THE youth revolution of the 1920s took its name from the 1923 novel *Flaming Youth* by Samuel Hopkins Adams. Young people engaged in wild parties, drank "bathtub" gin, and were promiscuous. They frequented illegal drinking clubs, known as "speakeasies" and roadhouses, doing "shimmy dances" like the Charleston and the Black Bottom to the wildly popular jazz music of performers such as Jelly Roll Morton and Louis Armstrong. Such activities earned the decade its appellation the "Roaring Twenties." A preoccupation with sex was evident in the confession magazines that filled stands, and on the silver screen where stars like Theda Bara and Clara Bow were given the nicknames the "Vamp" and the "It" girl. Women's skirts, which had been no more than six inches above the ground in 1919, were up to the knee in 1927.

The young women who carried the youth revolution and "new morality" the farthest were known as "flappers" for their habit of wearing galoshes with no laces. These girls cut their hair

There was a social revolution in the 1920s, which saw a more open-minded approach to previously taboo behavior ▶

short, rolled down their stockings, smoked cigarettes, wore lipstick, and competed with men on their own terms in speakeasies and at sporting events. A survey taken in the late 1930s showed that nearly half of college-educated women had lost their virginity before marriage but, of those, three-quarters had slept only with their future husbands.

1924   TEAPOT DOME SCANDAL

IN 1924, a Senate investigation revealed corruption in the Interior Department. Secretary Albert B. Fall signed contracts allowing private interests to exploit oil deposits under Teapot Rock in Wyoming. "Teapot Dome" had been set aside as a naval reserve, but Fall accepted "loans" of $400,000 from Harry Sinclair of the Mammoth Oil Company and $300,000 from Edward L. Doheny of Pan-American Petroleum and Transport Company. Fall was convicted of accepting bribes.

▲ *Johnny Scopes's lawyers during his trial in 1925*

1925   SCOPES TRIAL

FUNDAMENTALISM grew in America in the 1920s, focusing on combating the teaching of Charles Darwin's theory of evolution. In 1925 in Dayton, Tennessee, high school teacher John Scopes accepted a challenge issued by the American Civil Liberties Union, which offered to provide defense council for any teacher who would violate the state law against teaching evolution. Scopes was arrested and at his trial the agnostic labor lawyer Clarence Darrow defended him. William Jennings Bryan served as special prosecutor for the state. At the trial's climax, Bryan took the stand as a Biblical expert, affirming that a "big fish" swallowed Jonah, Joshua made the sun stand still, and that the world was made in seven days in 4004 B.C. Bryan's testimony became the object of ridicule for critics of fundamentalism, notably the acerbic newspaper columnist H. L. Mencken. Scopes was found guilty and fined $100. Bryan died of a heart attack a few days after the trial. Incidents like the Scopes "Monkey" Trial, as it became known, roused a liberal defense of academic freedom.

1926　　FLYING EXPEDITIONS

IN 1926, Richard Byrd became the first man to fly over the North Pole; a feat he recreated at the South Pole in 1929. Byrd also led five overland expeditions to Antarctica.

In May 1927, Colonel Charles A. Lindbergh, Jr. flew from New York to Paris, completing the first solo flight across the Atlantic in 33 hours and 30 minutes. Lindbergh was welcomed home with a thunderous tickertape parade in New York. The aviatrix Amelia Earhart became the first woman to fly the Atlantic in 1928. Joined by other famous aviators such as Jimmy Doolittle, Wiley Post, Richard Byrd, and Howard Hughes, they became the heroes of the air age.

Charles Lindbergh in his plane
Spirit of St Louis ▶

1926 HERBERT HOOVER AND BUSINESS

DURING the Harding and Coolidge Administrations, future president Herbert Hoover (1874–1964) served as Secretary of Commerce. He enlarged the Bureau of Foreign and Domestic Commerce and encouraged the Bureau of Standards Simplified Practices Division to host conferences on design, production, and distribution. Hoover's policies emphasized standardization in industry, and he supported the trade-association movement. His other innovations included the creation of the Bureau of Aviation in 1926 and the Federal Radio Commission the following year.

1927–29 INVESTMENT SPECULATION AND THE WALL STREET CRASH

AMERICA experienced a speculative mania in the 1920s, as evidenced by the Florida real estate boom. After 1927, the Stock Market became as much a social fad as a financial investment. Tax reductions freed up money for investments and buying stock on margin was popular; the investor made a down payment and borrowed the remainder from the broker, who held the stock as security. Despite warning signs, such as the saturation of the residential construction and automobile industries, and the slowed rate of consumer spending, the market continued to climb. Stock in Radio Corporation of America which had been under 100 in March 1928, stood at more than 500 on September 3, 1929, the day the market reached its peak. The bubble burst on October 29, 1929—"Black Tuesday"—when the share index dropped 43 points and 16.4 million shares traded hands; a normal day's trading would have been in the region of three million.

1929–39 THE GREAT DEPRESSION

AMERICA'S Gross National Product climbed from $88.9 billion in 1920 to $104.4 billion in 1929 on the eve of the Stock Market Crash, while the country's per capita income increased correspondingly, from $672 in 1922 to $857 in 1929.

The Great Depression and the New Deal

▲ *Panic on the streets after the Wall Street Crash*

The results of the Stock Market Crash were disastrous for Americans. Savings, and more than a few fortunes were wiped out overnight, unemployment skyrocketed, and suicides rose alarmingly. From 1929 to 1932, personal incomes dwindled from $82 million to $40 million. More than 9,000 banks closed, factories and mines shut down and thousands of farms were lost to foreclosures. The Great Depression lasted throughout the 1930s, gradually easing and eventually halted by the need for war materials during World War II.

1929   VOLUNTARISM

HERBERT Hoover, elected president in 1928, attempted to combat the economic crisis of the Stock Market Crash and the Great Depression with a spirit of "voluntarism." He did not believe in direct government intervention or relief as a solution. Under his leadership Congress did fund some public works projects—such as the construction of the Hoover Dam on the Colorado River between Nevada and Arizona—but such projects were too limited in scope to be of real assistance. In 1932, he supported the Reconstruction Finance Corporation, which provided aid to institutions and agencies but not to individuals. The idea was to get the economy going again, not just to give away money. The 1932 Federal Home Loan Bank Act provided government guaranteed loans for potential homeowners. Despite these measures, however, Hoover faced a hostile Democratic Congress demanding greater presidential action.

1930s   LEFTIST POLITICS

THE 1930s brought a renewed intellectual commitment, some of which was tied to revolutionary ideas. Leftist politics and rhetoric made inroads. In September 1932, 53 artists and intellectuals signed an open letter endorsing the Communist Party presidential candidate. Thousands of John Reed clubs formed, named after the American journalist who observed and wrote about the 1917 Russian Revolution. In 1935, the Communist party line switched to a broad "popular front," working with democratic and socialist groups that opposed fascism. John Reed clubs gave way to the League of American Writers. Other popular front groups

included the American Youth Congress, the American Negro Congress, and the American League for Peace and Democracy.

1931   ARCHITECTURE ☢

ARCHITECTURAL advances in the 1920s and 1930s, in particular the use of steel girders, sent the American city skyline soaring. On May 1, 1931, New York City's Empire State Building, built in less than a year, became the world's tallest building at 86 stories.

▼ *Skyscapers began to dominate the New York skyline from the 1930s*

1932   BONUS ARMY

IN 1924, Congress had voted endowment life insurance to World War I veterans, payable to those veterans or their heirs in 1945. During the Depression the veterans asked for the immediate payment of their bonuses. Throughout the spring of 1932, some 15,000 ex-soldiers poured into Washington, D.C., camping in vacant government buildings and a shantytown near the White House. When the Senate rejected a bill in their favor, many left; President Hoover persuaded Congress to buy train tickets for those who stayed. Three hundred or so had no place to go and, in an ugly confrontation with policemen sent to remove them, a stray shot was fired. The Secretary of War, Patrick J. Hurley, ordered the use of troops to remove the veterans. The shantytown was set on fire and tear gas employed to disperse the weary and desperate men. The public blamed Hoover for the incident. Herbert Hoover's handling of the Bonus Army ended his chances for reelection.

1933   NEW DEAL

THE administration of democratic president Franklin D. Roosevelt (1933–45) constructed programs that permanently altered the federal government and have shaped the nation's political life ever since. The New Deal was never committed to any particular philosophy, but was similar to the pragmatism of the 19th-century progressives, with an emphasis on experimentation to find the most effective solutions. The New Deal constructed the beginnings of the welfare system; extended areas of federal regulation; created a Democratic coalition that dominated American politics for 30 years; and produced a new liberal consensus in America. It did not, however, end the Great Depression, but merely stabilized the economy until the defense contracts of World War II brought renewed national prosperity.

Franklin D. Roosevelt meeting with farm laborers ▶

1933   FIRST HUNDRED DAYS

WITHIN the First Hundred Days of his administration following the 1933 inauguration, Franklin D. Roosevelt took sweeping measures to combat the nation's economic ills. He was inaugurated on March 4, 1933; just two days later all American banks were closed for four days and Congress was called into special session. On March 9th, the Emergency Banking Act provided for Treasury Department inspection of all banks before they could be reopened. Three-quarters of the banks reopened within three days and $1 billion in hoarded currency and gold were redeposited.

1933   ROOSEVELT'S CRITICS

A GROUP of dissident political movements
surfaced after 1933 in criticism of President
Franklin D. Roosevelt and his New Deal programs.
Dr. Francis E. Townsend, an elderly California
physician, led a movement to gain federal pensions
for the elderly, culminating in the 1935 Social
Security Act. Father Charles Coughlin broadcast
weekly radio sermons calling for monetary reforms and
the nationalization of the banking system. Senator
Huey P. Long of Louisiana advocated a program he
christened Share-Our-Wealth, in which surplus
riches would be confiscated and redistributed over the population.

▲ *President Roosevelt, who inaugurated the New Deal*

1933   RELIEF, RECOVERY, AND REFORM

IN retrospect, the New Deal legislation in 1933 can be classified as relief (getting
aid to suffering people); recovery (taking steps to get the economy going again),
and reform (preventing another financial crisis of similar magnitude). Notable
programs included the Agricultural Adjustment Act of 1933, placing production
limits on some crops and providing for subsidies; the National Industrial Recovery
Act, aiming at cooperation between labor and business; and the Federal Emergency
Relief Administration, which provided cash grants to states. Later measures included
the Tennessee Valley Authority (1933) to generate and sell reasonable electrical
power, the Rural Electrification Administration (1935) to bring power to isolated
regions, the Social Security Act (1935) to provide an income for elderly Americans,
and the Wagner Act (1935), known as labor's bill of rights.

1935–39 NEUTRALITY LAWS

BETWEEN 1935 and 1939, Congress passed neutrality laws forbidding the sale
of arms or the granting of loans to belligerents and warning Americans not to
travel on vessels owned by belligerent nations. Any other trade with nations at

war would be carried out on a strictly "cash and carry" basis. These blanket trade embargoes and similar requests by the American government carried little weight with the business community. Following the 1935 Italian annexation of Ethiopia, for instance, when Secretary of State Cordell Hull asked for a moral embargo on the sale of oil to Italy, Texas oilmen tripled their shipments.

1936   PROTESTANTS IN AMERICA

TRADITIONAL Protestant theology, though offering no answers during the Great Depression, regarded the interventionist New Deal as unscriptural and sinful. The great majority of Protestant periodicals and ministers, except in the South, supported the Republicans. A 1936 survey showed that more than 70 percent of 21,606 Protestant ministers voted for Alf Landon. Thus, the 1930s and 1940s marked a Protestant political retreat before a Democratic coalition in which Jews, Catholics, and progressives all had increasing roles.

1936   FASCIST SEIZURES

INTERNATIONAL relations continued to deteriorate in March 1936 when Hitler took control of the Rhineland and created the Rome–Berlin Axis with Benito Mussolini. That summer, civil war broke out in Spain, with Francisco Franco's forces fighting the Spanish Loyalists, who were aided by both the Italians and Germans. In the fall of 1937, Japan renewed its intervention in China. Hitler seized Austria in March 1938 and began exerting pressure on Czechoslovakia, which he took in 1939. In August 1939, Hitler signed a Non-Aggression Pact with the Russians preparatory to his September 1, 1939 invasion of Poland. Two days later England and France declared war on Germany.

Italian dictator Benito Mussolini ▶

CHAPTER 10

World War II

1939–45

1939   HITLER'S AGGRESSIVE MOVES

ADOLF Hitler (1889–1945) began his plan to seize all of Europe when he moved German troops into the demilitarized Rhineland on March 7, 1936. After seizing Austria and Czechoslovakia, he attacked Poland on September 1, 1939, eliciting a declaration of war from England and France. In May 1940, Hitler sent troops across Belgium, Holland, and Luxembourg, and drove the British and French forces back across France. The survivors of the British force literally fought in the surf at Dunkirk until evacuated by a concerted effort of British civilians, who crossed the English Channel in every vessel available in order to rescue the men. France surrendered to Germany on June 22, 1940.

▲ *German Nazi leader Adolf Hitler*

1939   PAYING FOR THE WAR

FROM 1939 to 1946, the United States' government covered 45 percent of its expenses with tax revenues. The remainder was raised in war bond drives, such as the 1945 Victory Drive, that raised $150 billion from patriotic Americans. Still, by the end of the war the government debt had risen to $260 billion.

In September 1940, Congress passed the Burke–Wadsworth Act, establishing the first peacetime draft in the history of the United States. At the same time the defense budget was increased from $2 billion to $10 billion.

1940s   CULT OF FDR

DURING World War II, Americans felt genuine affection for, and expressed great faith in, President Franklin D. Roosevelt, who provided a vital focal point in the war effort against Germany and Japan. The president's reassuring radio voice—coupled with his twinkling eyes, mischievous grin, and jaunty cigarette holder—conveyed optimism, courage, and good will and made the average American feel he had a personal friend in the White House. Although paralyzed from polio, Roosevelt projected an image of vitality. He was never photographed using his crutches, his wheelchair, or being supported when he walked. Many Americans had no idea their national leader was crippled. He used the press as an extension of the office of the presidency, often suggesting headlines and stories. His unexpected death in April 1945, five months after his election to a fourth term in office, left the nation stunned and bereft.

▼ *Franklin D. Roosevelt proved to be one of the most popular presidents in history*

▲ *Movie legend Humphrey Bogart, star of* Casablanca

1940s   MOTION PICTURE PROPAGANDA 🏛

IN 1941, President Franklin D. Roosevelt stated that, "The American motion picture is one of our most effective mediums in informing and entertaining our citizens. The motion picture must remain free insofar as national security will permit. I want no censorship of the motion picture." Some of the more inspiring war films produced in Hollywood during the war included *Across the Pacific* (1942), *Casablanca* (1942), *Mrs. Miniver* (1942), *Air Force* (1943), *Sahara* (1943), and *They Were Expendable* (1945).

1940s   AMERICANS OVERSEAS 🌍

FOR the thousands of young men and women who served in the American armed forces during World War II, the conflict was itself a period of exploration. The military fighting capacity of nearly half a million servicemen and women in 1940 climbed steadily: 1.8 million (1941); 3.8 million (1942); 9 million (1943); 11.4 million (1944); and 12 million (1945).

A generation that grew up on the quiet farms and Main Streets of the American countryside found themselves sent around the globe to Europe, Africa, and the islands of the Pacific Ocean in defense of their country. Entrusted with expensive equipment including airplanes, naval vessels, and tanks, their confidence expanded with their responsibility. These men and women returned to their homes at the war's end more cosmopolitan than any previous American generation. Given the opportunity to utilize the funds made available in the 1944 Servicemen's Readjustment Act known popularly as the G.I. Bill, returning servicemen and women sought college educations in unprecedented numbers. Their wartime experiences changed them, and they would change the face of America in the second half of the 20th century.

1940s   WOMEN IN THE ARMED SERVICE 🏛

AMERICAN women experienced a major social transformation during World War II. Approximately 200,000 served in the Women's Army Corps, the Women Accepted for Volunteer Emergency Service (the naval WAVES), the Marine Corps, Coast Guard, and the Army Air Force. By 1945, six million women entered the workforce, including 24 percent of the nation's married women. They became toolmakers, machinists, crane operators, lumberjacks, stevedores, blacksmiths, and railroad workers. The government launched an intense campaign to draw women into traditionally male occupations, christening the working woman contributing to the war effort "Rosie the Riveter."

▼ *The Women's Army Corps in 1945*

1940s   NATIVE AMERICANS IN WORLD WAR II   🏛

THE contribution of Native Americans during World War II was subject to less prejudice than that of African-Americans. Approximately 25,000 Indians served with distinction in the military, including the Pima Indian, Ira Hayes, one of the men who raised the American flag on Iwo Jima in the Pacific theater, becoming part of one of the war's most legendary photographs. Other Indians served as "code-talkers." They worked in military communications transmitting vital information in their own languages, and were successful in making these messages impenetrable to enemy espionage.

1940s   AFRICAN AMERICANS IN WORLD WAR II   🏛

ABOUT a million African Americans served in the armed forces, but in segregated units. The greatest departure from the segregation standard was the 1940 decision to integrate officer candidate schools in all branches of the service except the Air Force. Some two million African Americans worked in the war plants, reviving the migration out of the South that had lagged during the Depression years. The states that saw the greatest increase in black population were California, Michigan, Oregon, Washington, Utah, Colorado, Wisconsin, Illinois, and New York. Membership in the National Association for the Advancement of Colored Peoples rose to 450,000 during the war years, and African American participation in the conflict provided much of the impetus for the burgeoning civil rights movement in the late 1940s and '50s.

◀ *General MacArthur (center), military leader during World War II*

1940s   REFUGEE ARTISTS   🏛

IN the early 1940s, New York became a refuge for avant-garde artists, art dealers, art historians, museum curators, collectors, and writers fleeing Nazi-occupied Europe. The city became the artistic capital of the West, while the presence of the European artistic community had a catalytic effect on American art, allowing American modernists to move to the fore. The result was the Abstract Expressionism movement later christened the New York School, which vaulted American art into a position of international prominence after the war.

1940   RISING GNP   🏭

THE Gross National Product, which stood at $100.6 billion in 1940, rose to $213.6 billion in 1945, an increase of 112 percent. Government expenditures climbed accordingly, from $20 billion in 1941 to $97.2 billion in 1944. From July 1, 1940 to June 30, 1946 the total government expenditures rocketed to $337 billion, of which $304 billion went toward the war effort.

In January 1942, Congress authorized the Office of Price Administration to set price ceilings. The General Maximum Price Regulation of 1942 froze prices at the highest levels they had reached during the previous month. With prices frozen, goods were allocated through rationing, beginning with tires in December 1941 and extending to sugar, coffee, gasoline, and meats—all acquired through a system of ration coupons.

1940   ARSENAL OF DEMOCRACY   🗿

AFTER Franklin D. Roosevelt's election to a third term as president in 1940, his efforts to steer America toward intervention in the war in Europe grew bolder. He told the people that America must become an "arsenal of democracy" to help those nations whose survival was vital to American interests, and proposed a Lend-Lease program to make war materials and arms available to such nations. Congress approved the program with an initial appropriation of $7 billion. The ultimate cost of Lend-Lease was $50 billion.

1940   SHOOT ON SIGHT

BY endorsing a Lend
Lease program (1940)
and changing the
existing neutrality laws
to allow American
vessels to transport war
material to the British,
American ships in the
North Atlantic faced
the threat of German
submarines. After the
U.S. destroyer *Reuben
James* was hit by a

▲ *U.S. Navy ships entering the Golden Gate*

German torpedo and sank on October 21, 1941, President Franklin D. Roosevelt
issued a "shoot on sight" order, creating a state of undeclared naval war in the
North Atlantic.

In the summer of 1940, British Prime Minister Winston Churchill
(1874–1965), facing attacks by Adolf Hitler's forces from the continent, asked
President Roosevelt for replacement naval ships. In the "destroyers for bases"
deal the United States traded 50 old destroyers for rights to build eight naval
bases in the Atlantic and Caribbean.

1941   JAPANESE AGGRESSION

IN July 1941, Japanese troops pushed into Indochina, whereupon President
Roosevelt froze all Japanese assets in America, and all trade between the two
countries ceased. Up until this point, America had supplied more than half of
Japan's iron, steel, and oil. On November 20, Japan offered to cease aggressive
movements in the Pacific and to pull out of Indochina when peace in China
was restored. When the United States did not respond, the action in Indochina
continued. On November 26, Roosevelt sent a harsh note to the Japanese,

demanding troop withdrawal. The Japanese regarded the tone of the communiqué as an insult and, on December 7, planes of the Japanese Imperial Air Force bombed the American installation at Pearl Harbor, Hawaii.

The Japanese attack on U.S. ships at Pearl Harbor ▶

1941   ATLANTIC CHARTER

IN the fall of 1941 before the bombing of Pearl Harbor, President Franklin D. Roosevelt met with British Prime Minister Winston Churchill on an American ship off the coast of Newfoundland in order to establish joint war aims. The set of goals, known as the Atlantic Charter, outlined the requirements for "a better future for the world." They included the establishment of a permanent international peace organization, self-determination for all nations, and freedom of the seas. Shortly after the United States declared war in December 1941, Churchill flew to Washington, D.C. where the two leaders announced the formation of an alliance between the United States, Great Britain, and the Soviet Union on January 1, 1942.

1941   PEARL HARBOR

PLANES of the Japanese Imperial Air Force attacked the American installation at Pearl Harbor, Hawaii, at 7:55 a.m. Sunday, December 7, 1941; a second wave hit an hour later. The attack destroyed most of the American planes on the island of Oahu, and wrecked eight battleships, three destroyers, and three cruisers. The battleships *Oklahoma* and *Arizona* were completely destroyed. The American death toll stood at 2,323. In two hours the navy lost more men than it had in the Spanish—American War and World War I combined. The next day President Franklin D. Roosevelt spoke to a joint session of Congress, calling December 7th "a date that will live in infamy" and receiving confirmation of a declaration of war. On December 11th, Germany and Italy declared war on the U.S..

1941   PHILIPPINES

TWO hours after the 1941 attack on Pearl Harbor, the Japanese bombed Clark Field, the main U.S. base in the Philippines, and destroyed half of the Far East Air Force under the command of General Douglas MacArthur (1880–1964). Within three days, 43,000 Japanese troops landed 135 miles north of Manila. MacArthur withdrew the bulk of his forces to the Bataan Peninsula and the adjoining island of Corregidor. After a bitter struggle, MacArthur escaped to Australia and 76,000 American and Filipino troops surrendered to the Japanese. The remaining troops, under General Jonathan Wainwright, surrendered a month later.

General MacArthur, who heroically defended the Bataan Peninsula ▶

1941–42   MOBILIZING INDUSTRY 🏭

ALTHOUGH the American economy was partially mobilized for World War II as a result of the Lend-Lease program, the War Powers Act (1941) and the Second War Powers Act (1942) empowered the government to allot materials and facilities for defense. The War Production Board (1942) directed industrial conversion, with the end result being that auto makers turned out tanks, clothing manufacturers produced mosquito netting, toy factories rolled out hardware, and home appliance factories made munitions. It was this demand for war material and the host of new jobs thereby created that finally ended the Great Depression.

1941   MANHATTAN PROJECT ☢

WORRIED that Germany might successfully develop atomic weaponry, Albert Einstein (1879–1955) and other physicists persuaded President Roosevelt to begin a research endeavor that became the Manhattan Project. In June 1941, the government created the Office of Scientific Research and Development, headed by Dr. Vannevar Bush, to coordinate government-sponsored scientific efforts, including work on atomic fission. Teams were placed at a number of universities, among them Columbia, Princeton, California, and Chicago. Dr. Arthur Compton's team in Chicago produced the first

▲ *Albert Einstein encouraged the founding of the Manhattan Project*

chain reaction in uranium in December 1942. A laboratory was established in Los Alamos, New Mexico in 1943 for the express purpose of building an atomic bomb. The facility was under the direction of J. Robert Oppenheimer and General Leslie R. Groves. Over the next two years the endeavor employed 125,000 people at an expense of $2 billion. The first test explosion occurred at Alamogordo, New Mexico on July 16, 1945, and was a stunning—and frightening—success.

1942   PACIFIC OFFENSIVE

IN August 1942, American forces took the offensive in the Pacific, with assaults on the Japanese controlled islands of Gavutu, Tulagi, and Guadalcanal. The fighting on Guadalcanal was especially savage, lasting six months. Ultimately, the Japanese were forced to abandon the island, and with it their last chance of launching an effective offensive to the south.

The most crucial sea battle of the war in the Pacific occurred on June 4–6, 1942. The Japanese, determined to take the U.S. island of Midway, assembled 185 warships for the effort. The U.S. navy attacked the armada, and destroyed all four Japanese aircraft carriers while their aircraft were on deck refueling. The battle turned the tide of the Pacific war in favor of the United States.

▼ *The ships taking part in the Battle of Midway were supported by the airforce in planes such as the Grumman F4F Wildcat*

1942–43 NORTH AFRICA

ON November 8, 1942, British and American forces landed at Oran and Algiers in Algeria, and at Casablanca in Morocco, areas under the Nazi-controlled French government at Vichy. A controversial deal with French admiral and Nazi collaborator Jean Darlan enabled General Dwight D. Eisenhower (1890–1969) to begin moving his forces east toward the positions held by the Desert Fox, German Field Marshall Irwin Rommel (1891–1944). The Germans, having moved west from Egypt across Libya, threw the full weight of their forces against the inexperienced Americans, dealing a serious defeat at Kasserine Pass in Tunisia. General George S. Patton (1885–1945) regrouped the American troops and began an effective counteroffensive. With the help of Allied air and naval power, and of British forces attacking from the east under Field Marshall Bernard Montgomery (1887–1976), the American offensive drove the last Germans from Africa in May 1943.

1942 TURNING AWAY THE JEWS

AS early as 1942, officials in the United States government knew that Hitler and the Nazi government had put in force the extermination of the Jewish people, and were also rounding up other groups, such as Poles, homosexuals, and communists. The death toll in the concentration camps in eastern Germany and Poland ultimately reached 10 million, including six million Jews. As news of the atrocities reached the public, pressure built for some Allied action to end the killing and to rescue as many of the survivors as possible. The American government

The concentration camp at Buchenwald ▶

resisted such calls for actions. Although Allied bombers flew missions within a few miles of the Auschwitz death camp in Poland, raids to destroy the crematoria were rejected as militarily unfeasible, as were requests to bomb the rail lines leading to the camp. The United States further refused to admit large numbers of Jewish emigres. One vessel, the *St. Louis*, arrived off Miami carrying nearly 1,000 escaped German Jews, and was turned away. The State Department never used its full quota of visas during the war, leaving almost 90 percent of the allowed quota open, nor did it use up the number of visas permitted by law; almost 90 percent of the quota remained untouched.

1943   CASABLANCA CONFERENCE

IN January 1943, soon after the Allied landings in North Africa, President Roosevelt and British Prime Minister Winston Churchill met at the Moroccan port of Casablanca. There the two leaders committed their forces

to an invasion of Sicily and Italy, rather than an attack across the English Channel into France. A decision was also made to see an unconditional surrender from Germany.

1943–44 ITALIAN INVASION

THE Allied offensive on the Italian peninsula began on September 3, 1943, when soldiers faced entrenched Nazi positions. The Allies suffered a serious setback at Monte Cassino early in 1944, and the Allies did not capture the position until May 1944 at which time they resumed their move north. Rome fell on June 4, 1944. The Italian invasion postponed the invasion of France by at least a year, embittering the Soviet Union, and complicating its relations with the United States and Great Britain.

▼ *Franklin D. Roosevelt's leadership during World War II earned him the respect and support of the country*

1943 TEHRAN CONFERENCE

THE "Big Three"—President Franklin D. Roosevelt, British Prime Minister Winston Churchill, and Soviet leader Joseph Stalin (1879–1953)—met for the first time in the Iranian capital of Tehran in November 1943, at which time Roosevelt and Churchill promised an invasion of France across the English Channel in May or June 1944. Stalin reiterated his promise to enter the war with Japan but made it clear that he expected territorial concessions in return. The Soviet leader also made a vague commitment to the establishment of the United Nations.

▲ *Cartoon depicting Soviet leader Joseph Stalin*

1944 BATTLE OF LEYTE GULF

IN mid-June 1944, an American armada struck the heavily fortified Mariana Islands in the Pacific, and, after some of the bloodiest operations of the war, captured Tinian, Guam, and Saipan, 1,350 miles from Tokyo. In September, forces landed on the western Carolines. On October 20, General Douglas MacArthur's troops landed on Leyte Island in the Philippines. The Japanese prepared for a last defense of their empire, using their entire fleet against the Allied invaders in three major encounters known as the Battle of Leyte Gulf, the largest naval engagement in history. American forces held off the Japanese, sank four Japanese carriers, and destroyed Japan's capacity to continue a viable naval war.

1944 D-DAY AND THE GERMAN DEFEAT

ON June 6, 1944 the Allied forces staged the largest amphibious landing in history when they invaded German-held Normandy. Code-named D-Day, the attack against entrenched German positions succeeded, and within one week 326,00 men, 50,000 vehicles, and more than 100,000 tons of supplies had been landed. From the firm position thus established, the Allies swept across France and liberated Paris on August 25, 1944; by April 25, 1945, they successfully linked up with the Russians at the Elbe River for the final defeat of Germany.

1944 RECORDED SOUNDS ON D-DAY

IN the 1930s, American inventor Marvin Camras developed a wire recorder widely used by the military before and during World War II to train pilots. This recorder played a unique role in the 1944 invasion of Normandy (D-Day). Battle sounds were recorded, and equipment was developed to amplify it by thousands of watts. The recordings were then placed where the invasion was not going to take place, giving false information to the Germans.

1945 ROOSEVELT'S DEATH

BY 1945, President Roosevelt's health had deteriorated. He died of a stroke in Warm Springs, Georgia, on April 12, 1945, leaving Americans stunned and grieving. The only president elected four times (in 1932, 1936, 1940, and 1944), Roosevelt was the only national leader many Americans had ever known, and had inspired confidence and bravery during the Great Depression and World War II. Harry S. Truman (1884–1972), who became president on Roosevelt's death, did not inspire such feelings. The remark of Air Force Lieutenant Lloyd V. Williamson, on learning of Roosevelt's death, illustrated Truman's obscurity: "Who in the hell is Harry S. Truman?"

1945 UNITED NATIONS

AS the war came to a close in Europe, delegates from 50 nations met in San Francisco, in April 1945, to draft the charter of the United Nations. The U.N. basically consisted of a general assembly in which each member nation had one vote to act as a forum for world opinion. The decision-making authority resided with the Security Council consisting of five permanent member nations and six rotating ones. The permanent members were the United States, the Soviet Union, Britain, France, and China. Critical decisions of the Council required a unanimous vote.

1945 DAWN OF THE ATOMIC AGE AND JAPAN'S SURRENDER 🏛

WHILE at the Potsdam Conference (a conference between Allied leaders in Potsdam, Germany, in August 1945) President Truman was told that the atomic bomb was ready to be used on Japan. After lengthy discussion, Truman decided to use the bomb, after being told by his chiefs of staff that a million U.S. casualties would be caused if Japan were to be invaded. On August 6, 1945, a B-29 named the *Enola Gay*, with a crew commanded by Colonel Paul W. Tibbetts, dropped the atomic bomb on the Japanese city of Hiroshima. The resulting flash wiped out four square miles of the city, and killed more than 60,000 people.

On August 9, a second bomb was dropped on the port city of Nagasaki, killing 36,000 more. On August 14th, the Japanese emperor broke precedent and recorded a radio message announcing the surrender of his people. General Douglas MacArthur accepted the formal surrender on the deck of the battleship *Missouri* on September 2, 1945. The bomb not only marked the beginning of a new period in the history of mankind, but also increased the hostility between Truman and the Soviet leader Stalin, who had not been told about the bomb in advance. It became a factor in the development of the Cold War.

1945 RETURN TO CONSERVATISM ✡

THE liberals, who had been elevated to positions of power and influence by the New Deal in the 1930s, found themselves pushed aside to make room for the managers of wartime agencies drawn from the nation's industries and from Wall Street legal firms. Conservatives seized the opportunity to begin an onslaught on the liberal New Deal reforms. This shift paved the way for the rise of conservatism in America in the post–World War II years and into the 1950s.

The second atomic bomb was dropped on the Japanese city of Nagasaki in 1945, marking the dawn of the nuclear age ▶

CHAPTER 11

From Cold War to Kennedy

1945–63

1945   DISPUTE OVER GERMANY

AFTER 1945, the fundamental difference between East and West concerned attitudes toward Germany. Russia and the Soviet Union had been invaded twice by Germany during the first half of the 20th century, and Stalin felt the country remained a serious threat to be kept under control. The Soviet leader envisaged a Germany occupied by the Allies, paying reparations and subject to the tightest control. The West, on the other hand, believed that if Germany were treated too harshly there could be a reaction, as there had been after World War I. The Allies wanted an occupied Germany, but also wanted to offer the Germans help to recover from the damage inflicted upon it by the war.

**1945   YALTA CONFERENCE
AND THE START OF THE COLD WAR**

AT the Yalta conference in February 1945, the leaders of Britain, the United States, and the USSR met to decide the fate of Germany, which was to be divided into four zones, each to be occupied by one of the powers; France would occupy the fourth zone. Stalin promised to allow free elections in the Soviet-occupied Eastern

◄ *World leaders at the Yalta Conference*

European countries. He also agreed to allow exiled Poles to join the government that he had set up in Poland.

Five months later, at Potsdam President, Harry Truman took a much stronger line with Stalin, who had not allowed the promised elections. Stalin, in his turn, was angry that Truman had not informed him about the development of the atomic bomb. The Cold War had begun.

1945   IRON CURTAIN

FROM 1945, Soviet domination of eastern and central Europe increased, leading to what became known as the Iron Curtain, a thousand-mile barrier from the Baltic to the Adriatic that effectively cut Europe in two. Its purpose was to prevent any western influence from reaching the eastern European countries controlled by Stalin. In particular, it cut Germany into sections, the Soviet zone and the three western zones. The Iron Curtain received a hostile reception in the West, which surprised Stalin. At Yalta and Potsdam he had agreed that the West could do as it liked in western Europe, and he assumed he could do as he liked in the East. As always, Stalin's main preoccupation was security, and the Iron Curtain seemed to him a natural step. To the West, it correctly suggested the beginning of another form of dictatorship.

Soviet leader Stalin instigated the barrier across Europe that became known as the Iron Curtain ▶

1945 PRICE-WAGE SPIRAL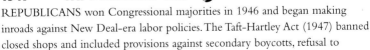

THOUGH prosperous, the American economy still presented a number of problems. The Truman administration faced postwar inflation and the need to curb wages, prices, and profits. The demands of organized labor ran counter to anti-inflationary policies. A series of labor strikes in 1945, including disruptions in the automobile and steel industries, were settled by allowing companies to raise prices in order to pay higher wages. This pattern was employed in other labor disputes, thus creating a problematic price-wage spiral.

The Servicemen's Readjustment Act of 1944, the "G.I. Bill of Rights," distributed $13 billion on education, vocational training, medical treatment, unemployment insurance, and home and business loans for returning World War II veterans.

1946 DR. SPOCK AND THE BABY BOOM

DOCTOR Benjamin Spock (1903–98) authored one of the most influential postwar books in America, *Baby and Child Care* (1946). His child-centered approach emphasized helping children to learn, grow, and realize their potential. According to Spock, all other considerations, including the mother's own physical and emotional requirements, must be subordinated to the needs of the child. The role of the father was, at best, modest.

Post-World War II America experienced large-scale population growth, known as the "baby boom." Of the total population, the birth rate per 1,000 grew from 19.4 in 1940 to more than 24 annually in 1946. It did not begin to decline until the 1960s.

Forrest M. Bird developed the first reliable, low-cost, mass-produced medical respirator in 1958. He followed with a respirator for infants in 1970, which reduced the worldwide infant mortality rate to less than 10 percent.

1947 TAFT-HARTLEY ACT

REPUBLICANS won Congressional majorities in 1946 and began making inroads against New Deal-era labor policies. The Taft-Hartley Act (1947) banned closed shops and included provisions against secondary boycotts, refusal to bargain in good faith, and political campaign contributions. Union leaders had to swear they were not members of the Communist party, and employers could sue unions for breaking contracts. Federal employees were forbidden to strike, and the president could impose an 80-day "cooling off" period in any strike dangerous to national health or safety. President Truman vetoed the bill, but Congress overrode it and the bill became law.

▼ *President Harry S. Truman*

1947   CONTAINMENT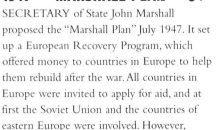

IN 1945, the United States was the only country that possessed atomic weapons, but by 1949, Soviet scientists duplicated the technology and detonated their first atomic bomb. The U.S. started work on a hydrogen fusion device, and both nations exploded hydrogen warheads in 1953–54. The next goal, rockets capable of delivering nuclear warheads, was reached in the early 1960s.

In an unsigned in July 1947 *Foreign Affairs* article, George F. Kennan, a member of the State Department, outlined a policy that defined America's Cold War policy. "It is clear," he wrote, "that the main element in any United States policy toward the Soviet Union must be that of a long-term, patient but firm and vigilant containment of Russian expansive tendencies . . . ." Containment infused America's Cold War actions well into the 1980s.

1947   MARSHALL PLAN

SECRETARY of State John Marshall proposed the "Marshall Plan" July 1947. It set up a European Recovery Program, which offered money to countries in Europe to help them rebuild after the war. All countries in Europe were invited to apply for aid, and at first the Soviet Union and the countries of eastern Europe were involved. However,

▲ *The nuclear arms race between the U.S. and the Soviet Union began after 1945*

when they discovered that Marshall Aid would involve membership of the Organization for European Economic Cooperation, the Soviets withdrew. Even so, Poland and Czechoslovakia still tried to obtain aid until Stalin banned their applications. Altogether about $13 billion was given out in aid from 1948–51.

1947   LIMITING PRESIDENTIAL POWER

DURING the Great Depression and World War II, Franklin D. Roosevelt stretched the power of the presidency more than any prior occupant of the Oval Office. Two postwar steps were taken to redefine some aspects of the presidency. The Presidential Succession Act (1947) allowed for the office to be passed in turn to the vice president, speaker of the house, president pro tempore of the Senate, and Secretary of State. This alignment was to insure elected rather than appointed officers led the government. The 22nd Amendment (1951) limited presidents after Harry Truman to two terms, a thinly veiled slap at Franklin Roosevelt's four terms.

▲ *Franklin D. Roosevelt's leadership during World War II earned him the admiration and support of the people*

1947   TRUMAN DOCTRINE

IN 1947 President Truman vocalized the Truman Doctrine, a major Cold War tenet to justify aid to Greece and Turkey, whose governments were in danger of becoming Communist. He said, "I believe that it must be the policy of the United States to support free peoples who are resisting attempted subjugation by armed minorities or by outside pressures."

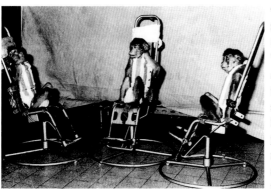

▲ *Monkeys were used initially in experiments with space exploration*

1947   RACE FOR SPACE

CAPTURED German V-2 missiles spurred American rocket technology. In 1947, a scientist at the White Sands, New Mexico, proving ground used monkeys to prove animals could survive rocket acceleration and brief periods of weightlessness.

Competition with the Soviet Union began in 1951, when the Russians launched a dog in the nose cone of a sounding rocket. In 1957, Russia placed *Sputnik*, the first artificial satellite, into orbit around the Earth, followed later in the year by the launch into space of a living creature, a small dog named

Yuri Gagarin, the first man in space ▶

Laika, who survived a week. On November 28, 1961, Enos, a five-and-a-half year old chimpanzee, made two orbits in an American Mercury spacecraft. The next day Enos returned safely. The first manned spaceflight carried Russian Yuri Gagarin (1934–68) in 1961. John Glenn became the first American to orbit the Earth in 1962.

1947 TIGHTENING NATIONAL SECURITY

CONGRESSIONAL investigations identified lack of coordination between the armed forces and intelligence services as a major factor in the Pearl Harbor disaster. The National Security Act of 1947 created a National Military Establishment, headed by a secretary of defense and with separate departments of the army, navy, and air force. The National Security Council was to be comprised of the president, heads of the defense departments, and the secretary of state. The wartime Joint Chiefs of Staff became permanent, and the Office of Strategic Service became the Central Intelligence Agency.

1948 BERLIN AIRLIFT

BERLIN, the capital of Germany, was divided into four sectors after the war. Each sector was governed by one of the Allies. In the British, U.S., and French sectors, people began to benefit from Allied rebuilding and Marshall Plan aid. As East Berliners from the Soviet sector were free to travel into the three western sectors, they were able to see the many advantages of life in the West. In June 1948, Stalin tried to cut off West Berlin from the Allied Zones in Germany, by stopping all traffic by road, rail, and canal. The Allies refused to be beaten and continued to supply Berlin by air. The Berlin Airlift lasted for ten and a half months and, at its peak, the Allies were carrying in 8,000 tons of supplies a day, twice what was required. In May 1949, Stalin gave up. The West had won the first real trial of strength of the Cold War.

1948 THE FAIR DEAL

BY the 1948 election, the Democratic party urged Harry Truman to step aside, but he refused and campaigned vigorously. He received the support of farmers, ethnic groups, labor, and—through his diplomatic recognition of Israel in 1948—the Jewish vote. He courted the African American vote by designating lynching as a federal crime and desegregating the armed forces. Truman defeated his Republican opponent Thomas Dewey and began work on his domestic program, the "Fair Deal." It called for national medical insurance, aid to education, regulation of discriminatory employment practices, and a better farm subsidy program. The program never got off the ground, blocked by a Congress dominated by Republicans and Southern Democrats.

1949 NATO

THE North Atlantic Treaty Organization was set up in 1949 after the Berlin Blockade. It was a military alliance involving countries on either side of the North Atlantic. It changed relations between East and West by uniting the countries of the West, leading to the stationing of U.S. forces in western

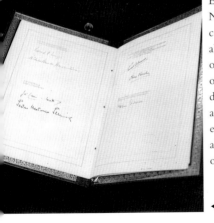

Europe. The most important clause in the NATO treaty was that an attack on one country was considered to be an attack on all. In other words, the East could not pick off democratic countries without the risk of a war with NATO. The Soviet Union did not react to NATO until the 1955 admission of West Germany. The Soviets established the Warsaw Pact, a military alliance between the Communist countries of eastern Europe.

◀ *The North Atlantic Treaty*

1950   POSTWAR PROSPERITY

THE Gross National Product in America reached $101 billion in 1940, and $347 billion by 1952. Unemployment, which in the 1930s averaged between 15–25 percent, remained throughout the 1950s and early 1960s at above five percent or lower. The suburban population grew 47 percent in the 1950s, stimulating growth in key economic sectors. In a boom even larger than that of the 1920s, the automobile industry saw private car ownership double within a decade. The suburban housing boom caused a vigorous construction industry, as did the demand for more and better roads. The average American in 1960 had over 20 percent more purchasing power than in 1945. Per capita income was more than $1,800, some $500 more than at the end of World War II. Americans had achieved the highest standard of living of any society in the history of the world.

1950s   TECHNOLOGICAL DEVELOPMENTS: TRANSISTORS, LASER AND ROBOTS

IN 1956, physicists John Bardeen, William Shockley, and Walter Brattain received the 1956 Nobel Prize for inventing the transistor to amplify electrical current with less energy than the vacuum tube in television and radio receivers. The transistor became the basis for modern electronics, and a primary foundation for microchip technology.

Gordon Gould's idea for the laser came to him in 1957. He wrote in his notebook,

Lasers were invented in 1957 by Gordon Gould ▶

"Some rough calculations on the feasibility of a LASER: Light Amplification by Stimulated Emission of Radiation." The devices are now widely used in industrial, commercial, and medical applications.

In 1961, General Motors pioneered the first industrial application of a robotic machine by introducing the Unimation 1900 into their car assembly line. By 1980, General Motors used a robot able to select and separate components. Robots have proved useful in projects too boring and laborious for humans and in dangerous situations such as bomb disposal and surface exploration of other planets.

1950s TELEVISION 🏛

TELEVISION made a rapid and pervasive impact on American life and had, by the end of the 1950s, replaced newspapers, magazines, and radios as the primary informational vehicle. Televised advertisements spread a demand for fashions and products, while sporting events became a favored source of entertainment. Three

national networks—the National Broadcasting Company, the Columbia Broadcasting System, and the American Broadcasting Company—controlled programing and supplanted the role of movies and radio.

1950s SELF-ACTUALIZATION

ABRAHAM Maslow and Carl Rogers founded the school of humanistic psychology in the United States in the 1950s. Maslow studied the behavior of

◄ *The popularity of television increased dramatically thoughout the 1950s*

people who were mentally healthier than average. His therapy aimed at removing all the inner obstacles to the open-ended process of "self-actualization": of achieving one's true potential. The theory was that human needs exist in a hierarchy; when lower needs, such as food and shelter, are satisfied then higher needs, such as love and acceptance, become the principal motivators. Maslow's study of self-actualizing people revealed that they were spontaneous, creative, lacked inhibitions, and were interested in the world rather than being self-centered.

The Reverend Norman Vincent Peale published *The Power of Positive Thinking* (1952), a book that remained a bestseller throughout the decade. A simple, how-to course on personal happiness, he drew on a long tradition of "positive thinking" in American social and religious thought. He offered a message of psychological security and material success that proved powerfully reassuring to many Americans.

1950   KOREA

AT the end of World War II, Korea had been divided into a Communist North and a non-Communist South. In 1950, North Korea invaded the South and quickly overran all but the very southernmost tip of the peninsula. The United States took the matter to the United Nations Security Council, which agreed to send a U.N. force to

Memorial to those killed in the Korean War ▶

support South Korea. U.N. forces landed in the South, and also behind North Korean lines at Inchon. The North Koreans were forced back, and retreated almost to the Chinese border. However, the Chinese army invaded to support them and the U.N. forces in turn were forced to retreat. A cease-fire was finally agreed in 1953. The border between the North and the South was then fixed at exactly the same point as it had been when the war began.

1950   McCARTHYISM   🏛

SENATOR Joseph McCarthy of Wisconsin achieved national prominence in February 1950. During a speech in Wheeling, West Virginia, he claimed knowledge of 205 communists in the State Department. After 1952, McCarthy served as chair of a special subcommittee, and the Republicans controlled the Senate. He conducted highly publicized investigations of subversion.

McCarthy relentlessly badgered witnesses, and excelled in the destruction of public careers. He never managed to produce evidence that a single federal employee had communist ties, and overreached himself in January 1954 by attacking President Dwight D. Eisenhower, Secretary of the Army Robert Stevens, and the armed services. The resulting Army v. McCarthy hearings, among the first to be nationally televised, destroyed McCarthy's public image. His bullying, groundless accusations, and cruel remarks made him out to be a villain and, finally, a fool. In December 1954, the Senate voted 67 to 22 to condemn him for "conduct unbecoming a senator." He died in 1957 of complications from alcoholism.

◀ *Senator Joseph McCarthy accused senior politicians of having communist sympathies*

1952   **MODERN REPUBLICANISM**

IN 1952, the American people elected to the White House Republican Dwight
D. Eisenhower (1890–1969), the former World War II Allied Supreme
Commander. He approved extensions of Social Security benefits, raised the
minimum wage to $1 an hour, and created the Department of Health,
Education, and Welfare in 1953 to act as a welfare clearing house. Eisenhower's
"modern Republicanism" worked for reduced federal spending, including
military appropriations. He favored private initiative and state-directed programs.

In 1956, he supported a Highway Act that provided funds for the
construction of a 41,000-mile interstate highway system. Reelected in 1956,
Eisenhower faced an economic recession in 1957, and switched to a policy of
greater federal spending. As a result, his dream of a balanced budget proved
elusive, and he left office with a $12 billion deficit.

▼ *General Dwight D. Eisenhower became President of the U.S. in 1952*

1953 COEXISTENCE

IN March 1953, Stalin died. After a period of rivalry, he was replaced by Nikita Khrushchev (1849–1971), who immediately brought about a change in East-West relations by introducing the policy of Coexistence. Khrushchev believed there was nothing to be gained by trying to destroy the West; the Soviet Union had to accept it existed, and had to try to compete with it and prove the Soviet system was superior. Competition took the form of the Space Race, which the Soviet Union won with the first satellite in 1957 and the first man in space in 1961. Soviet athletes also began to dominate the Olympic Games from 1956. Khrushchev was a lively character, who enjoyed travel and meeting people. He set out to make headlines and produce a popular image for Communism.

1953 & 1957 POLIO AND PENICILLIN

JONAS Salk (1914–95) developed the first successful vaccine for polio in 1953. Mass trials later that year on 1.83 million children proved the vaccine was safe and effective. He received a Congressional gold medal for his "great achievement in the field of medicine."

During World War II, more than 1,000 scientists throughout the U.S. worked unsuccessfully to synthesize the penicillin molecule. By 1948 only John Sheehan was continuing the research. In March 1957, while a professor at the Massachusetts Institute of Technology, Sheehan announced the first rational total synthesis of natural penicillin. The next year he reported a general total synthesis of penicillins.

◀ *Jonas Salk – the man who invented the polio vaccine*

1954   LITTLE ROCK   🏛

CIVIL Rights issues intensified in America in the 1950s. In 1954, the Supreme Court ruled in *Brown v. Board of Education of Topeka*, rejecting the doctrine of the 1896 *Plessy v. Ferguson* decision, which had established separate but equal facilities for the races. Because President Eisenhower did not actively endorse and support the decision, many branded him a racist. In actuality, the president did not believe real integration could be achieved by force. He worked for the desegregation of federal facilities, and when pushed to the wall, used the national guard to enforce the integration of Little Rock Central High School in 1957, when Arkansas governor Orville Faubus employed 270 armed troops to turn away nine black students.

1955   SUMMITS   🗡

FROM 1955, the leaders of the United States, the USSR, Britain and France began to meet regularly at "summits." Very little ever came of these meetings in terms of actual agreements, but they were a sign that relations between East and West were improving. In fact the Soviet prime minister, Nikita Khrushchev, used the meetings as a means of winning popular support throughout the world. When he visited Britain in 1957, he broke with protocol and shook hands with workers at a factory.

1959   CUBA   🗡

FROM 1952, Cuba was governed by pro-American dictator Fulgencio Batista, but in 1959 he was overthrown by rebels led by Fidel Castro. The United States cut off all aid

Cuban leader Fidel Castro ▶

to Cuba, and Castro in turn nationalized all US assets and property in Cuba. Khrushchev took advantage of the situation by agreeing to buy one million tons of Cuban sugar every year at inflated prices. This brought Cuba Soviet influence, and Castro set up a Communist regime. Many U.S. citizens were horrified. Communism now existed only 70 miles off the coast of Florida. President Eisenhower authorized an attempt to overthrow Castro by landing a force of Cuban exiles at the Bay of Pigs. The landing actually took place in April 1961, after Eisenhower had left office; it was a disaster, with all 1,500 Cubans either killed or captured.

1960　　NEW FRONTIER

IN 1960, American voters elected to office to a youthful, wealthy intellectual from Massachusetts, John Fitzgerald Kennedy (1917–63). His domestic program, the New Frontier, aspired to get America going again after the sluggish Republican moderation of the 1950s. He called for health care and aid to education, but his programs were blocked by an ultra-conservative majority in Congress in 1961, 1962, and 1963. Ironically, it was his "flexible response" foreign policy and the Soviet-inspired race for space that regenerated the economy through increased military appropriations.

Kennedy was assassinated in Dallas, Texas, on November 22, 1963. Although his death continued to generate conspiracy theories in the 1990s, the Warren Commission, charged with investigating the presidential murder, placed complete blame on a lone gunman, Lee Harvey Oswald.

1961　　BERLIN WALL

THE construction of the Berlin Wall was started in August 1961, separating families and trapping people who had crossed to the other side of Berlin. For 12 years people had been escaping from East Berlin to West Berlin and, by 1961, their numbers were reaching thousands every week. Most of the people

The wall dividing East and West Berlin ▶

who escaped were skilled workers, doctors, or engineers. The Wall was an attempt to stop the drain of people from East to West. It was very effective, but did not stop people trying to escape. The Wall also increased tension between the Superpowers. President Kennedy visited West Berlin to show his support for its citizens, making a speech containing the famous words "ich bin ein Berliner."

1962   KENNEDY AND CIVIL RIGHTS 🏛

CIVIL Rights issues exploded during President Kennedy's administration, as an angry response to the president's failure to meet campaign promises to work for African American rights.

Avoiding vigorous action in incidents like James Meredith's entrance to the University of Mississippi in 1962 and Governor George Wallace's attempt to halt the integration of the University of Alabama in 1963, Kennedy used the Justice Department to encourage blacks to register to vote, and engaged in under-funded ventures like the

Commission on Equal Employment Opportunities. African American activists led by the Reverend Martin Luther King (1929–68) exerted pressure on the administration. Following the Birmingham protests of 1963, during which the police used fire hoses and police dogs against demonstrators, Kennedy finally made a public stand for civil rights and proposed legislation calling for equal access to public facilities and increased black voting rights. Refusing to be lulled into complacency, the African American leaders staged a demonstration in Washington in August 1963 to keep up the pressure on Kennedy.

1962   CUBAN MISSILE CRISIS

ON October 17, 1962, President Kennedy was shown photographs of Soviet missile bases in Cuba. Their presence meant that Soviet missiles could be launched at most U.S. cities, and there was no defense against these attacks. After a week of discussions, Kennedy decided to blockade Cuba and stop any more Soviet ships going there. For a week U.S. forces were on full alert, and many people around the world expected that nuclear war would break out. In fact, Nikita Khrushchev, the Soviet prime minister, realized that he had made a mistake and sent two messages to Kennedy, one threatening, the other conciliatory. Kennedy replied to the conciliatory message and the crisis was settled peacefully. The Soviet bases in Cuba were destroyed and the United States agreed not to interfere in Cuban affairs.

1963   HOTLINE

AFTER the Cuban Missile Crisis, the leaders of the U.S. and the USSR realized such a situation could not be allowed to happen again. The first real sign of lessened tensions was the setting up of the Hotline in 1963, this was a direct teleprinter link between the Kremlin and the White House. It was hardly ever used, but it was a sign that the two sides were talking to each other.

◀ *Civil Rights' campaigner Martin Luther King*

CHAPTER 12

From Civil Rights to Clinton

1963–99

1963–69   LYNDON B. JOHNSON

LYNDON B. Johnson (1908–73) who became president following the Kennedy assassination on November 22, 1963, served as a Democratic Congressman from Texas for more than 30 years. As a memorial to the slain president, Johnson immediately went to Congress, asked for, and received passage of Kennedy's civil rights and tax legislation in 1964. The Civil Rights Act outlawed segregation in public facilities and established a Fair Employment Practices Committee; title VII of the act extended its protection to gender as well as race. The Tax Reduction Act cut personal income taxes by $10 billion giving the economy a needed boost and touching off $43 billion in increased consumer spending over the ensuing 18 months.

1963–73   VIETNAM

WHEN Lyndon Johnson became president in 1963, America was committed to the support of the democratic government of South Vietnam. Vietnamese rebels, the Viet Cong, worked to overthrow the government, aided by the Communist-backed leader of North Vietnam, Ho Chi Minh (1890–1960). Johnson believed the United States should honor its promises, but wanted to see the South Vietnamese carry out the bulk of economic and social reform in their country.

▲ *A U.S. soldier with a South Vietnamese refugee*

The number of American GIs in South Vietnam was raised in 1964 from 16,000 to almost 25,000, and they were increasingly drawn into the fighting. By August 1964, American planes raided North Vietnam following attacks on American naval vessels. Congress gave Johnson authority to take such actions as the situation required, which he did in February 1965 with enlarged air assaults. By the end of 1965, ground troops totaled 180,000; this number doubled in 1966, and by 1968 the level was close to 500,000. A major Viet Cong and North Vietnamese offensive in 1968 contradicted the optimistic assurances from the White House of an imminent victory. On March 31, 1968, Johnson announced both a pause in the bombing and his refusal to seek another term in office. The bombing was halted completely on November 1.

While North Vietnam continued pressure against South Vietnam and the neighboring countries of Laos and Cambodia, President Richard M. Nixon (1913–94), elected in 1968, gradually disengaged from the war. Troop strength fell to 30,000 in 1972. At the same time he approved an April 1970 attack on Communist sanctuaries in Cambodia. In February 1971, U.S. and South Vietnamese troops invaded Laos. The spring of 1972 brought increased bombings of the North Vietnamese capital, Hanoi. A cease-fire was finally achieved in 1972, and a peace agreement on January 28, 1973. Nearly 600 prisoners of war were returned to the U.S.. American involvement in Cambodia continued until August 15, 1973.

Soldiers in South Vietnam ▶

1964 GREAT SOCIETY

FOLLOWING his 1964 reelection triumph, President Johnson christened his legislative program the "Great Society." By the fall of 1965, his entire legislative shopping list moved through Congress; 89 bills found their way into law. Among the landslide of legislation came reforms such as Medicare and Medicaid (health insurance for the elderly); aid to education through the Elementary and Secondary Education Act; and increased voting protection for African Americans in the Voting Rights Act of 1965.

Johnson announced his war on poverty in his January 1964 State of the Union Address; at the time, some 35 million Americans qualified as impoverished. Between 1964 and 1967, the Johnson administration reduced this figure by 10 million, and as a result, American voters gave Johnson a landslide 1964 victory. He received 61.1 percent of the popular vote and 486 electoral votes to Republican opponent Barry Goldwater's 52.

President Johnson instigated a new legislative program known as the "Great Society" ▶

1965   VACCINATION NEEDLE ☢☢

IN 1965, microbiologist Benjamin A. Rubin ground the eyelet of a sewing machine needle into the shape of a fork, to create a vaccine delivery system that helped wipe out the killer disease smallpox. Before 1967, smallpox killed at least two million people annually worldwide. Rubin's innovation improved vaccinations to the point that the World Health Assembly declared smallpox defeated in 1980.

1967   EXPLORING SPACE 🌐🗺

THE Apollo space program began with the tragic deaths of those aboard Virgil I. "Gus" Grissom, Edward White, and Roger Chaffee were killed in a fire that swept their Block One Apollo spacecraft on January 27, 1967. Subsequently redesigned, the Apollo craft carried 47 men into space from October 1968 to July 1975. Twelve of those men walked on the moon, beginning with Neil Armstrong (1930–) in July 1969 and ending with Eugene Cernan in December 1972. Subsequent space exploration included the launch of the first space station by the Soviet Union in 1974, and the extensive use by the U.S. of the space shuttle. The shuttle *Columbia* took its first developmental flight in 1981, beginning a routine of satellite deployment and scientific experimentation. The program's success was marred on January 28, 1986, however, when the shuttle *Challenger* exploded 72 seconds after lift-off, killing all crew members.

Launch of the space shuttle Columbia ▶

In 1990, the shuttle *Discovery* deployed the Hubble Space Telescope and by 1998 the U.S. and Russia were at work on an international space station. On October 29, 1998, former Senator John Glenn (1921–) of Ohio—the first man to orbit the earth, in 1962, in the Mercury spacecraft Friendship—returned to space at age 78 as part of the shuttle *Discovery* crew.

1968 JOHNSON BOWS OUT

DURING the run-up to the 1968 presidential election, increased anti-war protests led Lyndon B. Johnson to announce he would not seek or accept his party's nomination. Hubert Humphrey received the nomination in the absence of his strongest opponent, Robert Kennedy, who had been assassinated in Los Angeles. Republican Richard M. Nixon (1913–94) capitalized on the anti-war discontent and cast himself as a peace candidate. The appeal of such promises, even from an archconservative and one-time Communist-hunter like Nixon, was undeniable. This Nixon appeared to be a moderate in the tradition of

▼ *President Richard Milhous Nixon*

Eisenhower, and many Americans yearned for the lost security of the 1950s. Nixon won by a slight popular majority, 31.8 million votes to Humphrey's 31.3 million. Nixon's victory is greatly credited to the presence of third-party candidate George Wallace, who picked up nearly 10 million votes.

1968   COUNTERCULTURE

IN the 1960s and early 1970s, the Vietnam War tore at the social fabric of the United States, and young Americans were further radicalized by social injustices and the fervor of the civil rights movement. Thousands of young men and women, hostile to the values of the middle-class, took their stand through rallies, protests, and concerts. Alternate lifestyles blossomed, with various experiments in communal living. Demonstrators chanted, "All we are saying is give peace a chance," and the phrase "Tune in, turn on, and drop out!", as advocated by academic and counterculture guru Timothy Leary, indicated the dramatic change in American youth. The long hair, rock and folk music, and drug use of the counterculture "flower children" threatened their elders in the "establishment."

▲ *The horrors of the Vietnam War caused young Americans to join the peace movement*

1969–74   RICHARD M. NIXON

AS Chief Executive, Richard Nixon exhibited a high degree of personal paranoia that led him to isolate himself in the Oval Office, appointing a corps of loyal watchdogs like H. R. Haldeman and John Ehrlichman. The president believed he could run the nation single-handedly, armed with sweeping executive powers and privileges, most of which existed only in his mind.

Nixon's forte was foreign policy, and during his two terms in office (1969–74) he made landmark trips to Communist China and Russia. Nixon concentrated his domestic efforts toward streamlining the federal bureaucracy. His plan for more efficient welfare distribution failed, but he did introduce the concept of revenue sharing, in which federal funds were dispersed to state, county, and city agencies to meet specific local needs. Nixon took a cautious line on civil rights, turning the thorny problem over to the federal courts. His presidency was destroyed by the constitutional crisis known as "Watergate," ultimately forcing him to resign.

1969   SALL

IN 1969, the Superpowers began Strategic Arms Limitation Talks aimed at limiting nuclear weapons. The first treaty, SALT 1, was signed in 1972. Its most important clause was a five-year moratorium on the building of strategic weapons. It did not lessen the risk of nuclear war or affect intermediate or tactical weapons, but it was the first agreement of its kind. SALT 2 (1979) was a more important treaty in that it limited the number of strategic weapons the two Superpowers could build; each would have no more than 2,500. Congress never ratified the treaty, however, due to the Soviet invasion of Afghanistan in December 1979.

1969 MICROPROCESSOR

FROM its inception in 1969, the microprocessor industry became one of the most important developments of the last half of the 20th century. Microprocessors in the form of single-chip general-purpose central processors

◀ *The microchip revolutionized technology from 1969*

(CPUs) are found in automobiles, medical devices, and computers. Stanley Mazor, Federico Faggin, and Marcian Hoff developed the microprocessor, and the first working CPU was delivered in February 1971; it had as much computing power as the first electronic computer, the room-sized ENIAC (1946).

1970   FORD, CARTER, AND THE ECONOMY

PRESIDENT Gerald R. Ford (1913–), who assumed the presidency upon the resignation of Richard M. Nixon in 1974, was a fiscal conservative. In fighting the nation's economic ills he resorted to such rhetoric as his WIN campaign, an acronym for "Whip Inflation Now." Ultimately, however, he followed Nixon's example and encouraged the Federal Reserve to tighten credit. The recession only deepened through the administration of Jimmy Carter (1924–), who was elected in November 1976.

In 1975 unemployment stood at 8.5 percent. For the fiscal year 1976–77, the federal deficit stood at $60 billion. The continued flight of the middle class to the suburbs wrecked the economy of many major cities. The government bailed out New York City in 1975 and in 1980 did the same for the Chrysler Corporation to the tune of $1.5 billion. Despite such efforts the recession deepened, with inflation reaching 13.4 percent in 1979 and unemployment standing at 7.5 percent in 1980.

President Gerald R. Ford ▶

1970   **INFLATION** 🏛

THE American economy in the 1970s suffered from a number of problems. As the economy became more service oriented, industrial output declined. Millions of "baby boomers," born in the population explosion at the end of World War II, hit the workforce at the same time sending unemployment figures upward, while the easy availability of credit drove inflation ever higher. Wages increased, but buying power did not. Farmers who stayed in business were forced to borrow heavily. Labor leaders blamed high foreign competition and called for raised tariffs. Businessmen blamed the federal government for imposing rigid health, safety, and environmental standards that increased their operating expenses. In truth, the greatest economic ill—spiraling inflation—could be attributed to the failure of both Lyndon B. Johnson and Richard M. Nixon to design sensible tax policies to pay for American involvement in the Vietnam War.

1970 **RELIGIOUS REVIVAL** ☖

IN the 1970s, approximately 70 million Americans experienced a religious revival as powerful as the second Great Awakening of the early 19th century. Various cults and sects rose in popularity including the Church of Scientology, the Unification Church of the Reverend Sun Myung Moon, and the People's Temple of the Reverend Jim Jones. This last developed into one of the tragedies of the decade, with its members ultimately committing mass suicide in Guyana in 1978, after drinking Kool-Aid laced with cyanide. The strongest impulse, however, was the rebirth of evangelical Christianity as evidenced by the founding of the Moral Majority in 1979 by the Reverend Jerry Falwell.

1970 "ME DECADE" 🏛

IN the 1970s, Americans turned inward and focused on personal improvement leading social commentators to dub the era the "Me Decade." Physical fitness fads were widespread, such as a new national addiction to jogging. The favored musical genre, disco, offered a flashy, bright-lights environment of dancing, strongly associated with casual sexual encounters and drug abuse, ironically coinciding with the "born again" spiritual revival. These trends slowed by 1980, when the census showed a population growing older and more conservative.

1970 FIBER OPTICS ☢

IN 1970, three employees of Corning Glass in New York—Robert Maurer, Donald Keck, and Peter Schultz—produced fiber-optic wire capable of carrying 65,000 times more information than conventional copper wire. Their development became the foundation of the global multimedia telecommunications network revolution of the late 1990s, with more than 90 percent of U.S. long-distance telephone traffic carried over fiber-optic lines in 1998.

◀ *Reverend Sun Myung Moon presiding over a wedding ceremony*

1971   NIXON AND THE ECONOMY

PRESIDENT Richard Nixon's economic performance was mediocre. He inherited a $25 billion budget deficit, much of which was created by the escalating Vietnam War, and a 5 percent inflation rate. Initially he attempted to

hold federal spending in check, and instructed the Federal Reserve Board to tighten the money supply; this led only to higher inflation. By 1971, the severe economic picture caused Nixon to alter his strategy. In mid-August, the president imposed a 90-day freeze on wages and prices, followed by imposed federal guidelines that helped to lessen the effects of the recession.

◄ *Nixon's involvement in the Watergate scandal resulted in his resignation*

1972   WATERGATE

THE Watergate scandal began with the 1972 break-in and electronic bugging of the Democratic National Committee headquarters in the Watergate apartment and office building in Washington, D.C.. The Committee for the Reelection of the President orchestrated the burglary. Before the scandal concluded, President Nixon was forced to resign (August 9, 1974), and more than 30 officials in his administration and campaign staffs pleaded to or were found guilty of breaking the law. Their transgressions included covering up the

White House involvement by destroying any incriminating documents, and lying to official investigators. In addition, many illegal campaign contributions were discovered. Nixon's resignation was prompted by his unwillingness to produce any recordings of Oval Office conversations.

▲ *President Jimmy Carter*

1973 ARAB OIL EMBARGO

DURING the 1973 Yom Kippur War, Egypt and Syria attacked Israel. The United States supplied the Israelis, and forced both sides to sign a truce by putting its forces on nuclear alert. In response, the Organization of Petroleum Exporting Countries (OPEC), cut back its oil production and exportation in an effort to force Israel to return seized territories. When President Nixon announced a $2.2 billion aid package to Israel in October, OPEC cut off all oil shipments to the United States. The Arab oil embargo forced Americans to realize they no longer lived in a nation with unlimited natural resources, and that the U.S. had, in fact, become dependant on other nations. It further signaled the end of the post-World War II economic boom.

1974–77 GERALD R. FORD

GERALD R. Ford (1913–) became the first vice-president to assume the Oval Office after a presidential resignation, on August 9, 1974. As chief executive, his personal integrity helped heal national discontent after the Watergate scandal. He inherited an economy plagued by inflation and unemployment, and pursued cautious fiscal policies, sought accommodations with the Soviet Union and China, and maintained the fragile Middle Eastern peace. The nation, however, craved vigorous leadership, leading to his 1976 defeat by Democrat Jimmy Carter.

▲ *Gerald Ford's integrity helped heal the public's outrage after Watergate*

1977–81 JIMMY CARTER

IN the election of 1976, Georgia Democrat Jimmy Carter (1942–) of Georgia presented himself as a man outside the Washington political infrastructure and thus untainted by corruption. He claimed to be a fiscal conservative who intended to curb government spending, but at the same time was a social liberal who would fight for the dispossessed. In the election, little over half of eligible voters participated, a frightening indication of the degree to which Americans were disenchanted with politics.

1978   CAMP DAVID

IN 1978, President Jimmy Carter invited Egyptian President Anwar Sadat and Israeli prime minister Menachem Begin to the presidential retreat in Maryland, Camp David, in order to attempt a solution to the continued hostility between their nations over the ownership of various territories seized by Israel in 1967. From this 13-day meeting came the Camp David accords, a set of agreements laying the groundwork for future negotiations. Although Israel and Egypt signed a treaty in 1979 providing for the gradual return of the Sinai to Egypt, the fate of the Palestinian Arabs was left unresolved, giving rise to radical terrorist groups like the Palestine Liberation Army under Yasser Arafat. Bitterly opposed by many Arab leaders and hated by Islamic fundamentalists, Sadat was assassinated in Cairo in 1981. Although Begin lived to retire and die in obscurity, the extent to which peace continued to elude the troubled Middle East became evident in November 1995, when Israeli Prime Minister Yitzhak Rabin was assassinated while leaving a public peace rally in the Middle East.

1979   IRANIAN HOSTAGE CRISIS

THE Iranian revolution in 1979 deposed the shah and placed the Ayatollah Ruhollah Khomeini, a fundamentalist Moslem leader, in control of the nation. On November 4, 1979, after President Carter allowed the exiled shah to enter the United States to seek medical treatment, the American embassy in Iran was seized.

Ayatollah Ruhollah Khomeini ▶

Diplomacy, economic pressure, and a show of naval strength in the Indian Ocean failed to secure the release of the Americans held hostage. In his State of the Union address in January 1980, President Carter pledged his determination to protect the flow of oil through the Persian Gulf and to secure the release of the hostages. Despite his strong words and a failed rescue mission in April 1980, however, the hostages were not released until January 20, 1981, the day of Ronald Reagan's inauguration.

1980   GRAYING OF AMERICA 🏛

THE 1990 census revealed the "graying of America": citizens in their 90s more than doubled in the 1980s, while the number of those over 100 grew by over three-quarters. Americans were healthier than ever, and they were also on the move with more and more being drawn from the Midwest and Northeast to the "Sunbelt"— the South and West—where they tended to settle in larger communities. The traditional family unit continued to decline, with more Americans living alone, opting not to have children, functioning as single parents, forming blended families, or openly choosing same-sex partners.

1981–89   RONALD REAGAN

AFTER a brief swing toward liberalism with the election of Jimmy Carter (1911–), the nation again turned to a strong Conservative

Republican president Ronald Reagan ▶

Republican, Ronald Reagan, in the 1980 election, at which time the combined rates of inflation and unemployment stood at 28 percent. Reagan blamed the situation on high federal spending and taxes and also claimed America's military had been dangerous weakened. He worked to reduce the growth of national government; restore the power of the states; expand the military and defense establishments; lower taxes; and bargain from a position of strength with the Soviet Union. He was reelected in 1984.

In 1986 the Reagan administration admitted to covert arms sales to Iran, with some of the profits possibly diverted to Nicarguan guerillas. Reagan denied knowledge of the Iran-Contra affair through a series of investigations. National security adviser Vice Admiral John Poindexter and his aide Lieutenant Colonel Oliver North were indicted in 1988.

1981 DETERIORATING RELATIONS WITH THE SOVIETS

WHEN Reagan, an arch anti-Communist, became president of the United States, relations with the Soviet Union deteriorated. In 1980 the United States had boycotted the Olympic Games in Moscow, and in 1984 the USSR staged a retaliatory boycott of the Games in Los Angeles. Disarmament talks made no progress for years. The situation was worsened by internal Soviet politics. Leonid Brezhnev, who had been president since 1964, was

▲ *Soviet president Leonid Brezhnev, whose death led to a protracted period of stagnation in the U.S.S.R.*

very ill and corruption was widespread. When he died in 1982, Yuri Andropov replaced him, but he fell ill and died in 1984. His successor, Konstantin Chernenko died in 1985. For five years there had been little prospect of real change, either internally or externally.

1982 BEIRUT

IN April 1982, the Israelis withdrew from the Sinai but continued to spread settlements into the West Bank despite the Camp David promise to pull back from this area, the proposed Palestinian homeland. On June 6, 1982, Israel began an invasion of southern Lebanon to secure the nation's northern border and crush the Palestine Liberation Organization. America allowed itself to be drawn into a civil war in Lebanon between Christian and Moslem forces. However, after Moslem terrorists drove a truck loaded with explosives into an American barracks, killing 239 soldiers in their sleep, the United States pulled out, with the last troops leaving Beirut in February 1984.

1982 REAGAN AND THE ECONOMY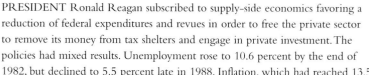

PRESIDENT Ronald Reagan subscribed to supply-side economics favoring a reduction of federal expenditures and revues in order to free the private sector to remove its money from tax shelters and engage in private investment. The policies had mixed results. Unemployment rose to 10.6 percent by the end of 1982, but declined to 5.5 percent late in 1988. Inflation, which had reached 13.5 percent in the Carter years, fell to 4–6 percent. The greatest economic shock occurred on October 19, 1987 with a 508 point stock market plunge ending a slide that began in August. In two months, stocks lost over a third of their value, though they recovered half the loss within a year.

1989–93 GEORGE BUSH

IN the 1988 presidential campaign future Republican president George Bush repeated the "no new tax" pledge, and promised to continue other Reagan-era economic policies that had brought general prosperity. He reaffirmed his predecessor's determination to negotiate with the Soviet Union only from a posture of strength. As president he faced a Democratic-controlled Congress, often leading him to often adopt middle-of-the road positions. In June 1990 Bush abandoned his "Read my lips. No new taxes" campaign pledge, and acknowledged that new or increased taxes were necessary. Many Republican

▲ *Republican president George Bush*

conservatives were critical of this shift, and his popularity ratings fell. The House, with many Republicans in opposition, defeated a compromise deficit-reduction plan. As a result, the government was almost forced to shut down for lack of money while a new budget proposal was drafted.

1990 PERSIAN GULF WAR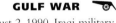

ON August 2, 1990, Iraqi military forces, on orders from President Saddam Hussein, invaded and occupied the neighboring country of Kuwait in less than four hours, thereby putting Iraq in control of nearly a quarter of the world's oil supplies.

Saddam's next target appeared to be Saudi Arabia, which issued a call for United States protection. The United States set a deadline, January 15, 1991, for all Iraq forces to be out of Kuwait, but Saddam ignored the deadline. The result was Operation Desert Shield, a troop build-up

▼ *Iraqi president Saddam Hussein*

in the region and eventually Operation Desert Storm, an all-out attack to free Kuwait. The Persian Gulf War was fought from January 16 to February 28, 1991, after which Saddam Hussein's troops were expelled from Kuwait.

1992　BUSH AND THE ECONOMY

THE unemployment rate climbed during the Bush administration (1988–92), though the president worked aggressively to create jobs through increased exports. In 1992, interest rates and inflation were at their lowest levels in years and unemployment stood at 7.8 percent, the highest level since 1984. The census bureau reported that 14.2 percent of all Americans lived in poverty.

▲ *Kuwaiti soldiers during the Gulf War*

1992　BILL CLINTON

BILL Clinton (1946–) was elected in 1992 on a wave of expectations for change. Early in his tenure he ended the federal prohibition on the use of fetal tissue for medical research, repealed restrictions on abortion counseling in federally funded health clinics, and placed women and minorities in prominent appointed positions. Congress altered his proposed ban on homosexuals in the military to a "don't ask, don't tell" policy. A much-hyped health-care reform package spearheaded by First Lady Hillary Clinton failed. Following President Clinton's 1996 reelection, questions over improprieties in an Arkansas land deal in the 1980s—the "Whitewater" affair—led to a special investigation that yielded evidence not of real estate fraud but of sexual improprieties with White House intern Monica Lewinsky. Allegations of perjury led the House of Representatives to start impeachment proceedings against Clinton in 1999, making him only the second president in the history of the United States to face such a process.

1997 CLINTON AND THE ECONOMY

PRESIDENT Bill Clinton managed a major tax-cut in 1997, the first since 1981, and was able to negotiate a deficit-reduction package that projected a balanced budget in 2002. Clinton's popularity increased as the apparent strength of the economy continued. His domestic record showed that he cut the deficit in half, expanded earned-income credit for the working poor, and significantly reduced the number of government workers.

▼ *President Bill Clinton being sworn in*

CHAPTER 13

Famous Americans

ALCOTT, LOUISA MAY

THE author Louisa May Alcott (1832–88) was part of the pre-Civil War Transcendentalist movement in America. She was a nurse in a Union hospital at Georgetown during the war, and published her letters from this period in 1863 as *Hospital Sketches*. It was followed by a novel, *Moods* (1864) after which she assumed the editorship of the children's magazine *Merry's Magazine*. She achieved great success with her books about the March family: *Little Women* (1868), *Good Wives* (1869), *Little Men* (1870), and *Jo's Boys* (1886). She counted Transcendentalist leaders Ralph Waldo Emerson and Henry David Thoreau among her friends.

ALI, MUHAMMAD

MUHAMMAD Ali is the adopted name of Cassius Clay (1942–), who was the Olympic light-heavyweight champion in 1960, and went on to become world professional heavyweight champion in 1964. Ali was known for his fast footwork and extrovert nature, and was the only man ever to regain the heavyweight title twice. He fought in the last of his 61 professional fights in 1981, against Trevor Berbick.

Ali, sadly, now suffers from Parkinson's disease. Since his retirement, he was honored at the 1996 Olympics held in Atlanta by lighting the Olympic flame.

◀ *Muhammad Ali*

▲ *Michael Collins, "Buzz" Aldrin, and Neil Armstrong—the first men to land on the moon*

ARMSTRONG, NEIL

ONE of the greatest endeavors of the 20th century was the "race" to the Moon. On July 20, 1969, the United States beat their Soviet rivals, when Neil Armstrong (1930–) and Edwin Aldrin (1930–) landed on lunar soil. Armstrong was the first man to walk on the moon, and Aldrin the second. The third member of the party, Michael Collins (1930–) remained in the shuttle, the *Apollo XI*. After a short time, Armstrong and Aldrin returned to the shuttle and made a successful flight back to Earth, bringing with them soil specimens.

BARNUM, PHINEAS T.

IN 1871, Phineas Taylor Barnum (1810–91), an American showman, founded a circus he billed as "The Greatest Show on Earth." Including the menagerie and freak show, Barnum's extravaganza traveled in 100 railroad cars. One of his most famous attractions was the midget Tom Thumb. In 1881 Barnum merged with his chief competitor, and the show continues today as the Ringling Brothers Barnum and Bailey Circus. Barnum attempted to change his image and become an art promoter. He coordinated the U.S. concert tour of Jenny Lind, the Swedish soprano he christened "The Swedish Nightingale."

BONNIE AND CLYDE

THE four-year criminal career of Bonnie Parker (1911–34) and Clyde Barrow (1909–34) ended in the most dramatic of ways in Louisiana. Apparently working on a tip-off, Texas Rangers ambushed the pair, riddling their bodies with more than 50 bullets. Bonnie and Clyde died as they had lived, with shotguns and revolvers in their hands. The criminal duo left a trail of robberies across the southwest of America, and are credited with the murder of at least 12 people. Both were still in their mid-20s when they were killed, and their exploits have passed into folklore around the world.

DEAN, JAMES

JAMES Dean (1931–55) has come to represent the epitome of 1950s youth culture. He lived on the edge, and died in a car accident at the age of 24. Had he lived, his film career would have been prolific. His early death, however, elevated him to the position of an icon of tragic youth, and has gained his three films a cult following. The most famous of these was *Rebel Without a Cause*, made in the year of his death, in which he co-starred with Natalie Wood and Sal Mineo.

DISNEY, WALT

WALT Disney (1901–1966) was a film producer and creator of animated cartoons featuring Mickey Mouse, a romping, rollicking rodent and Donald Duck the quintessential quacking dupe. Famous Disney productions include *Steamboat Willie* (1928), *Snow White and the Seven Dwarfs* (1937), *Pinocchio* (1940), *Fantasia* (1940), *Dumbo* (1941), *Cinderella* (1950), *Alice in Wonderland* (1951), and *Peter Pan* (1953). He built Disneyland amusement park in Anaheim, California and Disney World in Orlando, Florida.

Walt Disney ▶

DUBOIS, W. E. B.

WILLIAM Edward Burghardt DuBois (1868–1963) was a lifelong advocate of world peace and a leading champion of African-American liberation. DuBois was the first black to be awarded a Ph.D. from Harvard. In more than 20 books and 100 articles, DuBois championed the African American culture through historical and sociological studies. *The Souls of Black Folk* was a pioneering effort, arguing an educated black elite should lead blacks to liberation. In 1905, Du Bois founded the Niagara Movement, a forerunner of the National Association for the Advancement of Colored People (NAACP), which he helped organize in 1909.

EARHART, AMELIA

THE aviator Amelia Mary Earhart (1897–1937) became the first woman to cross the Atlantic in an airplane, in 1928, and the first woman to fly it solo in 1932. Other "firsts" included her 1935 flight from Hawaii to the mainland and her jaunt from Mexico City to New York City that same year. She was lost on an attempted around-the-world flight somewhere in the Pacific Ocean between New Guinea and Howland Island in 1937. Her published books include *20 Hrs., 40 Min.* (1928), *The Fun Of It* (1932), and *Last Flight* (1938), this last edited by her husband following her disappearance.

EDISON, THOMAS

THE inventor Thomas Edison (1847–1931) was granted his first patent in 1869 for a recording machine. The

Thomas Edison ▶

sale of his inventions helped him to establish his own workshop at Newark, New Jersey that was later moved to Menlo Park in California. Edison patented more than 1,000 inventions, including various telegraph devices, the phonograph (1877), and the incandescent electric lamp (1879). He constructed the first central power station and distribution system in New York City in 1881, and by 1913 was producing talking motion pictures. He worked on war problems for the government during World War I.

ELIOT, T. S.

THE poet and playwright T. S. Eliot (1888–1965) was born in America, but went to London in 1915. His poem cycle *The Waste Land* (1922) was one of the most influential examples of Modernist writing. Eliot's work became increasingly religious during the 1920s, culminating in *The Four Quartets*, first published together in 1943. Eliot demonstrated a whole new way of writing poetry, obscure and spiritual, but it was his *Old Possum's Book of Practical Cats* (1939) which became his greatest success after his death. It was turned into the musical *Cats* by English composer Andrew Lloyd Webber.

▲ *T. S. Eliot*

FITZGERALD, F. SCOTT

F. SCOTT Fitzgerald (1896–1940) enlisted in the U.S. Army during World War I and fell in love with Zelda Sayre. After he was discharged, he went to seek his literary fortune in New York City in order to marry her. His first novel, *This Side of Paradise* (1920), became a bestseller. Fitzgerald's secure place in American literature rests primarily on his novel *The Great Gatsby* (1925), a brilliantly written, economically structured story about the American dream of the self-made man. The protagonist, the mysterious Jay Gatsby, discovers the devastating cost of success in terms of personal fulfillment and love.

FORD, HENRY

THE automobile manufacturer Henry Ford (1863–1947) built his first car in 1896 and founded the Ford Motor Company in 1903. His Model T was the first car to be constructed solely by assembly-line methods and to be mass-marketed. It was designed to be affordable by the average person and, by 1927, 15 million had rolled out of his factories. In 1913, Ford introduced the first conveyor-belt assembly line and truly interchangeable parts, which revolutionized the car industry, as well as many others.

◄ *Henry Ford*

GATES, BILL

BILL Gates formed the computer company Microsoft with Paul Allen. They adapted the computer language BASIC to form an operating system MS-Dos, then sold it to IBM for the new personal computer on which they were working. Their system was an overnight success, arriving as it did on the brink of the technological revolution, and spawned an empire that no other computer company has been able to match since. Bill Gates was believed to be one of the richest men in the world by the end of the 1990s, although he faced problems with the United States government over alleged monopolistic practices.

GERSHWIN, GEORGE

IN the 1920s, the "Jazz Age" was swinging and George Gershwin (1898–1937) was right at its center. He composed vibrant, witty songs that had syncopated rhythms and expressive harmonies. In 1924, Gershwin bridged the gap between classical and popular music with *Rhapsody in Blue*, which captured the "tempo of modern living with its speed and chaos and vitality" but was performed as a serious piece of music. In the same year he wrote "Lady Be Good," with lyrics written by his brother Ira. It marked the advent of the Gershwin musical.

▼ *George Gershwin*

▲ *Betty Grable*

GRABLE, BETTY

ONE of the most enduring images of Betty Grable (1916–73) is as the armed force, favorite pin-up, looking back over her shoulder in a white swimsuit displaying her "million-dollar legs," the amount for which Lloyds of London insured them. For thousands of World War II veterans the photograph is an enduring image of the decade in which they served.

Grable was trained at Hollywood Professional School from the age of 12, and was in chorus lines before she was 14. She got her break at Fox studios, where she starred in 18 musicals, high on gloss and Technicolor.

HENDRIX, JIMI

JIMI Hendrix (1942–70) was born in Seattle, Washington, but started roaming after playing in local bands and serving in the army. Landing in London in 1966 he formed the Jimi Hendrix Experience. His electric-guitar playing was legendary, a kind of innovative buzz of controlled feedback and melodic riffs. He was also a dazzling showman, slinking on stage in outrageous velvet outfits, and then smashing or burning his guitar. His first album, *Are You Experienced?*, was a psychedelic blaze of chords with Dylan-inspired lyrics. His later recordings anticipated dub and ambient music. He died of a drugs overdose on September 18, 1970.

HITCHCOCK, ALFRED

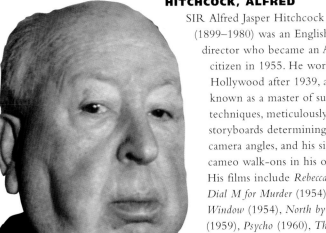

SIR Alfred Jasper Hitchcock (1899–1980) was an English film director who became an American citizen in 1955. He worked in Hollywood after 1939, and became known as a master of suspense, film techniques, meticulously drawn storyboards determining exact camera angles, and his signature cameo walk-ons in his own films. His films include *Rebecca* (1940), *Dial M for Murder* (1954), *Rear Window* (1954), *North by Northwest* (1959), *Psycho* (1960), *The Birds* (1963), and *Torn Curtain* (1966). He hosted a television mystery program (1955–65) and edited anthologies of mystery stories.

▲ *Alfred Hitchcock*

HOPPER, GRACE

GRACE Murray Hopper (1906–92) graduated from Vassar with a degree in math and physics. She received her masters degree from Yale and returned to Vassar as an instructor. She earned her Ph.D. and joined the Navy in 1934. Graduating at the top of her class from Midshipman's School, Hopper was assigned to the Bureau of Ordnance Computation Project. By the 1960s, with the rank of commander, she had been instrumental in the development of the COBOL programming language. In 1985, President Ronald Reagan named her a rear admiral. She retired in 1986 and died in her sleep in 1992.

JAMES, WILLIAM

WILLIAM James (1842–1910), the brother of the novelist Henry James, was a medical student turned philosopher and psychologist who concerned himself with religious issues throughout his life. In *The Varieties of Religious Experience* (1902) he studied the phenomena of mysticism and religious experience with an assessment of their validity. He developed a theory of a "mother sea of consciousness" which plays some of the roles of an infinite God or Absolute, while leaving humans with an independence and integrity of personal choice. He taught at Harvard from 1872 to 1907.

JORDAN, BARBARA

BARBARA Jordan (1936–96) became the first African-American congresswoman elected from the deep South when Texas sent her to the U.S. House of Representatives in 1972. In 1974, she served on the committee charged with evaluating the evidence bearing on Nixon's possible impeachment. Her incisive questioning and her impassioned defense of the Constitution captured national attention. In l976, Jordan became the first woman and first African-American to give the keynote speech at the Democratic National Convention. In 1978, she became a full professor at the Lyndon B. Johnson School of Public Affairs at the University of Texas.

KELLY, GRACE

GRACE Kelly (1929–82) came from a wealthy family, went to good schools, and was determined to prove that she could work. She modeled, did some commercial work, and acted in a few Broadway plays before Hollywood beckoned. She was spotted by Alfred Hitchcock who cast her with exquisite taste in *Dial M for Murder*, and opposite James Stewart in *Rear Window*. While working on her third Hitchcock film, *To Catch a Thief*, she met Prince Rainier III, the ruler of the small principality of Monaco. In 1956, she married the Prince in spectacular ceremony. She died in a car accident in 1982.

KING, BILLIE JEAN

BILLIE Jean King (1943–) was introduced to tennis by her parents in Long Beach, California, and rapidly rose to the top of her chosen profession. In 1967, she was selected as "Outstanding Female Athlete of the World" and, in 1972, was the first woman to be named *Sports Illustrated* "Sportsperson of the Year." She was the first female athlete to win more $100,000 prize money in a single season. King worked to break down gender barriers in sports. She established the first successful women's professional tennis tour, and founded tennis clinics for undeprivileged children.

▲ *Billie Jean King*

KING, MARTIN LUTHER

MARTIN Luther King (1929–68) was a civil-rights campaigner, black leader, Baptist minister, and founder and president of the Southern Christian Leadership Convention. An advocate of non-violence and racial brotherhood, he was awarded the Nobel Peace Prize in 1964 and used peaceful, but determined, methods to promote black equality. He was assassinated in Memphis, Tennessee, in 1968, but remains one of the most influential figures in the campaign for the rights of Black Americans; his famous "I Have a Dream" speech remains the greatest and most passionate call for human rights of the 20th century.

Martin Luther King ▶

KORESH, DAVID

DAVID Koresh formed the Branch Davidian religious sect in 1959, a splinter group that broke away from the Seventh Day Adventist Church. A charismatic leader, Koresh took his followers to Waco, Texas, and formed a commune. Koresh became more dictatorial, insisting that he was a messiah and that all the women in the group were his God-given wives. Authorities were alerted over the stockpiling of weapons there, and a siege was born. The fiery demise of the compound in 1993 claimed the lives of Koresh and 74 of his followers, with four federal agents killed in the preceding shoot-out.

KUBRICK, STANLEY

WRITER, director, and producer Stanley Kubrick (1928–) achieved legendary status in the American film business. His early work included *Fear and Desire* (1953) and *Killer's Kiss* (1955). *The Killing* (1956) caused critics to notice his brilliant style and bleakly cynical outlook, while *Paths of Glory* (1957) solidified his reputation as a filmmaker interested in depicting the individual at the mercy of a hostile world. The films *2001: A Space Odyssey* (1968) and *A Clockwork Orange* (1971), both made in England, where Kubrick has worked since 1961, engendered critical controversy, but the former has now become accepted as a landmark in modern cinema.

LAUREN, RALPH

ALTHOUGH the figure of a mallet-swinging polo player existed in various guises since its first use by the American Brooks Brothers in 1896, it did not become a trademark until the clothes designer Ralph Lauren (1937–) used it to launch a line of women's wear in 1971. The logo's appeal as a symbol of Ivy-league success was immediate, and it soon appeared on everything from Ralph Lauren men's wear (launched in 1967) to diffusion lines including fragrances, linens, and even housewares.

LEE, ROBERT E.

ROBERT E. Lee (1807–70) was a military strategist and Confederate general in the American Civil War. He sustained the South far beyond their true capacity, defeating numerous Union generals in decisive and well-managed battles. He failed to defeat the Union army at Gettysburg, and, in 1864, faced Ulysses S. Grant, the new Northern commander. Forced onto the defensive, he inflicted heavy losses on Grant at the battles of the Wilderness, Spotsylvania, and Cold Harbor. Early in April 1865, he met Grant at Appomattox and surrendered the army of Northern Virginia, ending the Civil War.

LEOPOLD, ALDO

ALDO Leopold (1887–1948) worked as a conservationist for the US Forest Service. His posthumously published work, *A Sand County Almanac* (1949), introduces the concept of the ecosystem as an interacting web of living organisms that has its own natural balance. Leopold wrote that to manage an ecosystem, it is necessary to "think like a mountain" and obtain an overview of the whole system. His "Land Ethic" was based on the moral maxim that "a thing is right when it tends to preserve the integrity, stability, and beauty of the biotic community. It is wrong when it tends otherwise."

LINDBERGH, CHARLES

AVIATOR Charles Lindbergh (1902–74) first achieved international fame in 1927 as the first person to fly alone across the Atlantic. He made the flight in the *Spirit of St Louis*, his single-engine monoplane, traveling from New York to Paris in $33\frac{1}{2}$ hours. In 1929, he married Anne Spencer Morrow, daughter of the US ambassador to Mexico, and she became his co-pilot and navigator on many subsequent expeditions, including the 1929 flight over the Yucatan peninsula, during which he photographed Mayan ruins. These photographs made an important contribution to the study of the Mayas and to the field of archeology.

MacARTHUR, DOUGLAS

DOUGLAS MacArthur (1880–1964) was a general during World War II, commander of the U.S. forces in the Far East and, from March 1942, of the Allied forces in the southwest Pacific. After his evacuation of the Philippines, he vowed he would return to liberate the country. True to his word, he achieved this, and was present at the formal capitulation of the Japanese armed forces in 1945. He served as the commander of United Nations forces in Korea (1950–51) but was dismissed by President Harry S. Truman for continued public statements which advocated the invasion of Communist China.

Douglas MacArthur ▶

MALCOLM X

MALCOLM Little (1926–65) became known as Malcolm X during his campaign for black equality in America. Exhorting these civil rights at the same time as Martin Luther King, Little's methods marked the opposite end of the scale to King. While King's campaign was characterized by "peaceful protest," Malcolm X preferred violent means to achieve black equality, suggesting the time for talk was past. Both men were extremely influential in their own ways, and both met the same end. Malcolm X was assassinated in 1965.

▲ *Malcolm Little, known as Malcolm X*

MARSHALL, GEORGE

GENERAL George Marshall (1880–1959) was a skilled officer and diplomat. During World War I, he served as an aide to General John J. "Black Jack" Pershing, and in World War II as Army Chief of Staff. In 1947, as Secretary of State, he announced the European Recovery Program, to help European reconstruction after the war. Known as the Marshall Plan (1948–53), it was drawn up under the leadership of the United States, Britain and France, and Congress made American funds available, gladly supporting the principle of giving aid to anti-Communist governments. Fourteen European nations accepted aid, including Britain.

MARSHALL, THURGOOD

THURGOOD Marshall (1908–93), the grandson of a slave, was one of the most well-known figures in civil rights history. As the first African-American Supreme Court Justice, he served on the Court for 24 years until June 28, 1991, when he retired due to advancing age and deteriorating health. Marshall's performance in the Supreme Court earned him the respect of his fellow justices. Through his objective arguments and decisions, he paved the way for much of the progress made in civil rights over the past two decades.

MCENROE, JOHN

NEW York tennis ace John McEnroe (1959–) earned himself a reputation as a bad-tempered, volatile player but, despite the nickname "Superbrat," McEnroe was arguably the best of his era. His victory over Björn Borg in 1981 was a momentous one, as it ended Borg's undisputed five-year reign as Wimbledon men's singles champion. Many felt the

John McEnroe ▶

volatile American's victory was poetic justice after the Swede had beaten him in the 1980 final. In 1981, McEnroe defeated the Swedish master in a riveting match, winning 4–6, 7–6, 7–6, 6–4 in three hours and 22 minutes.

MILLER, GLENN

ON December 16, 1944, en route to a concert in France, the aircraft carrying world-renowned band leader Colonel Glenn Miller (1904–44) disappeared. There was no sign of the wreckage and the pilot had not signaled that there was a problem. Miller had volunteered for service in 1941, but had been persuaded that the morale value of his music would be of more use to the war effort. From 1941 to 1944 his band played in almost every war zone in the world, from the Pacific to Europe. His music dominated broadcasting during the latter part of the war.

MONROE, MARILYN

MARILYN Monroe (Norma Jean Mortenson or Baker, 1926–62) was a film actress and the 20th century's ultimate tragic sex symbol. In many ways a victim of her own success, Marilyn struggled in the limelight. By the time of her best-loved film, *Some Like it Hot* (1959), stardom was beginning to affect her work, and director Billy Wilder took to writing her lines on the furniture to get her through the scenes. Eventually Marilyn took her own life at a tragically early age, though rumours still persist of her being "silenced" after affairs with President John F. Kennedy and his brother Robert. Among her other great films are *Gentlemen Prefer Blondes* and *The Seven Year Itch*.

◀ *Marilyn Monroe*

MORSE, SAMUEL

THE inventor of the Morse code, Samuel Morse (1791–1872) built the first electric telegraph in 1835. Electrical pulses were sent along the telegraph wire using his code; at the other end, a series of clicks were heard that had to be deciphered by the receiving operator. This was the first modern form of telecommunication. In 1843, Morse obtained financial support from the government to build a 35-mile-long demonstration telegraph system between Washington and Baltimore. Wires were attached by glass insulators to poles alongside a railroad.

◀ *Samuel Morse*

ONASSIS, JACQUELINE KENNEDY

JACQUELINE Lee Bouvier (1929–94) married Senator John F. Kennedy in 1953. When her husband was elected president in 1960, she proved to be a First Lady of unusual beauty, intelligence, and cultivated taste. "Jackie" devoted her time to developing the White House as a museum of history and arts for the American people. The gallant courage she displayed in the hours following her husband's 1963 assassination captured the admiration of the world. In 1968 she married Greek businessman, Aristotle Onassis, who died in March 1975. From 1978 until her death in 1994, she worked in New York City as a book editor.

OWENS, JESSE

TRACK and field star Jesse Owens (1913–80) had a sensational high school track career, and dozens of

Jesse Owens ▶

colleges courted the promising athlete before he chose Ohio State University. In 1936, Owens stood on the center tier of the awards platform of the Berlin Games to accept his fourth Olympic gold medal. In doing so, Owens—the son of a sharecropper and grandson of a slave—discredited Hitler and his Master Race by affirming that individual excellence, rather than race or national origin, distinguishes one man from another.

PERKINS, FRANCIS

FRANCIS Perkins (1882–1965) held a succession of posts in state regulatory agencies, and became a labor standards reformer. She served on the State Industrial Board from 1923 to 1929, when she was appointed industrial commissioner of New York. Perkins became the first female cabinet officer when she served as Franklin D. Roosevelt's secretary of labor from 1933 to 1945. Her work continued under the administration of Harry S. Truman, when she was a member of the civil service commission until 1953.

RODGERS, JIMMIE

JIMMIE Rodgers (1897–1933), "The Singing Brakeman," became known as the "Father of Country Music." His first two recordings in the 1920s were a ballad, "The Soldier's Sweetheart," and a lullaby, "Sleep, Baby, Sleep." His songs told stories of the "singing" rails, the steam locomotives, and the railroad people he loved so well. Rodgers never appeared on any major radio show or even played the *Grand Ole Opry*, but he, Fred Rose, and Hank Williams were the first persons to be elected to the Country Music Hall of Fame in 1961.

ROOSEVELT, ELEANOR

ELEANOR Roosevelt (1884–1962), the niece of President Theodore Roosevelt, married her distant cousin and future president, Franklin D. Roosevelt, in 1905. She was admired for championing liberal causes and humanitarian concerns and, after her husband's death in 1945, was considered the leader of the liberal wing of the Democratic party. She served as a United

▲ *Eleanor Roosevelt*

Nations delegate (1945, 1949–52, and 1961), and chaired the UN Commission on Human Rights (1946–51). In 1936, she began writing the syndicated column "My Day," and authored *This is My Story* (1937), *i* (1940), and *On My Own* (1958).

WILLIAMS, TENNESSEE

TENNESSEE Williams (1911–83), a native of Mississippi, was one of the more complex literary figures of the mid-20th century, and one of the first to live openly as a homosexual. He focused on disturbed emotions and unresolved sexuality within southern families. He was known for incantatory repetitions, a poetic southern diction, weird Gothic settings, and Freudian exploration of sexual desire. He wrote more than 20 full-length dramas, many of them autobiographical. He reached his peak in the 1940s with *The Glass Menagerie* (1944) and *A Streetcar Named Desire* (1947).

◄ *Tennessee Williams*

CHAPTER 14

Presidents of the United States

1789 GEORGE WASHINGTON

George Washington (1732–99), the "father of his country," commanded the Continental Army (1775–83). He served as 1st U.S. president (1789–97).

1797 JOHN ADAMS

John Adams (1735–1826), signer of the American Declaration of Independence, served as George Washington's vice-president (1789–97) and as 2nd U.S. president (1797–1801).

1801 THOMAS JEFFERSON

Thomas Jefferson (1743–1826), author of the American Declaration of Independence (1776) and founder of the Democratic-Republican party, served as 3rd U.S. president (1801–09).

1809 JAMES MADISON

Democratic-Republican James Madison (1751–1836), the 4th U.S. president (1809–17), is regarded as the father of the federal Constitution (1787) and the Bill of Rights.

1817 JAMES MONROE

The 5th U.S. president (1817–25), Democrat-Republican James Monroe (1758–1831) negotiated the 1803 Louisiana Purchase and vocalized the Monroe Doctrine (1823), opposing further European intervention.

1825 JOHN QUINCY ADAMS

Before serving as 6th U.S. president (1825–29), John Quincy Adams (1767–1848) negotiated an end to the War of 1812 and formulated the 1823 Monroe Doctrine.

1829 ANDREW JACKSON

Hero of the War of 1812, Andrew Jackson (1767–1845) represented the frontier New Democracy. He served as 7th U.S. president (1829–37).

1837   MARTIN VAN BUREN

While serving as 8th U.S. president (1837–41), Democrat Martin Van Buren's (1782–1862) laissez-faire policies complicated the Panic of 1837. He blocked Texas annexation and supported states' rights.

1841   WILLIAM HENRY HARRISON

The 9th U.S. president, William Henry Harrison (1773–1841), was the oldest president to take office. He caught a chill at his inauguration on March 4th, 1841, and died a month later.

1841   JOHN TYLER

When William Henry Harrison died, Vice-President John Tyler assumed office. As 10th U.S. president (1841–45) he annexed Texas and settled Canadian boundary disputes.

1845   JAMES POLK

James Polk (1795–1849), the 11th U.S. president (1845–49) resolved the Oregon border dispute with Britain and entered the Mexican War (1848).

1849   ZACHARY TAYLOR

A Mexican War general (1848), Whig Zachary Taylor (1785–1850), the 12th U.S. president (1849–50), favored free soil views (the prohibition of slavery in regions acquired through the Mexican Cession), but he died after 16 months in office.

1850   MILLARD FILLMORE

Millard Fillmore (1800–74) became 13th U.S. president (1850–53) upon Zachary Taylor's death. He signed the Compromise of 1850 and enforced the Fugitive Slave Act.

1853   FRANKLIN PIERCE

Franklin Pierce (1804–1869), 14th U.S. president (1853–57), failed to unite the Democrats. He backed the Kansas – Nebraska Act (1850), causing fighting in Kansas over slavery.

1857   JAMES BUCHANAN

15th U.S. president (1857–61), James Buchanan (1791–1868) believed that slavery was wrong but constitutional. He failed to maintain a balance of power and lost the 1860 election to Abraham Lincoln.

1861 ABRAHAM LINCOLN

Republican Abraham Lincoln (1809–65) was 16th U.S. president (1861–65) and led the North against the South during the Civil War. He was the first president to be assassinated.

1865 ANDREW JOHNSON

Democrat Andrew Johnson (1808–75), a former Tennessee governor, became 17th U.S. president (1865–69) following Abraham Lincoln's assassination. He later escaped impeachment by a single vote.

1869 ULYSSES S. GRANT

Union Civil War commander Ulysses S. Grant (1822–85), 18th U.S. president (1869–77), was overwhelmed by government corruption but attempted liberal Reconstruction of the South.

1877 RUTHERFORD B. HAYES

Republican Rutherford B. Hayes (1822–93), became 19th U.S. president (1877–81) through a disputed election settled by the Compromise of 1877 ending southern Reconstruction.

1881 JAMES GARFIELD

Republican James Garfield (1831–81) served as 20th U.S. president (1881) for four months before his assassination. He was the second American president to be murdered.

1881 CHESTER A. ARTHUR

When James Garfield was assassinated in 1881, Chester A. Arthur (1830–86) became 21st U.S. president

(1881–85). He emphasized civil
service reform.

1885 GROVER CLEVELAND

Grover Cleveland (1837–1908) served
as 22nd and 24th U.S. president
(1885–89, 1893–97). He was the first
Democrat elected after the Civil War.

1889 BENJAMIN HARRISON

Republican Benjamin Harrison
(1833–1901) served as 23rd U.S.
president (1889–93). He dealt with
currency reform and worked to
broaden Latin American relations.

1897 WILLIAM McKINLEY

William McKinley (1843–1901), 25th
U.S. president (1897–1901), led the
nation into the Spanish–American War
(1898). He was assassinated in Buffalo,
New York.

1901 THEODORE ROOSEVELT

Theodore Roosevelt (1858–1919),
26th U.S. president (1901–09),
campaigned against business trusts

choking American free trade, and
followed a nationalistic foreign policy.

1909 WILLIAM HOWARD TAFT

William Howard Taft (1857–1930),
27th U.S. president (1909–13),
angered Progressive reformers with
his conservatism and was a one-
term president.

1912 WOODROW WILSON

Woodrow Wilson (1856–1924), 28th
U.S. president (1912–24), kept the
country out of World War I until
1917. His Fourteen Points were the
basis for
peace.

1921 WARREN HARDING

Warren Harding (1865–1923), though honest himself, presided over a corruption-filled administration as 29th U.S. president (1921–23). He died in office.

1923 CALVIN COOLIDGE

Known popularly as "Silent Cal," Calvin Coolidge (1872–1933), 30th U.S. president (1923–29), presided over a period of economic prosperity.

1929 HERBERT HOOVER

Republican Herbert Hoover (1874–1964), 31st U.S. president (1929–33), was vilified by the public for his cautious policies after the 1929 Stock Market Crash.

1933 FRANKLIN D. ROOSEVELT

Democrat Franklin D. Roosevelt (1882–1945) was 32nd U.S. president (1933–45). Elected four times, he led the country through the Great Depression and World War II.

1945 HARRY S. TRUMAN

Harry S. Truman (1884–1972), 33rd U.S. president (1945–53), made the crucial decision to use the atomic bomb to end World War II in the Pacific.

1953 DWIGHT D. EISENHOWER

Dwight D. Eisenhower (1890–1969), 34th U.S. president (1953–60), was Supreme Allied Commander in World War II, promoted business, and dealt with the Cold War.

1961 JOHN F. KENNEDY

John F. Kennedy (1917–63), 35th U.S. president (1960–63) and the first Roman Catholic elected, grappled with the Cold War and civil rights before his assassination.

1963 LYNDON B. JOHNSON

Lyndon B. Johnson (1908–73), 36th U.S. president (1963–69), advocated programs to combat poverty and address civil rights, but was vilified for the Vietnam War.

1969 RICHARD M. NIXON

Richard M. Nixon (1913–94), 37th U.S. president (1969–74), resigned during his second term as a result of the Watergate scandal.

1974 GERALD R. FORD

Gerald R. Ford (1913–), 38th U.S. president (1974–77), was nominated vice-president after Spiro Agnew's 1973 resignation and became president after Richard Nixon's resignation. He was the only president not actually elected to that post.

1977 JIMMY CARTER

Jimmy Carter (1924–), 39th U.S. president (1977–81), is known for negotiating the Camp David Middle Eastern peace agreements. A Washington outsider, he served one term.

1981 RONALD REAGAN

Ronald Reagan (b. 1911–), 40th U.S. president (1981–89) and former Hollywood actor, was a conservative who touched off a wave of nationalism.

1989 GEORGE BUSH

George Bush (1924–), 41st U.S. president (1989–93), led the UN Coalition that sent forces against Iraq (1991) over the annexation of Kuwait.

1993 BILL CLINTON

The 42nd U.S. President (1993–) Bill Clinton (1946–) is the first reelected Democrat since Roosevelt; in December 1998, he also became the first president to be impeached since Andrew Johnson.

CHAPTER 15

Reference

The Declaration of Independence

WHEN in the course of human events, it becomes necessary for one people to dissolve the political bands which have connected them with another, and to assume among the powers of the earth, the separate and equal station to which the Laws of Nature and of Nature's God entitle them, a decent respect to the opinions of mankind requires that they should declare the causes which impel them to the separation.

WE hold these truths to be self-evident, that all men are created equal, that they are endowed by their Creator with certain unalienable Rights, that among these are Life, Liberty, and the pursuit of Happiness. That to secure these rights, Governments are instituted among Men, deriving their just powers from the consent of the governed. That whenever any Form of Government becomes destructive of these ends, it is the Right of the People to alter or to abolish it, and to institute new Government, laying its foundation on such principles and organizing its powers in such form, as to them shall seem most likely to effect their Safety and Happiness. Prudence, indeed, will dictate that Governments long established should not be changed for light and transient causes;

and accordingly all experience hath shown, that mankind are more disposed to suffer, while evils are sufferable, than to right themselves by abolishing the forms to which they are accustomed. But when a long train of abuses and usurpations, pursuing invariably the same object evinces a design to reduce them under absolute Despotism, it is their right, it is their duty, to throw off such Government, and to provide new Guards for their future security. Such has been the patient sufferance of these Colonies; and such is now the necessity which constrains them to alter their former Systems of Government. The history of the present King of Great Britain is a history of repeated injuries and usurpations, all having in direct object the establishment of an absolute Tyranny over these States. To prove this, let Facts be submitted to a candid world.

HE has refused his Assent to Laws, the most wholesome and necessary for the public good.

HE has forbidden his Governors to pass Laws of immediate and pressing importance, unless suspended in their operation till his Assent should be obtained, and when so suspended, he has utterly neglected to attend to them.

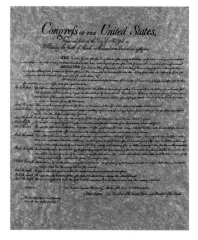

▲ *The Bill of Rights*

HE has refused to pass other Laws for the accommodation of large districts of people, unless those people would relinquish the right of Representation in the Legislature, a right inestimable to them and formidable to tyrants only.

HE has called together legislative bodies at places unusual, uncomfortable, and distant from the depository of their public Records, for the sole purpose of fatiguing them into compliance with his measures.

HE has dissolved Representative Houses repeatedly, for opposing with manly firmness his invasions on the rights of the people.

HE has refused for a long time, after such dissolutions, to cause others to be elected; whereby the Legislative powers, incapable of Annihilation, have returned to the People at large for their exercise; the State remaining in the meantime exposed to all the dangers of invasion from without, and convulsions within.

HE has endeavoured to prevent the population of these States; for that purpose obstructing the Laws for Naturalization of Foreigners; refusing to pass others to encourage their migrations hither, and raising the conditions of new Appropriations of Lands.

HE has obstructed the Administration of Justice, by refusing his Assent to Laws for establishing Judiciary powers.

HE has made Judges dependent on his Will alone, for the tenure of their offices, and the amount and payment of their salaries.

HE has erected a multitude of New Offices, and sent hither swarms of Officers to harass our people, and eat out their substance.

He has kept among us, in times of peace, Standing Armies, without the consent of our legislatures.

HE has affected to render the Military independent of and superior to the Civil power.

HE has combined with others to subject us to a jurisdiction foreign to our constitution and unacknowledged by our laws; giving his Assent to their Acts of pretended Legislation.

FOR protecting them by a mock Trial from punishment for any Murders which they should commit on the Inhabitants of these States.

FOR cutting off our Trade with all parts of the world:

FOR imposing Taxes on us without our Consent.

FOR depriving us in many cases of the benefits of Trial by Jury.

FOR transporting us beyond Seas to be tried for pretended offences.

FOR abolishing the free System of English Laws in a neighboring Province, establishing therein an Arbitrary government, and enlarging its Boundaries

so as to render it at once an example and fit instrument for introducing the same absolute rule into these Colonies.

FOR taking away our Charters, abolishing our most valuable Laws, and altering fundamentally the Forms of our Governments.

FOR suspending our own Legislatures, and declaring themselves invested with power to legislate for us in all cases whatsoever.

HE has abdicated Government here by declaring us out of his Protection and waging War against us.

HE has plundered our seas, ravaged our Coasts, burnt our towns, and destroyed the lives of our people.

HE is at this time transporting large Armies of foreign Mercenaries to complete the works of death, desolation and tyranny, already begun with circumstances of cruelty and perfidy scarcely paralleled in the most barbarous ages, and totally unworthy of the Head of a civilized nation.

HE has constrained our fellow Citizens taken Captive on the high Seas to bear Arms against their Country, to become the executioners of their friends and Brethren, or to fall themselves by their Hands.

HE has excited domestic insurrections amongst us, and has endeavored to bring on the inhabitants of our frontiers, the merciless Indian Savages, whose known rule of warfare is an undistinguished destruction of all ages, sexes and conditions.

IN every stage of these Oppressions We have Petitioned for Redress in the most humble terms. Our repeated Petitions have been answered only by repeated injury. A Prince, whose character is thus marked by every act which may define a Tyrant, is unfit to be the ruler of a free people.

NOR have We been wanting in attentions to our British brethren.

WE have warned them from time to time of attempts by their legislature to extend an unwarrantable jurisdiction over us.

WE have reminded them of the circumstances of our emigration and settlement here.

WE have appealed to their native justice and magnanimity, and we have conjured them by the ties of our common kindred to disavow these usurpations, which would inevitably interrupt our connections and correspondence.

THEY too have been deaf to the voice of

▲ *Thomas Jefferson*

justice and of consanguinity. We must, therefore, acquiesce in the necessity, which denounces our Separation, and hold them, as we hold the rest of mankind, Enemies in War, in Peace Friends.

WE, THEREFORE, the Representatives of the UNITED STATES OF AMERICA, in General Congress, Assembled, appealing to the Supreme Judge of the world for the rectitude of our intentions, do, in the Name, and by the authority of the good People of these Colonies, solemnly publish and declare That these United Colonies are, and of Right ought to BE FREE AND INDEPENDENT STATES; that they are Absolved from all

Allegiance to the British Crown, and that all political connection between them and the State of Great Britain is and ought to be totally dissolved; and that as Free and Independent States, they have full Power to levy War, conclude Peace, contract Alliances, establish Commerce, and to do all other Acts and Things which Independent States may of right do. And for the support of this Declaration, with a firm reliance on the protection of Divine Providence, we mutually pledge to each other our Lives, our Fortunes, and our sacred Honor.

The foregoing Declaration was, by order of Congress, engrossed, and signed by the following members:

New Hampshire:
Josiah Bartlett, William Whipple, Matthew Thornton
Massachusetts:
John Hancock, Samuel Adams, John Adams, Robert Treat Paine, Elbridge Gerry
Rhode Island:
Stephen Hopkins, William Ellery
Connecticut:
Roger Sherman, Samuel Huntington, William Williams, Oliver Wolcott
New York:
William Floyd, Philip Livingston, Francis Lewis, Lewis Morris
New Jersey:
Richard Stockton, John Witherspoon,

Francis Hopkinson, John Hart, Abraham Clark
Pennsylvania:
Robert Morris, Benjamin Rush, Benjamin Franklin, John Morton, George Clymer, James Smith, George Taylor, James Wilson, George Ross
Delaware:
Caesar Rodney, George Read, Thomas McKean
Maryland:
Samuel Chase, William Paca, Thomas Stone, Charles Carroll of Carrollton
Virginia:
George Wythe, Richard Henry Lee, Thomas Jefferson, Benjamin Harrison, Thomas Nelson, Jr., Francis Lightfoot Lee, Carter Braxton
North Carolina:
William Hooper, Joseph Hewes, John Penn
South Carolina:
Edward Rutledge, Thomas Heyward, Jr., Thomas Lynch, Jr., Arthur Middleton
Georgia:
Button Gwinnett, Lyman Hall, George Walton

RESOLVED: That copies of the Declaration be sent to the several assemblies, conventions, and committees, or councils of safety, and to the several commanding officers of the continental troops; that it be proclaimed in each of the United States, at the head of the army.

The United States Constitution

WE THE PEOPLE of the United States, in order to form a more perfect Union, establish Justice, insure domestic Tranquility, provide for the common defence, promote the general Welfare, and secure the Blessings of Liberty to ourselves and our Posterity, do ordain and establish this Constitution for the United States of America.

ARTICLE. I.

Section. 1.

All legislative Powers herein granted shall be vested in a Congress of the United States, which shall consist of a Senate and House of Representatives.

Section. 2.

The House of Representatives shall be composed of Members chosen every second Year by the People of the several States, and the Electors in each State shall have the Qualifications requisite for Electors of the most numerous Branch of the State Legislature.

No Person shall be a Representative who shall not have attained to the Age of twenty five Years, and been seven Years a Citizen of the United States, and who shall not, when elected, be an Inhabitant of that State in which he shall be chosen.

Representatives and direct Taxes shall be apportioned among the several States which may be included within this Union, according to their respective Numbers, which shall be determined by adding to the whole Number of free Persons, including those bound to Service for a Term of Years, and excluding Indians not taxed, three fifths of all other Persons. The actual Enumeration shall be made within three Years after the first Meeting of the Congress of the United States, and within every subsequent Term of ten Years, in such Manner as they shall by Law direct. The Number of Representatives shall not exceed one for every thirty Thousand, but each State shall have at Least one Representative; and until such enumeration shall be made, the State of New Hampshire shall be entitled to chuse three, Massachusetts eight, Rhode-Island and Providence Plantations one, Connecticut five, New-York six, New Jersey four, Pennsylvania eight, Delaware one, Maryland six, Virginia ten, North Carolina five, South Carolina five, and Georgia three.

When vacancies happen in the Representation from any state, the Executive Authority thereof shall issue Writs of Election to fill such Vacancies.

The House of Representatives shall chuse their Speaker and other Officers; and shall have the sole Power of Impeachment.

Section. 3.

The Senate of the United States shall be composed of two Senators from each State, chosen by the legislature thereof, for six Years; and each Senator shall have one Vote.

Immediately after they shall be assembled in Consequence of the first Election, they shall be divided as equally as may be into three Classes. The Seats of the Senators of the first Class shall be vacated at the Expiration of the second Year, of the second Class at the Expiration of the fourth Year, and of the third Class at the Expiration of the sixth Year, so that one third may be chosen every second Year; and if Vacancies happen by Resignation, or otherwise, during the Recess of the Legislature of any State, the Executive thereof may make temporary Appointments until the next Meeting of the Legislature, which shall then fill such Vacancies.

No Person shall be a Senator who shall not have attained to the Age of thirty Years, and been nine Years a Citizen of the United States, and who shall not, when elected, be an Inhabitant of that State for which he shall be chosen.

The Vice President of the United States shall be President of the Senate, but shall have no Vote, unless they be equally divided.

The Senate shall chuse their other Officers, and also a President *pro tempore*, in the Absence of the Vice President, or when he shall exercise the Office of President of the United States.

The Senate shall have the sole Power to try all Impeachments. When sitting for that Purpose, they shall be on Oath or Affirmation. When the President of the United States is tried, the Chief Justice shall preside: And no Person shall be convicted without the Concurrence of two thirds of the Members present.

Judgment in Cases of Impeachment shall not extend further than to removal from Office, and disqualification to hold and enjoy any Office of Honor, Trust or Profit under the United States: but the Party convicted shall nevertheless be liable and subject to Indictment, Trial, Judgment and Punishment, according to Law.

Section. 4.
The Times, Places and Manner of holding Elections for Senators and Representatives, shall be prescribed in each State by the Legislature thereof; but the Congress may at any time by Law make or alter such Regulations, except as to the Places of chusing Senators.

The Congress shall assemble at least once in every Year, and such Meeting shall be on the first Monday in December, unless they shall by Law appoint a different Day.

Section. 5.
Each House shall be the Judge of the Elections, Returns and Qualifications of its own Members, and a Majority of each shall constitute a Quorum to do Business; but a smaller Number may adjourn from day to day, and may be authorized to compel the Attendance of absent Members, in such Manner, and under such Penalties as each House may provide.

Each House may determine the Rules of its Proceedings, punish its Members for disorderly Behaviour, and, with the Concurrence of two thirds, expel a Member.

Each House shall keep a Journal of its Proceedings, and from time to time publish the same, excepting such Parts as may in their Judgment require Secrecy; and the Yeas and Nays of the Members of either House on any question shall, at the Desire of one fifth of those Present, be entered on the Journal.

Neither House, during the Session of Congress, shall, without the Consent of the other, adjourn for more than three days, nor to any other Place than that in which the two Houses shall be sitting.

Section. 6.
The Senators and Representatives shall receive a Compensation for their Services, to be ascertained by Law, and paid out of the Treasury of the United States. They shall in all Cases, except Treason, Felony and Breach of the Peace, be privileged from Arrest during their Attendance at the Session of their respective Houses, and in going to and returning from the same; and for any Speech or Debate in either House, they shall not be questioned in any other Place.

No Senator or Representative shall, during the Time for which he was elected, be appointed to any civil Office under the Authority of the United States, which shall have been created, or the Emoluments whereof shall have been encreased during such time; and no Person holding any Office under the United States, shall be a Member of either House during his Continuance in Office.

Section. 7.
All Bills for raising Revenue shall originate in the House of Representatives; but the Senate may propose or concur with Amendments as on other Bills.

Every Bill which shall have passed the House of Representatives and the Senate, shall, before it become a Law, be presented to the President of the United States; If he approve he shall sign it, but if not he shall return it, with his Objections to that House in which it shall have originated, who shall enter the Objections at large on their Journal, and proceed to reconsider it. If after such Reconsideration two thirds of that House shall agree to pass the Bill, it shall be sent, together with the Objections, to the other House, by which it shall likewise be reconsidered, and if approved by two thirds of that House, it shall become a Law. But in all such Cases the Votes of both Houses shall be determined by yeas and Nays, and the Names of the Persons voting for and against the Bill shall be entered on the Journal of each House respectively. If any Bill shall not be returned by the President within ten Days (Sundays excepted) after it shall have been presented to him, the Same shall be a Law, in like Manner as if he had signed it, unless the Congress by their Adjournment prevent its Return, in which Case it shall not be a Law.

Every Order, Resolution, or Vote to which the Concurrence of the Senate and House of Representatives may be necessary (except on a question of Adjournment) shall be presented

to the President of the United States; and before the Same shall take Effect, shall be approved by him, or being disapproved by him, shall be repassed by two thirds of the Senate and House of Representatives, according to the Rules and Limitations prescribed in the Case of a Bill.

Section. 8.

The Congress shall have Power to lay and collect Taxes, Duties, Imposts and Excises, to pay the Debts and provide for the common Defence and general Welfare of the United States; but all Duties, Imposts and Excises shall be uniform throughout the United States;

To borrow Money on the credit of the United States;

To regulate Commerce with foreign Nations, and among the several States, and with the Indian Tribes;

To establish an uniform Rule of Naturalization, and uniform Laws on the subject of Bankruptcies throughout the United States;

To coin Money, regulate the Value thereof, and of foreign Coin, and fix the Standard of Weights and Measures;

To provide for the Punishment of counterfeiting the Securities and current Coin of the United States;

To establish Post Offices and Post Roads;

To promote the Progress of Science and useful Arts, by securing for limited Times to Authors and Inventors the exclusive Right to their respective Writings and Discoveries;

To constitute Tribunals inferior to the supreme Court;

To define and punish Piracies and Felonies committed on the high Seas, and Offences against the Law of Nations;

To declare War, grant Letters of Marque and Reprisal, and make Rules concerning Captures on Land and Water;

To raise and support Armies, but no Appropriation of Money to that Use shall be for a longer Term than two Years;

To provide and maintain a Navy;

To make Rules for the Government and Regulation of the land and naval Forces;

To provide for calling forth the Militia to execute the Laws of the Union, suppress Insurrections and repel Invasions;

To provide for organizing, arming, and disciplining, the Militia, and for governing such Part of them as may be employed in the Service of the United States, reserving to the States respectively, the Appointment of the Officers, and the Authority of training the Militia according to the discipline prescribed by Congress;

To exercise exclusive Legislation in all Cases whatsoever, over such District (not exceeding ten Miles square) as may, by Cession of Particular States, and the Acceptance of Congress, become the Seat of the Government of the United States, and to exercise like Authority over all Places purchased by the Consent of the Legislature of the State in which the Same shall be, for the Erection of Forts, Magazines, Arsenals, dock-yards, and other needful Buildings; – And

To make all Laws which shall be necessary and proper for carrying into Execution the foregoing Powers, and all other Powers vested by this Constitution in the Government of the United States, or in any Department or Officer thereof.

Section. 9.

The Migration or Importation of such Persons as any of the States now existing shall think proper to admit, shall not be prohibited by the Congress prior to the Year one thousand eight hundred and eight, but a Tax or duty may be imposed on such Importation, not exceeding ten dollars for each Person.

The Privilege of the Writ of *Habeas Corpus* shall not be suspended, unless when in Cases of Rebellion or Invasion the public Safety may require it.

No Bill of Attainder or *ex post facto* Law shall be passed.

No Capitation, or other direct, Tax shall be laid, unless in Proportion to the Census or Enumeration herein before directed to be taken.

No Tax or Duty shall be laid on Articles exported from any State.

No Preference shall be given by any Regulation of Commerce or Revenue to the Ports of one State over those of another: nor shall Vessels bound to, or from, one State, be obliged to enter, clear, or pay Duties in another.

No Money shall be drawn from the Treasury, but in Consequence of Appropriations made by Law; and a regular Statement and Account of the Receipts and Expenditures of all public Money shall be published from time to time.

No Title of Nobility shall be granted by the United States: And no Person holding any Office of Profit or Trust under them, shall, without the Consent of the Congress, accept of any present, Emolument, Office, or Title, of any kind whatever, from any King, Prince, or foreign State.

Section. 10.

No State shall enter into any Treaty, Alliance, or Confederation; grant Letters of Marque and Reprisal; coin Money; emit Bills of Credit; make any Thing but gold and silver Coin a Tender in Payment of Debts; pass any Bill of Attainder, *ex post facto Law*, or Law impairing the Obligation of Contracts, or grant any Title of Nobility.

No State shall, without the Consent of the Congress, lay any Imposts or Duties on Imports or Exports, except what may be absolutely necessary for executing its inspection Laws: and the net Produce of all Duties and Imposts, laid by any State on Imports or Exports, shall be for the Use of the Treasury of the United States;

and all such Laws shall be subject to the Revision and Control of the Congress.

No State shall, without the Consent of Congress, lay any Duty of Tonnage, keep Troops, or Ships of War in time of Peace, enter into any Agreement or Compact with another State, or with a foreign Power, or engage in War, unless actually invaded, or in such imminent Danger as will not admit of delay.

ARTICLE. II.
Section. 1.

The executive Power shall be vested in a President of the United States of America. He shall hold his Office during the Term of four Years, and, together with the Vice President, chosen for the same Term, be elected, as follows:

Each State shall appoint, in such Manner as the Legislature thereof may direct, a Number of Electors, equal to the whole Number of Senators and Representatives to which the State may be entitled in the Congress: but no Senator or Representative, or Person holding an Office of Trust or Profit under the United States, shall be appointed an Elector.

The Electors shall meet in their respective States, and vote by Ballot for two Persons, of whom one at least shall not be an Inhabitant of the same State with themselves. And they shall make a List of all the Persons voted for, and of the Number of Votes for each; which List they shall sign and certify, and transmit sealed to the Seat of the Government of the United States, directed to the President of the Senate. The President of the Senate shall, in the Presence of the Senate and House of Representatives, open all the Certificates, and the Votes shall then be counted. The Person having the greatest Number of Votes shall be the President, if such Number be a Majority of the whole Number of Electors appointed; and if there be more than one who have such Majority, and have an equal Number of Votes, then the House of Representatives shall immediately chuse by Ballot one of them for President; and if no Person have a Majority, then from the five highest on the List the said House shall in like Manner chuse the President. But in chusing the President, the Votes shall be taken by States, the Representation from each State having one Vote; A quorum for this Purpose shall consist of a Member or Members from two thirds of the States, and a Majority of all the States shall be necessary to a Choice. In every Case, after the Choice of the President, the Person having the greatest Number of Votes of the Electors shall be the Vice President. But if there should remain two or more who have equal Votes, the Senate shall chuse from them by Ballot the Vice President.

The Congress may determine the Time of chusing the Electors, and the Day on which they shall give their Votes; which Day shall be the same throughout the United States.

No Person except a natural born Citizen, or a Citizen of the United States, at the time of the Adoption of this Constitution, shall be eligible to the Office of President; neither shall any Person be eligible to that Office who shall not have attained to the Age of thirty five Years, and been fourteen Years a Resident within the United States.

In Case of the Removal of the President from Office, or of his Death, Resignation, or Inability to discharge the Powers and Duties of the said Office, the Same shall devolve on the Vice President, and the Congress may by Law provide for the Case of Removal, Death, Resignation or Inability, both of the President and Vice President, declaring what Officer shall then act as President, and such Officer shall act accordingly, until the Disability be removed, or a President shall be elected.

The President shall, at stated Times, receive for his Services, a Compensation, which shall neither be encreased nor diminished during the Period for which he shall have been elected, and he shall not receive within that Period any other Emolument from the United States, or any of them.

Before he enters on the Execution of his Office, he shall take the following Oath or Affirmation: – "I do solemnly swear (or affirm) that I will faithfully execute the Office of President of the United States, and will to the best of my Ability, preserve, protect and defend the Constitution of the United States."

Section. 2.

The President shall be Commander in Chief of the Army and Navy of the United States, and of the Militia of the several States, when called into the actual Service of the United States; he may require the Opinion, in writing, of the principal Officer in each of the executive Departments, upon any Subject relating to the Duties of their respective Offices, and he shall have Power to grant Reprieves and Pardons for Offences against the United States, except in Cases of Impeachment.

He shall have Power, by and with the Advice and Consent of the Senate, to make Treaties, provided two thirds of the Senators present concur; and he shall nominate, and by and with the Advice and Consent of the Senate, shall appoint Ambassadors, other public Ministers and Consuls, Judges of the supreme Court, and all other Officers of the United States, whose Appointments are not herein otherwise provided for, and which shall be established by Law: but the Congress may by Law vest the Appointment of such inferior Officers, as they think proper, in the President alone, in the Courts of Law, or in the Heads of Departments.

The President shall have Power to fill up all Vacancies that may happen during the Recess of the Senate, by granting Commissions which shall expire at the End of their next Session.

Section. 3.

He shall from time to time give to the Congress Information of the State of the Union, and recommend to their Consideration such Measures as he shall judge necessary and expedient; he may, on extraordinary Occasions, convene both Houses, or either of them, and in Case of Disagreement between them, with Respect to the Time of Adjournment, he may adjourn them to such Time as he shall think proper; he shall receive Ambassadors and other public Ministers; he shall take Care that the Laws be faithfully executed, and shall Commission all the Officers of the United States.

Section. 4.
The President, Vice President and all civil Officers of the United States, shall be removed from Office on Impeachment for, and Conviction of, Treason, Bribery, or other high Crimes and Misdemeanors.

ARTICLE. III.
Section. 1.
The judicial Power of the United States, shall be vested in one supreme Court, and in such inferior Courts as the Congress may from time to time ordain and establish. The Judges, both of the supreme and inferior Courts, shall hold their Offices during good Behaviour, and shall, at stated Times, receive for their Services, a Compensation, which shall not be diminished during their Continuance in Office.

Section. 2.
The judicial Power shall extend to all Cases, in Law and Equity, arising under this Constitution, the Laws of the United States, and Treaties made, or which shall be made, under their Authority; – to all Cases affecting Ambassadors, other public Ministers and Consuls; – to all Cases of admiralty and maritime Jurisdiction; – to Controversies to which the United States shall be a Party; – to Controversies between two or more States; – between a State and Citizens of another State; – between Citizens of different States, – between Citizens of the same State claiming Lands under Grants of different States, and between a State, or the Citizens thereof, and foreign States, Citizens or Subjects.

In all Cases affecting Ambassadors, other public Ministers and Consuls, and those in which a State shall be Party, the supreme Court shall have original Jurisdiction. In all the other Cases before mentioned, the supreme Court shall have appellate Jurisdiction, both as to Law and Fact, with such Exceptions, and under such Regulations as the Congress shall make.

The Trial of all Crimes, except in Cases of Impeachment, shall be by Jury; and such Trial shall be held in the State where the said Crimes shall have been committed; but when not committed within any State, the Trial shall be at such Place or Places as the Congress may by Law have directed.

Section. 3.
Treason against the United States, shall consist only in levying War against them, or in adhering to their Enemies, giving them Aid and Comfort. No Person shall be convicted of

Treason unless on the Testimony of two Witnesses to the same overt Act, or on Confession in open Court.

The Congress shall have Power to declare the Punishment of Treason, but no Attainder of Treason shall work Corruption of Blood, or Forfeiture except during the Life of the Person attainted.

ARTICLE. IV.

Section. 1.

Full Faith and Credit shall be given in each State to the public Acts, Records, and judicial Proceedings of every other State. And the Congress may by general Laws prescribe the Manner in which such Acts, Records and Proceedings shall be proved, and the Effect thereof.

Section. 2.

The Citizens of each State shall be entitled to all Privileges and Immunities of Citizens in the several States.

A Person charged in any State with Treason, Felony, or other Crime, who shall flee from Justice, and be found in another State, shall on Demand of the executive Authority of the State from which he fled, be delivered up, to be removed to the State having Jurisdiction of the Crime.

No Person held to Service or Labor in one State, under the Laws thereof, escaping into another, shall, in Consequence of any Law or Regulation therein, be discharged from such Service or Labor, but shall be delivered up on Claim of the Party to whom such Service or Labor may be due.

Section. 3.

New States may be admitted by the Congress into this Union; but no new State shall be formed or erected within the Jurisdiction of any other State; nor any State be formed by the Junction of two or more States, or Parts of States, without the Consent of the Legislatures of the States concerned as well as of the Congress.

The Congress shall have Power to dispose of and make all needful Rules and Regulations respecting the Territory or other Property belonging to the United States; and nothing in this Constitution shall be so construed as to Prejudice any Claims of the United States, or of any particular State.

Section. 4.

The United States shall guarantee to every State in this Union a Republican Form of Government, and shall protect each of them against Invasion; and on Application of the Legislature, or of the Executive (when the Legislature cannot be convened) against domestic Violence.

ARTICLE. V.

The Congress, whenever two thirds of both Houses shall deem it necessary, shall propose Amendments to this Constitution, or, on the Application of the Legislatures of two thirds of the several States, shall call a Convention for proposing Amendments, which, in either Case, shall be valid to all Intents and Purposes, as Part of this Constitution, when ratified by the Legislatures of three fourths of the several States, or by Conventions in three fourths thereof, as the one or the other Mode of

Ratification may be proposed by the Congress; Provided that no Amendment which may be made prior to the Year One thousand eight hundred and eight shall in any Manner affect the first and fourth Clauses in the Ninth Section of the first Article; and that no State, without its Consent, shall be deprived of its equal Suffrage in the Senate.

ARTICLE. VI.

All Debts contracted and Engagements entered into, before the Adoption of this Constitution, shall be as valid against the United States under this Constitution, as under the Confederation.

This Constitution, and the Laws of the United States which shall be made in Pursuance thereof; and all Treaties made, or which shall be made, under the Authority of the United States, shall be the supreme Law of the Land; and the Judges in every State shall be bound thereby, any Thing in the Constitution or Laws of any State to the Contrary notwithstanding.

The Senators and Representatives before mentioned, and the Members of the several State Legislatures, and all executive and judicial Officers, both of the United States and of the several States, shall be bound by Oath or Affirmation, to support this Constitution; but no religious Test shall ever be required as a Qualification to any Office or public Trust under the United States.

ARTICLE. VII.

The Ratification of the Conventions of nine States, shall be sufficient for the Establishment of this Constitution between the States so ratifying the Same. Done in Convention by the Unanimous Consent of the States present the Seventeenth Day of September in the Year of our Lord one thousand seven hundred and Eighty seven and of the Independence of the United States of America the Twelfth In witness whereof We have hereunto subscribed our Names,

GO WASHINGTON –
Presidt. and deputy from Virginia
[Signed also by the deputies of twelve States.]
Delaware
Geo: Read
Gunning Bedford jun
John Dickinson
Richard Bassett
Jaco: Broom
Maryland
James McHenry
Dan of ST ThoS. Jenifer
DanL Carroll.
Virginia
John Blair –
James Madison Jr.
North Carolina
WM Blount
RichD. Dobbs Spaight
Hu Williamson
South Carolina
J. Rutledge
Charles Cotesworth Pinckney
Charles Pinckney
Pierce Butler

Georgia
William Few
Abr Baldwin
New Hampshire
John Langdon
Nicholas Gilman
Massachusetts
Nathaniel Gorham
Rufus King
Connecticut
WM. SamL. Johnson
Roger Sherman
New York
Alexander Hamilton
New Jersey
Wil: Livingston
David Brearley.
WM. Paterson.
Jona: Dayton
Pennsylvania
B Franklin
Thomas Mifflin
RobT Morris
Geo. Clymer
ThoS. FitzSimons
Jared Ingersoll
James Wilson
Gouv Morris
Attest William Jackson Secretary

BILL OF RIGHTS

Amendment I

Congress shall make no law respecting an establishment of religion, or prohibiting the free exercise thereof; or abridging the freedom of speech, or of the press; or the right of the people peaceably to assemble, and to petition the Government for a redress of grievances.

Amendment II

A well regulated Militia, being necessary to the security of a free State, the right of the people to keep and bear Arms, shall not be infringed.

Amendment III

No Soldier shall, in time of peace be quartered in any house, without the consent of the Owner, nor in time of war, but in a manner to be prescribed by law.

Amendment IV

The right of the people to be secure in their persons, houses, papers, and effects, against unreasonable searches and seizures, shall not be violated, and no Warrants shall issue, but upon probable cause, supported by Oath or affirmation, and particularly describing the place to be searched, and the persons or things to be seized.

Amendment V

No person shall be held to answer for a capital, or otherwise infamous crime, unless on a presentment or indictment of a Grand Jury, except in cases arising in the land or naval forces, or in the Militia, when in actual service in time of War or public danger; nor shall any person be subject for the same offence to be twice put in jeopardy of life or limb; nor shall be compelled in any criminal case to be a witness against himself, nor be deprived of life, liberty, or property, without due process of law; nor shall private property be taken for public use, without just compensation.

Amendment VI

In all criminal prosecutions, the accused shall enjoy the right to a speedy and public trial, by an impartial jury of the State and district wherein the crime shall have been committed, which district shall have been previously ascertained by law, and to be informed of the nature and cause of the accusation; to be confronted with the witnesses against him; to have compulsory process for obtaining witnesses in his favor, and to have the Assistance of Counsel for his defence.

Amendment VII

In Suits at common law, where the value in controversy shall exceed twenty dollars, the right of trial by jury shall be preserved, and no fact tried by a jury, shall be otherwise re-examined in any Court of the United States, than according to the rules of the common law.

Amendment VIII

Excessive bail shall not be required, nor excessive fines imposed, nor cruel and unusual punishments inflicted.

Amendment IX

The enumeration in the Constitution, of certain rights, shall not be construed to deny or disparage others retained by the people.

Amendment X

The powers not delegated to the United States by the Constitution, nor prohibited by it to the States, are reserved to the States respectively, or to the people.

Subsequent Amendments to the Constitution:

Amendment XI

The Judicial power of the United States shall not be construed to extend to any suit in law or equity, commenced or prosecuted against one of the United States by Citizens of another State, or by Citizens or Subjects of any Foreign State.

Amendment XII

The Electors shall meet in their respective states, and vote by ballot for President and Vice-President, one of whom, at least, shall not be an inhabitant of the same state with themselves; they shall name in their ballots the person voted for as President, and in distinct ballots the person voted for as Vice-President, and they shall make distinct lists of all persons voted for as President, and of all persons voted for as Vice-President, and of the number of votes for each, which lists they shall sign and certify, and transmit sealed to the seat of the government of the United States, directed to the President of the Senate; – The President of the Senate shall, in the presence of the Senate and House of Representatives, open all the certificates and the votes shall then be counted; – The person having the greatest number of votes for President, shall be the President, if such number be a majority of the whole number of Electors appointed; and if no person have such majority, then from the persons having the highest numbers not exceeding three on the list of those voted for as President, the House of Representatives shall choose immediately, by ballot, the President. But in choosing the President, the votes shall be taken by states, the representation from each state having one vote; a quorum for this purpose

shall consist of a member or members from two-thirds of the states, and a majority of all the states shall be necessary to a choice. And if the House of Representatives shall not choose a President whenever the right of choice shall devolve upon them, before the fourth day of March next following, then the Vice-President shall act as President, as in the case of the death or other constitutional disability of the President. – The person having the greatest number of votes as Vice-President, shall be the Vice-President, if such number be a majority of the whole number of Electors appointed, and if no person have a majority, then from the two highest numbers on the list, the Senate shall choose the Vice-President; a quorum for the purpose shall consist of two-thirds of the whole number of Senators, and a majority of the whole number shall be necessary to a choice. But no person constitutionally ineligible to the office of President shall be eligible to that of Vice-President of the United States.

Amendment XIII

Section 1. Neither slavery nor involuntary servitude, except as a punishment for crime whereof the party shall have been duly convicted, shall exist within the United States, or any place subject to their jurisdiction.

Section 2. Congress shall have power to enforce this article by appropriate legislation.

Amendment XIV

Section 1. All persons born or naturalized in the United States, and subject to the jurisdiction thereof, are citizens of the United States and of the State wherein they reside. No State shall make or enforce any law which shall abridge the privileges or immunities of citizens of the United States; nor shall any State deprive any person of life, liberty, or property, without due process of law; nor deny to any person within its jurisdiction the equal protection of the laws.

Section 2. Representatives shall be apportioned among the several States according to their respective numbers, counting the whole number of persons in each State, excluding Indians not taxed. But when the right to vote at any election for the choice of electors for President and Vice President of the United States, Representatives in Congress, the Executive and Judicial officers of a State, or the members of the Legislature thereof, is denied to any of the male inhabitants of such State, being twenty-one years of age, and citizens of the United States, or in any way abridged, except for participation in rebellion, or other crime, the basis of representation therein shall be reduced in the proportion which the number of such male citizens shall bear to the whole number of male citizens twenty-one years of age in such State.

Section 3. No person shall be a Senator or Representative in Congress, or elector of President and Vice President, or hold any office, civil or military, under the United States, or under any State, who, having previously taken an oath, as a member of Congress, or as an officer of the United States, or as a member of any State legislature, or as an executive or judicial officer of any State, to support the Constitution of the United States, shall have engaged in insurrection or rebellion against the same, or given aid or comfort to the enemies thereof. But Congress may by a vote of two-thirds of each House, remove such disability.

Section 4. The validity of the public debt of the United States, authorized by law, including debts incurred for payment of pensions and bounties for services in suppressing insurrection or rebellion, shall not be questioned. But neither the United States nor any State shall assume or pay any debt or obligation incurred in aid of insurrection or rebellion against the United States, or any claim for the loss or emancipation of any slave; but all such debts, obligations and claims shall be held illegal and void.

Section 5. The Congress shall have power to enforce, by appropriate legislation, the provisions of this article.

Amendment XV
Section 1. The right of citizens of the United States to vote shall not be denied or abridged by the United States or by any State on account of race, color, or previous condition of servitude.

Section 2. The Congress shall have power to enforce this article by appropriate legislation.

Amendment XVI
The Congress shall have power to lay and collect taxes on incomes, from whatever source derived, without apportionment among the several States, and without regard to any census or enumeration.

Amendment XVII
The Senate of the United States shall be composed of two Senators from each State, elected by the people thereof, for six years; and each Senator shall have one vote. The electors in each State shall have the qualifications requisite for electors of the most numerous branch of the State legislatures.

When vacancies happen in the representation of any State in the Senate, the executive authority of such State shall issue writs of election to fill such vacancies: Provided, That the legislature of any State may empower the executive thereof to make temporary appointments until the people fill the vacancies by election as the legislature may direct.

This amendment shall not be so construed as to affect the election or term of any Senator chosen before it becomes valid as part of the Constitution.

Amendment XVIII
Section 1. After one year from the ratification of this article the manufacture, sale, or transportation of intoxicating liquors within, the importation thereof into, or the exportation thereof from the United States and all territory

subject to the jurisdiction thereof for beverage purposes is hereby prohibited.

Section 2. The Congress and the several States shall have concurrent power to enforce this article by appropriate legislation.

Section 3. This article shall be inoperative unless it shall have been ratified as an amendment to the Constitution by the legislatures of the several States, as provided in the Constitution, within seven years from the date of the submission hereof to the States by the Congress.

Amendment XIX

The right of citizens of the United States to vote shall not be denied or abridged by the United States or by any State on account of sex.

Congress shall have power to enforce this article by appropriate legislation.

Amendment XX

Section 1. The terms of the President and Vice President shall end at noon on the 20th day of January, and the terms of Senators and Representatives at noon on the 3rd day of January, of the years in which such terms would have ended if this article had not been ratified; and the terms of their successors shall then begin.

Section 2. The Congress shall assemble at least once in every year, and such meeting shall begin at noon on the 3rd day of January, unless they shall by law appoint a different day.

Section 3. If, at the time fixed for the beginning of the term of the President, the President elect shall have died, the Vice President elect shall become President. If a President shall not have been chosen before the time fixed for the beginning of his term, or if the President elect shall have failed to qualify, then the Vice President elect shall act as President until a President shall have qualified; and the Congress may by law provide for the case wherein neither a President elect nor a Vice President elect shall have qualified, declaring who shall then act as President, or the manner in which one who is to act shall be selected, and such person shall act accordingly until a President or Vice President shall have qualified.

Section 4. The Congress may by law provide for the case of the death of any of the persons from whom the House of Representatives may choose a President whenever the right of choice shall have devolved upon them, and for the case of the death of any of the persons from whom the Senate may choose a Vice President whenever the right of choice shall have devolved upon them.

Section 5. Sections 1 and 2 shall take effect on the 15th day of October following the ratification of this article.

Section 6. This article shall be inoperative unless it shall have been ratified as an amendment to the Constitution by the legislatures of three-fourths of the several States within seven years from the date of its submission.

Amendment XXI
Section 1. The eighteenth article of amendment to the Constitution of the United States is hereby repealed.

Section 2. The transportation or importation into any State, Territory, or possession of the United States for delivery or use therein of intoxicating liquors, in violation of the laws thereof, is hereby prohibited.

Section 3. This article shall be inoperative unless it shall have been ratified as an amendment to the Constitution by conventions in the several States, as provided in the Constitution, within seven years from the date of the submission hereof to the States by the Congress.

Amendment XXII
Section 1. No person shall be elected to the office of the President more than twice, and no person who has held the office of President, or acted as President, for more than two years of a term to which some other person was elected President shall be elected to the office of the President more than once. But this Article shall not apply to any person holding the office of President when this Article was proposed by the Congress, and shall not prevent any person who may be holding the office of President, or acting as President, during the term within

which this Article becomes operative from holding the office of President or acting as President during the remainder of such term.

Section. 2. This article shall be inoperative unless it shall have been ratified as an amendment to the Constitution by the legislatures of three-fourths of the several States within seven years from the date of its submission to the States by the Congress.

Amendment XXIII
Section 1. The District constituting the seat of Government of the United States shall appoint in such manner as the Congress may direct: A number of electors of President and Vice President equal to the whole number of Senators and Representatives in Congress to which the District would be entitled if it were a State, but in no event more than the least populous State; they shall be in addition to those appointed by the States, but they shall be considered, for the purposes of the election of President and Vice President, to be electors appointed by a State; and they shall meet in the District and perform such duties as provided by the twelfth article of amendment.

Section 2. The Congress shall have power to enforce this article by appropriate legislation.

Amendment XXIV
Section 1. The right of citizens of the United States to vote in any primary or other election for President or Vice President, for electors for President or Vice President, or for Senator or Representative in Congress, shall not be denied or abridged by the United States or any State by reason of failure to pay any poll tax or other tax.

Section 2. The Congress shall have power to enforce this article by appropriate legislation.

Amendment XXV

Section 1. In case of the removal of the President from office or of his death or resignation, the Vice President shall become President.

Section 2. Whenever there is a vacancy in the office of the Vice President, the President shall nominate a Vice President who shall take office upon confirmation by a majority vote of both Houses of Congress.

Section 3. Whenever the President transmits to the President *pro tempore* of the Senate and the Speaker of the House of Representatives his written declaration that he is unable to discharge the powers and duties of his office, and until he transmits to them a written declaration to the contrary, such powers and duties shall be discharged by the Vice President as Acting President.

Section 4. Whenever the Vice President and a majority of either the principal officers of the executive departments or of such other body as Congress may by law provide, transmit to the President *pro tempore* of the Senate and the Speaker of the House of Representatives their written declaration that the President is unable to discharge the powers and duties of his office, the Vice President shall immediately assume the powers and duties of the office as Acting President.

Thereafter, when the President transmits to the President *pro tempore* of the Senate and the Speaker of the House of Representatives his written declaration that no inability exists, he shall resume the powers and duties of his office unless the Vice President and a majority of either the principal officers of the executive department or of such other body as Congress may by law provide, transmit within four days to the President *pro tempore* of the Senate and the Speaker of the House of Representatives their written declaration that the President is unable to discharge the powers and duties of his office. Thereupon Congress shall decide the issue, assembling within forty-eight hours for that purpose if not in session. If the Congress, within twenty-one days after receipt of the latter written declaration, or, if Congress is not in session, within twenty-one days after Congress is required to assemble, determines by two-thirds vote of both Houses that the President is unable to discharge the powers and duties of his office, the Vice President shall continue to discharge the same as Acting President; otherwise, the President shall resume the powers and duties of his office.

Amendment XXVI

Section 1. The right of citizens of the United States, who are eighteen years of age or older, to vote shall not be denied or abridged by the United States or by any State on account of age.

Section 2. The Congress shall have power to enforce this article by appropriate legislation.

Amendment XXVII

No law, varying the compensation for the services of the Senators and Representatives, shall take effect, until an election of Representatives shall have intervened.

Political Institutions

THE CONSTITUTION

DEVISED by a 1787 convention meeting in Philadelphia under the leadership of George Washington, the Constitution replaced the earlier and ineffectual Articles of Confederation. The world's longest-lived national constitution, it establishes a republican government meshing decisions achieved through the popular will with those made by appointed representatives: the Electoral college used to select the Chief Executive and the Congress comprised of the House of Representatives and the Senate. Both legislative bodies are elected, though originally state legislatures appointed the Senators until the passage of the 17th Amendment in 1913.

The Constitution provides for three governmental branches—legislative, executive, and judicial—interacting through powers that provide "checks and balances," including the presidential veto, congressional override, presidential nomination of federal judges, and senatorial consent for high ranking appointment and for treaty ratification. Article V allows for the document to be amended by a two-thirds vote of Congress and a three-fourths vote of the states.

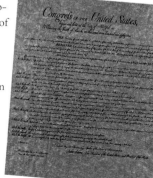

Made up of seven articles and 26 amendments, the Constitution stipulates power sharing between federal and state governments, an arrangement clarified in the 10th amendment: "The powers not delegated to the United States by the Constitution, nor prohibited by it to the States, are reserved to the States respectively, or to the people."

The first 10 amendments, known as the Bill of Rights, which protect personal liberties like freedom of speech, press and religion, were added by the First Congress. Their addition honored a promise made by the Federalist supporters of the Constitution. To gain ratification of the document over the fears of opponents, they pledged the addition of amendments safeguarding the citizen from potential government tyranny. A reflection of the British heritage of the new United States, the Bill of Rights' roots stretch as far back in Anglo history as the 1215 Magna Carta.

THE PRESIDENCY

THE federal constitution, Article II (1787), established the Presidency. Presidents serve a maximum of two four-year terms and are chosen by an electoral college selected by the state legislatures. The president heads the executive branch of the government and is commander-in-chief of the armed forces. He has the power to veto legislation passed by the Congress and to appoint judges.

As the office has evolved, the president heads his political party, directs foreign policy, and serves as a point of national focus. In addition, he has been given authority beyond the constitutionally outlined powers to manage trade relations, to protect natural resources, and to mediate in extreme labor disputes. The president's wife, or First Lady, also a national figure, usually identifies herself with a specific cause or issue during her husband's tenure in office.

America's first president, George Washington, established precedents of executives working with department heads as a body known as the "cabinet," of communicating with Congress in writing, and of delivering a farewell address upon leaving office. Constitutional amendments affecting the presidency include the 12th (1804), calling for the president and vice-president to be chosen in separate electoral college ballots; the 20th (1933), which moved inauguration day from March 4 to January 20; the 22nd (1951), limiting an individual to only two presidential terms; and the 25th (1967), dealing with potential presidential disability.

The line of succession in the event of a president's death (redefined in 1947) passes in turn to the vice-president, Speaker of the House of Representatives, president *pro tempore* of the Senate, and the cabinet officers beginning with the Secretary of State.

If the House of Representatives finds a president guilty of "high crimes or misdemeanors" he is "impeached": he is tried before the Senate, which decides if he is to be removed from office.

CONGRESS

THE bicameral United States Congress consists of an upper house, known as the Senate and a lower, the House of Representatives. Together these bodies seek answers to issues that confront the country, and when necessary propose laws.

Based on population, each state sends representatives to the House, which has exclusive power to tax and to formulate spending legislation. Members serve two-year terms. In the event of a disputed presidential election, the House chooses who will assume the office. The Speaker of the House is the presiding officer of the body and second in line to the presidential succession, often the vice-president. The speaker influences committee assignments and controls floor deliberations. Committees accomplish much of the body's work before bills are put to a vote of the entire membership. The use of permanent standing committees began after the War of 1812 and was well-established by the 1848 Mexican War, at which time each committee held exclusive jurisdiction over some area of government policy.

The Senate, in which each state has two representatives, advises the president on issues of foreign policy and chooses the vice-president in disputed elections. Members serve six-year terms, with one-third of the body elected every two years. The Senate established permanent committees in 1816. Since the 1920s, Senate committees have assumed a largely investigatory role into matters such as oil leases (1920s), securities regulation (1930s), war profiteering (1940s), organized crime

(1950s), the Vietnam War (1960s), the Watergate scandal (1970s), and covert intelligence operations (1980s). The Senate provides advice and consent to nominations and treaties. Closest scrutiny has been reserved for judicial appointees, with presidents given a fair amount of latitude in selecting the members of their cabinets. In the event of a presidential impeachment trial, the Senate members serve as jurors with the Chief Justice of the Supreme Court presiding.

SUPREME COURT

THE Judiciary Act of 1789 implemented the judicial branch designed by Article III of the Constitution creating the Supreme Court and subordinate courts. A Chief Justice presides, assisted by eight associate justices; appointments are for life. The court's principal role, defined by Chief Justice John Marshall in *Marbury v. Madison* (1803), is judicial review, deciding legislative and judicial constitutionality. If a president is impeached and tried before the Senate, the Chief Justice serves as presiding officer.

For its first 135 years, the court played a key role in arbitrating disputes arising under the federal system, especially those dealing with nationalism versus those of states rights. Under the influential administration of Marshall, the court affirmed the supremacy of the national government in cases like *Fletcher v. Peck* (1810), forbidding states to impair contracts and *McCulloch v. Maryland* (1819), in which the court ruled that a state may not tax a federal entity.

Such decisions did not always soothe national feelings, however, as in *Dred Scott v. Sanford* (1857) in which Chief Justice Roger Taney ruled that blacks could not be citizens and that Congress had no power to limit the extension of slavery into the western territories. In one decision, he destroyed the fragile sectional truce achieved in the 1820 Missouri Compromise and speeded the coming of the Civil War. In the similarly destructive case *Plessy v. Ferguson* (1896), the court held that separate but equal facilities for the races were constitutional. Since World War II, the court has concerned itself with limiting the power of the government to infringe on individual rights, and of monitoring the government's commitment to and success in seeing the individual fully enjoy those rights. An exemplar case of this nature was Brown v. Board of Education of Topeka (1974), ending racial segregation in public facilities.

ELECTORAL SYSTEM

FROM its earliest national period, the United States has emphasized frequent elections and, since 1888, the "Australian" or secret ballot has been utilized. Presidential elections are held every four years, with the next scheduled for the year 2000. The major political parties hold a nominating convention attended by state delegates to choose their candidates for president and vice-president. Most states have statutes limiting campaign funding by political parties, but such laws have not always been effectively enforced. Statewide elections called "primaries" are held prior to the presidential election to decide the candidates for the major political parties. Voters then designate their presidential choice in November of the election year. The candidate with the majority receives the state's electoral votes. In December, the electoral college meets and votes accordingly. The tradition that a president should not serve more than two terms was only broken by the enormously popular Franklin D. Roosevelt, elected four times (1932, 1936, 1940, and 1944).

Critics point to a major flaw in the electoral college system: a president can be elected with a majority of electoral votes even if his opponent has the lion's share of the popular vote. This last occurred in 1888, when Republican Benjamin Harrison defeated Democrat Grover Cleveland. Reformers have urged the electoral college be abolished in favor of direct election, a prospect that would have horrified the Founding Fathers, who feared the rule of the mob. Defenders of the system praise it, insisting it has served the country far better than could ever have been expected when it was devised.

POLITICAL PARTIES

POLITICAL parties developed in the United States during the George Washington (1789–97) presidential administration under the leadership of Thomas

Jefferson and Alexander Hamilton. Traditionally traced to Thomas Jefferson, the liberal Democratic party was originally identified with strict constitutional interpretation, states rights, and minimal government. With its roots in the philosophy of Alexander Hamilton, who favored a loose constitutional interpretation, the modern Republican party, founded in 1854 to oppose slavery, has a conservative reputation.

Initially the Hamiltonian faction, known as the Federalists, emerged as proponents for the ratification of the federal constitution of 1787. They disappeared as a coherent group early in the 19th century. The Jeffersonian Republicans dominated during the Era of Good Feelings (1817–24). Two party politics reemerged with the candidacy of Andrew Jackson in 1824. Jackson, a candidate of the New Democracy movement that sought wider citizen participation in the political process, was one of the first politicians to campaign on emotional rather than intellectual appeal. In opposition to the Jacksonian Democrats, the Whigs evolved, and remained on the scene until they were subsumed by the emerging Republican party, which placed Abraham Lincoln in the White House in 1860.

In the 1820s, the first "third" parties began to surface in American politics, beginning with the Anti-Masonic and Workingmen's parties. The Anti-Masons were the first party to use the nominating convention to select their candidates, a method adopted by the major parties. The third party group that came closest to capturing the White House were the agricultural Populists who supported William Jennings Bryan in the election of 1896. The most recent third party to attract a wide following in America is the Reform party organized by Texas tycoon H. Ross Perot, active in the elections of 1992 and 1996.

DEMOCRATS

THE modern Democratic party was formed after the War of 1812 in opposition to the more aristocratic Federalists. Using nominating conventions, party platforms, and institutionalized

campaigning, the party solidified under the leadership of
Martin Van Buren, James K. Polk, and Franklin Pierce.
Andrew Jackson was the party's national symbol from
1824, and was elected president in 1832 and 1836, by
which time the Democrat's organizational structure was solid.

The core of the party's support lay in the slave-holding
south, on the nation's farms, and with immigrants in eastern cities.
Democrats tended to come from groups of "outsiders," non-conforming ethnic
or religious groups. They feared a powerful central government, and adopted the
stance of egalitarians fighting a government elite.

From the mid-1830s to the Civil War, the Democrats were the nation's
majority party. They began to lose support in the 1850s, and split into northern
and southern wings during the war. During Reconstruction, southern whites
who had not been Democrats before the war converted in massive numbers, and
the Solid (Democratic) South became part of the political landscape in the last
years of the 19th century.

Courtesy of their high percentage of immigrant members and toleration of
Catholics, the Democrats lost ground in the 1890s, regaining ascendancy with
the 1912 election of Woodrow Wilson. The 1920 election put Republican
Warren G. Harding in office, repudiating Wilson, the Democrats, and Progressive
reform. Throughout the early half of the 20th century the party split into urban
and rural wings. The great height of Democratic power occurred in Franklin D.
Roosevelt's four terms of office (1932, 1936, 1940, and 1944). Eastern, urban
liberals dominated the party in the 1960s, and into the 1990s the party
maintained its liberal image. In 1996, Bill Clinton became the first Democrat
reelected president since Roosevelt but by 1998 was embroiled in an
impeachment controversy.

REPUBLICANS

THE Republican party first appeared on a presidential ballot in 1856. With the
disintegration of the Whig party after the 1854 Kansas–Nebraska Act, the

Republicans formalized their organization in opposition to the spread of slavery into the western territories. By 1860, the new group had also absorbed the Know-Nothing Party and, with Abraham Lincoln as their candidate, captured the White House.

The Civil War made the Republicans the avowed enemies of the South for the next century, during which the Republicans promoted industrial development through high tariffs. In the 1865–1900 period, when eastern, corporate Republicans dominated with laissez-faire economic policies, farmers dropped their support.

After William McKinley defeated Democrat William Jennings Bryan in 1896 and 1900, the Republican party won every presidential election until 1932, with the exception of the Woodrow Wilson victories in 1912 and 1916. Republicans controlled Congress from 1896 to 1930, with the exception of the period 1910–18.

Three Republicans were elected president in the 1920s by comfortable margins, Warren G. Harding, Calvin Coolidge, and Herbert Hoover. After initially supporting the policies of Franklin Roosevelt in the frightening days of the Great Depression, the Republicans became unremittingly hostile to the New Deal. They did not regain the White House until 1952, however, when General Dwight D. Eisenhower entered the Oval Office.

The Watergate scandal during the Richard Nixon administration reflected badly on all elements of the party. With the election of Ronald Reagan in 1980 and the new president's vigorous pursuit of a conservative New Right agenda, the party began a three-administration White House, run with two terms for Reagan and one for George Bush, who was defeated by Democrat Bill Clinton in 1992. During Clinton's two terms, the Republicans were accused of organizing a conservative conspiracy to destroy the Democratic president and his policies.

Power and Politics

JULY 4, 1776
Britain's American colonies declared their independence.

1787
Constitutional Convention drafted a new constitution for the United States.

1791–94
Two U.S. political parties, Federalists and Republicans, emerged.

FEBRUARY 24, 1803
In Marbury v. Madison the Supreme Court established judicial review.

MARCH 2, 1820
The Missouri Compromise made Missouri and Maine slave free states.

NOVEMBER 6, 1860
Abraham Lincoln's presidential election prompted seven Southern secessions.

FEBRUARY 24, 1868
The Senate tried President Andrew Johnson, acquitting him by one vote.

1876
The disputed Hayes-Tilden presidential election caused a constitutional crisis.

JULY 2, 1881
An assassin shot President James Garfield, who died Sept. 19.

JANUARY 16, 1883
The Pendleton bill reformed United States civil service.

FEBRUARY 4, 1887
Interstate Commerce Commission created for railroad regulation.

JULY 2, 1890
The Sherman Anti-Trust Act forbade monopolies in industry.

MARCH 3, 1891
Office of the Superintendent of Immigration created to manage immigration.

MAY 19, 1891
Farmers and laborers founded the Populist Party.

FEBRUARY 14, 1903
The Department of Commerce and Labor created.

OCTOBER 25, 1923
Teapot Dome Scandal prompts investigations of Harding administration.

MARCH 6, 1933
Franklin Roosevelt began his First Hundred Days assault on the Depression.

JULY 22, 1937
Senate overturned Franklin Roosevelt's Court Packing Scheme.

NOVEMBER 7, 1944
Franklin Roosevelt elected to an unprecedented fourth term.

APRIL 12, 1945
Franklin Roosevelt died, making Harry S. Truman president.

JANUARY 3, 1951
22nd Amendment limited presidents to two terms.

NOVEMBER 22, 1963
President John F. Kennedy assassinated in Dallas, Texas.

MARCH 31, 1968
Lyndon Johnson announced he will not seek a second term.

AUGUST 9, 1974
Richard M. Nixon resigned the presidency over the Watergate scandal.

MARCH 30, 1981
Ronald Reagan wounded in an assassination attempt.

JULY 12, 1984
Geraldine Ferarro became the first female vice-presidential candidate.

AUGUST 12, 1987
Ronald Reagan accepted responsibility for Iran-Contra Affair.

MARCH 15, 1989
Veterans' Administration made a Cabinet department.

JANUARY 22, 1993
Bill Clinton overturned abortion restrictions passed by Reagan and Bush.

DECEMBER 1998
House of Representatives impeached Bill Clinton.

War and Peace

1763
Colonial relations deteriorated after the French and Indian War.

1775–83
Britain's thirteen colonies waged the War of American Independence.

JUNE 19, 1812
The United States declared war on Britain over maritime disputes.

MAY 13, 1846
Congress declared war on Mexico over a border dispute.

APRIL 12, 1861
Civil War broke out at Ft. Sumter in Charleston, South Carolina.

JULY 1–3, 1863
George Meade defeated Robert E. Lee at Gettysburg.

APRIL 9, 1865
Robert E. Lee surrendered to Ulysses S. Grant at Appomattox.

DECEMBER 29, 1890
Last major conflict with Indians fought at Wounded Knee.

FEBRUARY 15, 1898
The *USS Maine* exploded in Havana Harbor killing 260.

APRIL 24, 1898
Congress declared war on Spain.

MAY 7, 1915
A German submarine sank the *Lusitania* with 128 Americans aboard.

MARCH 15, 1916
U.S. troops entered Mexico in pursuit of bandit Pancho Villa.

MARCH 1, 1917
Zimmermann Telegram suggesting a Mexican-German alliance made public.

APRIL 6, 1917
The U.S. declared war on Germany.

JUNE 28, 1919
The Treaty of Versailles ended World War I.

SEPTEMBER 16, 1940
The first peace-time draft enacted.

DECEMBER 7, 1941
The Japanese Imperial Air Force bombed Pearl Harbor, Hawaii.

MAY 7, 1945
Germany surrendered unconditionally.

AUGUST 6, 1945
The United States dropped an atomic bomb on Hiroshima, Japan.

AUGUST 14, 1945
Japan surrendered unconditionally.

JULY 1, 1950
The first American troops landed in Korea.

JULY 27, 1953
The war in Korea ended with the Panmunjon armistice.

JULY 8, 1959
Two American advisors killed in Vietnam.

AUGUST 7, 1964
Congress awarded President Johnson wide powers to act in Vietnam.

MARCH 8, 1965
The first American combat troops landed in Vietnam.

JANUARY 30, 1968
The Tet Offensive illustrated America was not winning in Vietnam.

JANUARY 27, 1973
A peace agreement was signed in the Vietnam War.

JANUARY 1991
Americans participated in UN bombings against Iraq.

FEBRUARY 23, 1991
A land offensive was launched against Iraq.

FEBRUARY 28, 1991
President Bush ordered a cease fire in the Persian Gulf War.

Foreign Affairs

1783
Treaty of Paris ended the American Revolution.

FEBRUARY 1785
Diplomatic relations established with Great Britain.

1814
Treaty of Ghent ended the War of 1812.

DECEMBER 2, 1823
The Monroe Doctrine became the American foreign policy.

1846
Treaty with Britain settled The Oregon boundary at 49th parallel.

1848
Treaty of Guadalupe Hidalgo ended Mexican War.

1867
Treaty with Russia to acquire Alaska.

1893
Hawaii became a U.S. protectorate.

1898
Treaty with Spain ended Spanish–American War.

1901
Hay–Pauncefote Treaty paved way for construction of Panama Canal.

MARCH 2, 1901
Plat Amendment made Cuba an American protectorate.

SEPTEMBER 16, 1915
Haiti became an American protectorate.

MARCH 2, 1917
Puerto Rico became a United States territory.

NOVEMBER 19, 1919
Senates refuses to ratify the Treaty of Versailles.

1920
U.S. boycotted the first meeting of the League of Nations.

1927
U.S. citizenship granted to Virgin Islanders.

1941
Britain and the U.S. announced war goals in the Atlantic Charter.

1943
Casablanca Conference of wartime allies.

1945
Yalta agreement with wartime allies on the future of Germany.

1949
U.S. was a founding member of the United Nations.

1958
NORAD, North American Air Defense Command established.

1963
"Hotline" agreement reached between the U.S. and Russia.

1968
Nuclear Non-Proliferation Treaty agreed and opened for signature.

1973
Agreement reached to end the war in Vietnam.

1976
U.S.–Soviet Treaty restricted nuclear explosions for peaceful purposes.

1978
Camp David agreements between Israel and Egypt.

1980
Agreement reached for normalization of relations with China.

1990
Treaty on the Final Settlement with Respect to Germany signed.

1992
North American Free Trade Association settled with Canada and Mexico.

1995
U.S. hosted Dayton Agreements on Bosnia-Herzegovina future.

Economics

FEBRUARY 25, 1791
Bank of the United States chartered.

1792
Coinage Act established bimetallism.

1794
First American trade union established in Philadelphia.

APRIL 1816
First protective U.S. tariff established.

OCTOBER 1836
Massachusetts enacted first child labor law.

1837
Financial depression followed Andrew Jackson's destruction of the National Bank.

1840
Independent Treasury Bill enacted.

JANUARY 1848
Gold discovered at Sutter's Mill, California.

1863
The National Bank Act laid foundation for national banking system.

1879
Standard Oil of Ohio formed as the first trust.

1890
The McKinley Act raised duties 50%.

MAY 20, 1895
Congress declared the income tax unconstitutional.

1900
Agricultural employment fell to 37% of the workforce.

FEBRUARY 25, 1913
Federal income tax introduced

DECEMBER 23, 1913
Federal Reserve system created.

1922
First nationwide railroad strike occurred.

OCTOBER 24, 1929
Wall Street stock market crash began an economic panic.

1932
Unemployment stood at 23.6 %.

1933
The Federal Deposit Insurance Corporation established.

1935
The Wagner Act created the National Labor Relations Board.

1944
Unemployment stood at 1.2 %.

1947
The U.S. initiated the Marshall Plan for European financial aid.

1950
Agricultural employment fell to 11.6% of the workforce.

1974
U.S. International Trade Commission formed.

1978
U.S. domestic air transportation de-regulated.

1987
Dow fell 508 points on "Black Monday."

1988
Unemployment stood at 5.5%.

1990
Agricultural employment fell to 2.4% of the workforce.

1993
NAFTA agreement established between Mexico, Canada, and U.S. common market.

1994
National debt totalled $4.6 trillion.

1994
Unemployment stood at 6.1%

Science and Technology

1751
Benjamin Franklin conducted his experiments with electricity.

1776
David Bushnell developed a hand-powered wooden submarine.

1784
Dispersal of horses to Indians of American Plains completed.

1791
Samuel Slater established the first productive American factory.

1794
Eli Whitney developed the cotton gin to extract fiber cleanly.

1831
Cyrus McCormick developed a machine to reap grain.

1835
Samuel Morse built the first electric telegraph.

1836
Samuel Colt patented his revolver.

1846
William Morton developed the anesthetic ether.

1851
Isaac Singer patented an improved mechanical sewing machine.

1876
Alexander Graham Bell invented the telephone.

1903
First controlled air flight by Orville and Wilbur Wright.

1908
Henry Ford introduces the Model T winning wide support for automobiles.

1926
Warner Brothers produced the first talking motion picture.

1931
At 86 stories the Empire State Building became the world's tallest.

1945
First nuclear explosion at Alamagordo, New Mexico.

1946
J. Presper Eckert and J. Mauchly developed ENIAC, first electronic computer.

1951
UNIVAC 1 was the first commercially available electronic computer.

1955
The Salk vaccine for polio came into use.

1959
Grace Hopper invented COBOL, a high-level business computing language.

1960
The U.S. launched the first weather satellite.

1968
Douglas Engelbart at Stanford invented the computer mouse.

1971
American Intel corporation introduced the first microprocessor.

1971
The first personal computer, the Altair 8800, sold in the U.S..

1977
The Apple II, a fully assembled personal computer, sold in the U.S..

1981
AIDS recognized for the first time.

1982
IBM introduced the first laser printer.

1989
Doppler radar used for weather forecasting.

1990
The first pen-based computers were introduced.

1990
Hubble Space Telescope placed in Earth Orbit.

Slavery and Abolition

1775
Formation of Pennsylvania Society for Promoting the Abolition of Slavery.

1776
Continental Congress calls for end to importation of slaves.

1780–84
Abolition bills passed by Pennsylvania, Maryland, Rhode Island, and Connecticut.

1785
New York Society promoting freedom of slaves formed.

1786
First slaves began to escape north by "underground railroad."

1787
Northwest Ordinance excluded slavery from north of Ohio River.

1788–92
Abolition societies formed in Delaware, Maryland, Rhode Island, Connecticut, and Virginia.

1793
Federal Fugitive Slave law passed. Eli Whitney invented cotton gin.

1800
Suppression of planned slave revolt by Gabriel Prosser of Virginia.

1803
South Carolina opened slave trade from Caribbean and South America.

1805
Slaves emancipated required by law to leave Virginia.

1807
Importation of slaves from Africa banned by Congress.

1816
Establishment of American Colonization Society in Washington forming Liberia colony.

1820
Missouri admitted as slave state; slavery forbidden north of 36–30 Line.

1827
First black newspaper, the *Freedom's Journal*, begins publication.

1831
Nat Turner slave rebellion in Virginia kills 57 whites.

1832
The New England Anti-Slavery Society was formed.

1833
The National Anti-Slavery Society was formed in Philadelphia.

1835
The New York Anti-Slavery Society was organized.

1835
Oberlin College became the first to admit blacks.

1838
Frederick Douglass escaped slavery to become an abolitionist author and speaker.

1839
The Liberty Party formed to bring slavery into political debate.

1846
The Senate defeated Wilmot's Provision banning slavery in the Mexican Cession.

1852
Harriet Beecher Stowe published the inflammatory *Uncle Tom's Cabin*.

1854
The Republican party formed to oppose the extension of slavery.

1855
Massachusetts schools abolished segregation.

1857
The Supreme Court ruled in *Dred Scot v. Sanford*.

1859
Abolitionist John Brown's plans for a slave uprising failed.

1861
The seceding states formed a provisional government.

1865
The abolition of slavery became formally effective.

Black American Chronology

1868
14th Amendment granted all citizens equal protection under the law.

1870
15th Amendment stated the vote may not be denied by race.

1881
"Jim Crow" era began with laws providing for racial segregation.

1896
Supreme Court approved separate but equal facilities for the races.

1909
National Association for the Advancement of Colored People founded.

1911
National Urban League founded for equal conditions for black workers.

1915
Supreme Court rulings outlawed Jim Crow housing.

1917-1921
Race riots in Houston, Chicago, and Tulsa County, Oklahoma.

1930
Black Muslims (Nation of Islam) founded in Detroit by Wali Farad.

1938
Integration of Missouri Law School ordered, Texas and Oklahoma followed.

1942
Congress of Racial Equality (CORE)

for non-violent protest founded.

1944
Black leader Adam Clayton Powell elected to Congress.

1954
Supreme Court ruling declared segregated education unconstitutional and unequal.

1957
Southern Christian Leadership Conference (SCLC) founded by Martin Luther King.

1960
Student Nonviolent Coordinating Committee (SNCC) founded for biracial student protest.

1961
Attack on Freedom Riders traveling by bus to Birmingham, Alabama.

1963
Civil rights march of 250,000 to Washington for peaceful demonstration.

1964
Civil Rights Act and Voting Rights Act became law.

1965
Riots in Los Angeles triggered by arrest of black motorist.

1966
Black Panthers founded, demanding equal opportunities, and an end to police brutality.

1967
Thurgood Marshall appointed first black Associate Justice of the Supreme Court.

1968
Assassination of Martin Luther King. Eldridge Cleaver, Panther leader, arrested.

1969
FBI intensifies campaign against Black Panthers.

1972
Barbara Jordan of Texas first black woman chairing state legislature.

1980
Rioting after all-white jury acquitted police of fatal beating.

1988
Rioting in Miami after police killed black motorcyclist.

1989
Barbara Harris, first black woman appointed Episcopal bishop.

1990
Virginians elect first black governor, New York first black mayor.

1992
Los Angeles riots after police acquitted in Rodney King case.

1994–95
Murder trial of sports star O.J. Simpson reawakens racial tension.

Native American Chronology

1778
First US Treaty with an Indian tribe, the Delaware.

1779
Smallpox epidemics spread in native tribes.

1785
Cherokee ceded lands in North Carolina, Tennessee, and Kentucky.

1790
Conflict with Indians broke out in Ohio Valley.

1794
Battle of Fallen Timbers ended resistance in northwest Ohio.

1795
Indians ceded southern and eastern Ohio.

1809–1810
Shawnee Tecumseh leads native resistance against the whites.

1824
Office of Indian Affairs organized by War Department.

1830
Andrew Jackson signed the Indian Removal Act.

1832
Black Hawk War fought in Illinois and Wisconsin.

1835
Outbreak of Second Seminole War.

1849
Office of Indian Affairs transferred to Department of the Interior.

1864
More than 450 Cheyenne and Arapaho massacred at Sand Creek.

1867
Establishment of Board of Indian Commissioners.

1870
First Congressional appropriation for Indian education.

1876
Defeat of Custer, "Custer's Last Stand."

1881
Helen Hunt Jackson cataloged ill-treatment of Indians.

1882
Foundation of Indian Rights Association.

1884
Traditional Indian religious practices made a criminal offense.

1890
Two hundred Sioux massacred at Wounded Knee.

1911
Foundation of Society of American Indians.

1924
Passage of American Indian Citizenship Act.

1935
Establishment of Indian Arts and Crafts Board.

1964
Foundation at Santa Fe of Institute of American Indian Arts.

1968
Indian Bill of Rights passed by Congress.

1970
Publication of *Bury My Heart at Wounded Knee*.

1972
Indian militants occupy Washington headquarters of Bureau of Indian Affairs.

1978
Passage of American Indian Religious Freedom Act.

1988
Indian Gaming Act had huge cultural effect on reservations.

1990
Total Indian population reported as 1,959,000.

Equality for Women

1821
Emma Willard founded Troy Female Seminary (New York), a women's college.

1835
Oberlin College in Ohio admitted women.

1848
New York gave women the right to own property.

1865
American Woman Suffrage Association founded by Lucy Stone and Julia Ward.

1869
Wyoming territorial legislature enacted first law giving women the vote.

1872
Victoria Woodhall became the first female presidential candidate.

1874
The National Women's Christian Temperance Union founded in Cleveland, Ohio.

1883
Francis E. Willard founded the World's Women's Christian Temperance Union.

1887
Susanna Madora Salter elected America's first woman mayor in Argonia, Kansas.

1890
The Wyoming constitution granted women equal voting rights.

1895
Mary Church Terrell founded the Colored Woman's League of Washington.

1906
Susan B. Anthony, the leader of the women's movement died.

1913
Illinois, the first state east of the Mississippi, granted women suffrage.

1916
Jeannette Rankin of Montana was first woman elected to Congress.

1920
The 19th Amendment gave women the national vote.

1924
Nellie Taylor Ross of Wyoming became the first woman governor.

1932
Hattie Wyatt Carraway became the first woman elected to the Senate.

1933
Frances Perkins became the first woman Cabinet officer as Secretary of Labor.

1962
Betty Friedan published *The Feminine Mystique*.

1966
Betty Friedan founded the National Organization of Women.

1971
The Women's National Political Caucus was organized.

1973
Roe v. Wade caused the repeal of abortion laws in 46 states.

1974
Supreme Court ruled the genders must be paid equal wages.

1980
The first women officers graduated from U.S. military academies.

1981
Sandra Day O'Connor became first female Supreme Court justice.

1983
Cabinet appointments included Elizabeth Dole (Transportation) and Ann McLaughlin (Labor).

1984
Democrat Geraldine A. Ferraro ran for the vice-presidency with Walter Mondale.

1989
Barbara Harris was appointed the first African American female bishop.

1993
Cabinet appointments included Janet Reno (Attorney General) and Hazel O'Leary (Energy).

1996
Madeleine Albright became the first female Secretary of State.

Religion and Belief

1777
New York became the first state to enfranchise Jews completely.

1784
Methodist Church in America founded in Baltimore, Maryland.

1791
Article I of the Bill of Rights granted freedom of religion.

1804
Church of Christ emerged in Kentucky.

1822
First Roman Catholic newspaper founded in Charleston, South Carolina.

1827
Joseph Smith received revelation of the Book of Mormon.

1833
Massachusetts officially abandoned Congregationalism.

1844
Methodist Church fractured into three divisions over slavery.

1945
Southern Baptist Convention founded.

1847
Mormons founded Salt Lake City, Utah.

1850
Immigration made Roman Catholicism America's largest religious group.

1873
Rabbi Isaac Mayer Wise founded Union of American Hebrew Congregations.

1875
Mary Baker Eddy founded Christian Science movement.

1875
John McCloskey, Archbishop of New York, became first American Cardinal.

1877
New Hampshire became the last state to enfranchise Jews.

1890
National Baptist Convention of America founded.

1889
Central Conference of American Rabbis organized.

1901
Pentecostalism emerged in Kansas.

1907
Northern Baptist convention founded.

1909
Scofield Reference Bible, a bestseller, published.

1918
United Lutheran Church founded.

1930
American Lutheran Church formed.

1939
Convention became American Baptist Convention

1950
Northern Baptist Convention became American Babtist Convention.

1956
Methodists and Presbyterians ordain women.

1962–65
Second Vatican Council generated major changes in Catholicism.

1963
Supreme Court banned school prayer.

1974
First female Episcopal priest ordained in U.S.

1980
Fundamentalists staged a "Washington for Jesus" rally.

1989
First female African-American Episcopal bishop ordained in U.S.

Labor

1780S
Short-lived craft groups emerged.

1792
Groups like Philadelphia shoemakers developed more permanent protective organizations.

1824
First recorded strike of women workers in Pawtucket, Rhode Island.

1834
Andrew Jackson ordered military intervention in Irish worker strike in Maryland.

1830S-1840S
Groups work for legislated 10-hour day.

1842
Commonwealth v. Hunt affirmed right to strike for closed-shop recognition.

1852
National Typographical Union founded followed by others in 1850s.

1866
National Labor Union founded.

1868
Federal employees granted eight-hour day.

1876
Ten Irish miners, the "Molly maguires," hanged in Pennsylvania.

1877
Socialist Labor Party organized.

1883
House of Representatives established Standing Committee on Labor.

1884
Bureau of Labor established to gather data.

1886
American Federation of Labor founded in Columbus, Ohio.

1890
United Mine Workers founded.

1894
Federal troops intervened in Pullman railroad strikes.

1901
Socialist Party of America founded.

1902
Maryland passed first state worker's compensation laws.

1911
Improved factory laws follow tragic "Triangle Fire" in New York.

1913
Department of Labor became the tenth executive department.

1919
National Labor Party formed; organized workers reach 4.25 million.

1929
Great Depression caused decline in union membership.

1933
National Recovery Administration fixed minimum wages and maximum hours.

1935
Wagner Act, known as labor's "Bill of Rights," enacted.

1938
Fair Labor Standards Act established 40-hour week.

1942
National War Labor Board created.

1947
Taft-Hartley Act condemned as "slave labor" act.

1955
AFL and CIO merged to create membership of 16 million.

1957
AFL-CIO expelled Teamsters Union for corrupt practices.

1959
Landgrum-Griffin Act curbed abuses of labor union officials.

Popular Protest

1786–87
Western Massachusetts farmers protested taxes and foreclosures in Shay's Rebellion.

1794
On Pennsylvania frontier the Whiskey Rebellion protested federal excise tax.

1800
A thousand black slaves revolted and moved toward Richmond, Virginia.

1822
Slave revolt led by Denmark Vesey aborted in South Carolina

1831
Nat Turner's Virginia slave revolt caused stringent slavery laws.

1859
Abolitionist John Brown attempted seizure of Harpers ferry federal arsenal.

1861–65
Civil War riots erupted in New York.

1877
Riots in San Francisco against Chinese immigrant workers.

1886
Chicago Haymarket Riot destroyed Knights of Labor.

1898
Race riot erupted in Wilmington, North Carolina over black franchise.

1906
Atlanta race riots prompted removal of blacks from electoral rolls.

1914
National Guardsmen killed 17 women and children during Colorado coal strike.

1919
Chicago race riots lasted thirteen days, leaving 1,000 families homeless.

1920
Bloody race riot left 79 dead in Tulsa, Oklahoma.

1932
Veterans marched on Washington seeking ÒbonusÓ payment.

1943
Federal troops were deployed in Detroit race riot.

1957
Troops used to force school integration in Little Rock, Arkansas.

1966
Race riots erupted in more than a dozen U.S. cities.

1968
Violence swept the nation following the Martin Luther King assassination.

1970
Anti-war protests at Kent State University caused student deaths.

1971
Attica prison revolt termed world in U.S. history.

1975
A bomb in New York's La Guardia Airport killed 11.

1980
Miami rioting erupted following aquittal of white police officers.

1990S
Right to Life protestors harrassed and bombed abortion clinics.

1991
Hispanics in Washington rioted in Mount Pleasant following police shooting.

1992
Los Angeles race riots left 58 dead.

1993
World Trade Center bombing in New York injured 1,000.

1993
FBI assault on Waco Brance Davidian compound killed 80.

1995
Terrorist bombed federal building in Oklahoma City.

1996
Terrorist bombed Centennial Olympic Park in Atlanta, Georgia.

The States

ALABAMA

THE French discovered Alabama in the 18th century, which became British (1763), U.S. (1783), and a state (1819). A population of 4,040,600 (1990) resides on 51,994 sq mi/134,700 sq km, and produces cotton, soybeans, peanuts, lumber, coal, livestock, poultry, iron, chemicals, textiles, and paper. Negro Leader Booker T. Washington established Tuskegee Institute (1881), but by the 1960s Alabama was a civil rights battleground.

ALASKA

EUROPEANS first visited rugged, mountainous Alaska in 1741. The U.S. voided Russia's claim (1744–1867) with an 1867 purchase ($7.2 m). Alaska entered the union in 1959. Its 591,004 sq mi/1,530,700 sq km produce oil, natural gas, coal, copper, iron, gold, tin, furs, lumber, and fish. A population of 550,000 (1990) experience cold winters and brief summers.

ARIZONA

ORIGINALLY Spanish, the U.S. acquired Arizona after the Mexican War in 1848. It became a state in 1912. Arizona's 113,500 sq mi/ 294,100 sq km occupies the arid Colorado Plateau with southern and western deserts. The economy features irrigated crops, livestock, copper, molybdenum, silver, electronics, and aircraft and supports 3,665,000 (1990). Arizona boasts the Grand Canyon (up to 1.1 mi/1.7 km deep).

ARKANSAS

SPANIARDS explored Arkansas (1541) which became U.S. territory in 1803 and a state in 1836. Dominated by the Ozark Plateau and Ouachita mountains in the west, the 53,191 sq mi/137,800 sq km region produces cotton, soybeans, rice, oil, natural

gas, bauxite, timber, and processed foods for a population of 2,350,700 (1990). Native sons include President Bill Clinton and General Douglas MacArthur.

CALIFORNIA

THE U.S. gained California after the

Mexican War (1848). A gold rush ensued (1849–56). California joined the Union under the Compromise of 1850, which involved the controversial western extension of slavery. Its 29,760,000 population (1990) resides on 158,685 sq mi/411,100 sq km, producing fruit, nuts, wheat, vegetables, cotton, rice, cattle, timber, fish, petroleum, technology, food processing, entertainment, and geothermal energy.

COLORADO

COLORADO'S 104,104 sq mi/269,700 sq km with eastern plains and western Rocky Mountain foothills, was part of the 1803 Louisiana Purchase and 1848 Mexican Cession. Colorado became a state in 1876. It generates cereal, meat, dairy products, oil, coal, molybdenum, uranium, iron, steel, and machinery. Tourism regularly swells the 3,294,400 population (1990) at sites like Mesa Verde National Park.

CONNECTICUT

CONNECTICUT, one of America's original 13 colonies, covers 5,018 sq mi/13,000 sq km. Coastal plains give way to rolling hills and mountains. Explored in 1614 and settled in 1633 by the Dutch, the former whaling and shipbuilding center became a state in 1788. It produces varied items from watches and jets to livestock and tobacco, for a population of 3,287,000 (1990).

DELAWARE

DELAWARE settlers included the Dutch (1631), Swedes (1638), and Britons (1664). An original colony, it was the first to ratify the U.S. Constitution (1787). The second-smallest state (2,046 sq mi/5,300 sq km), it has a population of 666,200 (1990). Highly industrialized, the economy includes agriculture, motor vehicles, and textiles, and is the home of the DuPont chemical empire.

FLORIDA

SPANIARD Ponce de Leon claimed Florida (1513–1763) which is home to the oldest U.S. city, St. Augustine (1565). The U.S. gained the 58,672 sq-mi/152,000 sq-km region in the 1819 Adams-Onis Treaty. Florida became a state in 1845. Hills and lakes dominate the central area, the Everglades the southern. A 12,937,900 population (1990) generates chemical, technological, citrus, and fish products.

GEORGIA

FOUNDED by James Oglethorpe in 1733, Georgia's northern rolling hills and southern coastal plain cover 26,911 sq mi/69,700 sq km. Home to 6,480,000 (1990), the region became a state in 1788 and saw a great deal of action in the Civil War. It produces tobacco, tea, citrus and orchard fruits, tung oil, vines, silk, and hydroelectricity. The Okefenokee National Wildlife Refuge covers 656 sq mi/1,700 sq km.

HAWAII

THE opening site of World War II in the Pacific, with the 1941 Japanese bombing of Pearl Harbor. The seven Hawaiian islands have been American controlled since 1900, and a state since 1959 – planters overthrew the Polynesian kingdom in 1893. The population of 1,108,200 live on 6,485 sq mi/16,800 sq km) and depend on tourism, coffee, pineapple, sugar, and flower plantations.

IDAHO

MORMONS settled Idaho in 1860 which became a state in 1890. The government controls two-thirds of the 83,569 sq mi /216,500 sq km, covered by mountains and dense forests. The population of 1,006,700 (1990) depend on potato, wheat, livestock, timber, silver, lead, zinc, and antimony production. The Snake River carves Hells Canyon, the deepest in North America (7,646 ft/2,330 m).

ILLINOIS

EXPLORED by Louis Joliet and Jacques Marquette (1673), Illinois grew quickly after the Erie Canal opened (1825). A state since 1818, its 53,395 sq mi/146,100 sq km are drained by 275 rivers, and support 11,430,6000 (1990) on an economy of soybeans, cereals, meat and dairy products, machinery, electrical, and electronics equipment. It contains the U.S. largest prehistoric earthworks, Cahokia Mounds.

INDIANA

FRENCH settled in 1731–35, Indiana became British in 1763, and a U.S. state in 1816. It remained a third rural into the 1980s. A 1990 population of 5,544,200 lived on 36,168 sq mi/93,700 producing corn, pigs, soybeans, limestone, machinery, electrical goods, coal, steel, iron, and chemicals. The state is known for the Indiana Dunes National Lakeshore, and the Indianapolis Motor Speedway.

IOWA

IOWA, part of the Louisiana Purchase (1803), became a state in 1846. Monetary and agricultural reformers were active in the late 19th century. Rolling prairies lying between the Mississippi and Missouri river bluffs form 56,279 sq mi/145,800 sq km supporting 2,776,800 (1990). The economy includes the growing of cereals, soybeans, and livestock, chemicals, farm machinery, electrical goods, lumber, and minerals.

KANSAS

KANSAS "bled" in the 1850s slavery controversy, and during the Civil War suffered the highest Union casualties. A state since 1861, blizzards, tornadoes, and thunderstorms plague its vast, flat seas of wheat. The 1930s Dust Bowl hit Kansas hard. The 2,477,600 (1990) population live on 82,296 sq mi/ 213,200 sq km, producing wheat, cattle, coal, petroleum, natural gas, minerals, and aircraft.

KENTUCKY

KENTUCKY, the first region settled west of the Alleghenies, and a state since 1792, was torn by Civil War guerilla fighting. The economy of tobacco, cereals, textiles, coal, whiskey, horses, and transport vehicles supports 3,365,300 (1990) living on 40,414 sq mi/ 104,700 sq km. The state is home to the Kentucky Derby, first jewel in U.S. horse racing's Triple Crown.

LOUISIANA

LOUISIANA explorers included Alonso Alvarez de Pineda (1519) and Cabeza de Vaca (1528). Acquired by the U.S. in 1803 and a state since 1812, the Civil War destroyed its sugar and cotton plantations. Famed for the French-speaking, Creole, bayou culture, Louisiana covers 52,457 sq mi/135,900 sq km, supporting 4,219,970 (1990) on rice, cotton, sugar, petroleum, chemicals, fish, timber, and paper.

MAINE

MAINE, a British settlement after 1623, was part of Massachusetts. It became a state in 1820, under the Missouri Compromise. Its heavily forested 33,273 sq mi/86,200 sq km boast 5,000 streams and rivers. Dairy and market garden produce, lumber products, textiles, and fishing support a population of 1,228,000 (1990). Tourists enjoy sites like Campobello International Park, Franklin D. Roosevelt's summer home.

MARYLAND

LORD Baltimore organized Maryland (1634) as a refuge for English Roman Catholics. A state since 1788, it joined with Virginia to contribute land in 1791 for the capital, Washington, D.C.. Its 591,004 sq mi/1,530,700 sq km supports 550,000 (1990) on poultry, dairy products, machinery, steel, automobiles, electronics, chemicals, and fishing. The U.S. Naval Academy is located at Annapolis.

MASSACHUSETTS

THE American Revolution began in Massachusetts at Lexington and Concord (1775). An 18th-century trading center, the state was home to 19th-century philosophical and social movements. The coastline offers numerous natural harbors. A population of 6,016,400 (1990) lives on 8,299 sq mi/21,500 sq km, generating electronics, communications and optic equipment, precision instruments, fish, cranberries, and dairy products.

MICHIGAN

FRENCH-settled Michigan (1668), became British in 1763, and a state in 1837. Captured in the War of 1812, the 58,518 sq mi/151,600 sq km region's Lower Peninsula is bordered by Lakes Huron and Erie on the east, the Upper by Lakes Michigan (south) and Superior (north). A population of 9,295,300 (1990), generates motorized

equipment, iron and steel, chemicals, pharmaceuticals, and dairy products.

MINNESOTA

THOUGH explored by Frenchmen in the 17th century and U.S.-acquired in 1803, Scandinavian settlements shaped Minnesota, which entered the Union in 1858. Glacier carved lakes and boulder-strewn hills lie in the north, prairies in the south of the 84,418 sq mi/218,700 sq km region. It supports 4,375,200 (1990) on cereals, soybeans, livestock, machinery, and two-thirds of the annual U.S. iron ore output.

MISSISSIPPI

THE French settled Mississippi (1699), followed by Spain (1795), and the U.S. (1795). A state since 1817, it joined the Civil War Confederacy, and saw bitter 1960s Civil Rights conflicts. Its 47,710 sq mi/123,600 sq km supports 2,573,200 (1990), generating cotton, rice, soybeans, chickens, fish, lumber, petroleum, chemicals, and transport equipment. The Vicksburg National Military Park and Natchez mansions draw tourists.

MISSOURI

CLAIMED by France in 1862, Missouri became U.S. territory in 1803, and a state in 1820. Its admission generated the first national slavery debate. Its 69,712 sq mi/180,600 sq km supports 5,117,100 (1990). The economy includes meat and processed food production, aerospace and transport equipment, lead and zinc. The birthplace of outlaw Jesse James, Missouri houses the Truman presidential library (Independence).

MONTANA

U.S.-HELD since 1803 and a state since 1889, Montana initially attracted fur trappers. Gold mining and ranching (1860s) led to Indian wars and the 1876 Battle of Little Big Horn commemorated today at the Custer Battlefield National Monument. Montana's 799,100 (1990) live on 147,143 sq mi/318,100 sq km, and generate irrigated wheat, cattle, coal, copper, oil, natural gas, and lumber.

NEBRASKA

VISITED by Spanish explorer Coronado (1451), Nebraska became U.S. territory in 1803 and a state in 1867. The 1862 Homestead Act, and the arrival of railways in 1867, caused a land rush. Its 77,354 sq mi/200,400 sq km support 1,578,300 (1990) and generate cereals, livestock, processed foods, fertilizers, oil, and natural gas. Nebraska has the U.S.'s only unicameral state legislature.

NEVADA

MEXICO ceded Nevada to the U.S. in 1846. Discovery of the Comstock Lode silver streak (1858) inspired support of the Free Silver currency reform (1890s). A state since 1864, its 110,550 sq mi/286,400 sq km support 1,201,800 (1990) on legalized gambling and prostitution (in some counties), and mercury, barite, and gold mining. Both Las Vegas and Reno are entertainment and gambling centers.

NEW HAMPSHIRE

SETTLED by Massachusetts Puritans (1620s–1630s), New Hampshire became a separate colony in 1741, and was first to declare independence from Britain (1776). With 9,264 sq mi/24,000 sq km, New Hampshire supports 1,109,200 (1990) on dairy products, poultry, fruit and vegetables, electrical and other machinery, pulp and paper. The state's Mount Washington is the highest peak east of the Rocky Mountains.

NEW JERSEY

THE Dutch settled New Jersey in 1660. The British seized control in 1664. An original American colony, it was a post-Revolutionary textile center. Some 7,562,000 (1990) live on 7,797 sq mi/20,200 sq km producing fruits, vegetables, fish, shellfish, chemicals, pharmaceuticals, soap and cleansers, transport equipment, and petroleum refining. The state is home to Princeton University and the Edison National Historic Site.

NEW MEXICO

INDIANS resisted 16th-century settlement of New Mexico. Fighting continued after U.S. acquisition (1848) and until 1886. A state since 1912, its 121,590 sq mi/315,000 sq km support 1,515,000 (1990) generating uranium, potash, copper, oil, natural gas, petroleum, coal, sheep, cotton, pecans, and vegetables. It is home to Carlsbad Caverns (the largest known), and Los Alamos atomic and space research center.

NEW YORK

DUTCH-held New York became British in 1667. The site of a third of American Revolutionary battles, its 49,099 sq mi/127,200 sq km support 17,990,400 (1990) on dairy products, apples, clothing, printing and publishing, office machines and computers, communication equipment, motor vehicles, aircraft, and pharmaceuticals. Home to West Point Military Academy.

NORTH CAROLINA

THE 1580s saw British settlement attempted in North Carolina. A state since 1789, it joined the Civil War Confederacy and experienced forced Indian removal (1835). Some 6,628,600 (1990) live on 52,650 sq mi/136,400 sq km producing tobacco, corn, soybeans, livestock, poultry, textiles, clothing, furniture, chemicals, and machinery. It houses the Duke, North Carolina State, and University of North Carolina research triangle.

NORTH DAKOTA

NORTHWEST North Dakota was part of the 1803 Louisiana Purchase; the southeast was acquired from Britain in 1818. A state since 1889, its settlement was hampered by Indian wars in the 1860s. Its 70,677 sq mi/183,100 sq km are home to 638,800 (1990) and the economy includes cereals, meat products, farm equipment, oil, and coal. The state contains Theodore Roosevelt's Elkhorn Ranch.

OHIO

THE French claimed Ohio in 1669, but lost the area to the British in 1763. Indian resistance ended in 1793. A state since 1803, Ohio became a post-Civil War petroleum center. Its 41,341 sq mi/107,100 sq km support 10,847,100 (1990) on coal, cereals, livestock, dairy foods, machinery, chemicals, steel, automotive and aircraft industries, rubber products, office equipment, and petroleum.

OKLAHOMA

OKLAHOMA became U.S. territory in 1803. It received relocated Indian tribes until 1889 when land opened for American settlement. Oil was discovered in the 1890s and Oklahoma entered the Union in 1907. Its 69,905 sq mi/181,100 sq km support 3,145,600 (1990) living on cereals, peanuts, cotton, livestock, oil, natural gas, helium, machinery, and metal parts.

OREGON

THE American Fur Company established Oregon's first settlement (1811). Waves of settlers arrived (1842–43), joint U.S.–British control lasted until 1846, and Oregon became a state in 1859. Its 97,079 sq mi/251,500 sq km support 2,842,300 (1990) on wheat, livestock, timber, and electronics. The state contains Crater Lake, the deepest in the US at 1,933 ft/589 m.

PENNSYLVANIA

SWEDES settled Pennsylvania (1643), followed by Dutch (1655), and British (1664).

A Quaker refuge, it contains Philadelphia, the center of the American Revolution. Its 45,316 sq mi/117,400 sq km support 11,881,600 (1990) on agricultural products, cement, coal, steel, petroleum, pharmaceuticals, motor vehicles and equipment, electronics, and textiles. The Valley Forge National Historical Park, and Gettysburg Civil War battlefield both lie in Pennsylvania.

RHODE ISLAND

PURITAN Roger Williams purchased Rhode Island from Narragansett Indians (1635). In 1790 it became a state and Samuel Slater built the first successful American textile mill. Its 1,197 sq mi/3,100 sq km support 1,003,464 (1990) on poultry, jewelry, silverware, textiles, machinery, metals, rubber products, and submarine assembly. Famous mansions stand in Newport. Narragansett Bay hosts the America's Cup yacht race.

SOUTH CAROLINA

SOUTH Carolina, British settled in 1670, and a state since 1788, was the first to secede before the Civil War (1860). The war's first battle occurred there in 1861. Its 31,112 sq mi/ 80,600 sq km support 3,486,700 (1990) on tobacco, soybeans, lumber, textiles, paper, wood pulp, chemicals, non-electrical machinery, and metals. It is home to resorts on Myrtle Beach, and Hilton Head Islands.

SOUTH DAKOTA

SOUTH Dakota, sparsely settled until gold discoveries in 1868, entered the Union in 1890 prompting Indian wars and the massacre of The Sioux at Wounded Knee. Its 77,123 sq mi/199,800 sq km support 696,000 (1990) on cereals, hay, livestock, and the U.S.' second largest gold production. Mount Rushmore's carved face commemorating presidents Washington, Jefferson, Lincoln, and T. Roosevelt lies in the Black Hills.

TENNESSEE

AFTER the American Revolution, Tennessee was briefly independent (1784–88) and became a state in 1796. In the 1830s, native tribes were removed to Oklahoma. Its 42,151 sq mi/109,200 sq km supports 4,877,200 (1990) on cereals, cotton, tobacco, soybeans, livestock, timber, coal, zinc, copper, and chemicals. The state is home to country music's Grand Ole Opry in Nashville.

TEXAS

AMERICANS began to enter Mexican-held Texas in 1821, starting the Texas Revolution (1835) and leading to an independent republic

until U.S. annexation in 1845. Its 266,803 sq mi/691,200 sq km support 16,986,500 (1990) on rice, cotton, sorghum, wheat, livestock, shrimp, lumber, paper, petroleum products, sulfur, salt, uranium, chemicals, petrochemicals, machinery, metal products, and transport equipment.

UTAH

EXPLORED by Spanish missionaries (1776), Mormons under Brigham Young shaped Utah in 1847. Annexation to the U.S. occurred after the church renounced polygamy (1890). Its 84,881 sq mi/219,900 sq km support 1,722,900 (1990) on wool, gold, silver, copper, coal, salt, and steel production. Utah is home to five national parks, and the Mormon temple and tabernacle in Salt Lake City.

VERMONT

VERMONT, explored by Samuel Champlain in 1609, was claimed by both New York and New Hampshire. Partisan feelings led to an independent state (1781–91). Its 9,611 sq mi/24,900 sq km support 562,800 (1990) on apples, maple syrup, dairy products, kaolimite, granite, marble, slate, business machines, paper, and tourism. Vermont is best known for small rural villages and brilliant autumn foliage.

VIRGINIA

THE British established Jamestown, Virginia in 1607 – their first permanent American settlement. First to declare independence (1776), the Civil War saw Richmond function as the Confederate capital. Virginia's 40,762 sq mi/105,600 sq km support 6,187,400 (1990) on varied agricultural and industrial products. Virginia is home to Arlington National Cemetery, Mount Vernon (George Washington's home), and Monticello (home of Thomas Jefferson).

WASHINGTON

CAPTAIN James Cook explored Washington in 1778. The U.S. and Britain settled their boundary dispute in 1846. A state since 1889, its 68,206 sq mi/176,700 sq km support 4,866,700 (1990) on agricultural, fishing,

wood, paper, aircraft, aerospace, and aluminum products. The state houses the Olympic mountains, Mount Rainier National Park, and the Microsoft corporation's home "campus" in Richmond.

WEST VIRGINIA

GERMAN families settled the West Virginia area (c. 1730), a region that opposed slavery and broke off from Virginia to form a separate state (1863). Its 24,279 sq mi/62,900 sq km support 1,793,500 (1990) on agricultural, chemical, petroleum, plastic, steel, and glass products. The state features the restored port at Harper's Ferry seized in 1859 by abolitionist John Brown.

WISCONSIN

FRENCH fur trader Jean Nicolet claimed Wisconsin in 1634, followed by the British (1763) and U.S. (1783). A state since 1848, large-scale settlement began when the Erie Canal opened (1820s). Its 56,163 sq mi/145,500 sq km support 4,891,800 (1990) on corn, hay, industrial and agricultural machinery, engines, turbines, precision instruments, paper, automotive products, and dairy farming.

WYOMING

THE railroad arrived in Wyoming in 1868. The Indians were subdued (1870s), opening the way for cattle ranchers who clashed with sheep farmers (1892). A state since 1890, its 97,812 sq mi/253,400 sq km support 453,600 (1990) on oil, natural gas, sodium salts, coal, uranium, and sheep. Yellowstone National Park is situated in Wyoming, the first state to grant women the vote (1869).

Glossary

ABOLITION

In the first half of the 19th century, the abolition movement, led by men like William Lloyd Garrison, worked for the extinction of Negro slavery.

APPEASEMENT

In historical terms, appeasement refers to the 1937 Munich conference during which the British and French capitulated to German dictator Adolf Hitler's demands for the Sudeten region of Czechoslovakia.

BICAMERALISM

The American tradition of representative assemblies with two houses. – bicameral legislatures, began in England's Atlantic seaboard colonies in the 17th century and were modeled after the English Parliament.

BOLSHEVISM

After the 1917 Russian revolution, Americans used the term "bolshevik" to describe any individual with a suspected Communist tie. The term fell into disuse after World War II.

BRINKSMANSHIP

Brinksmanship, a Cold War term from President Dwight D. Eisenhower's "massive retaliation" foreign policy, referred to American willingness to go to the brink of nuclear war in confrontations with Soviet Russia.

CAUCUS

A caucus is a meeting of local political party members to nominate candidates or elect convention delegates. The term also refers to Congressmen of the same party who act as a group.

CIVIL DISOBEDIENCE

Civil Disobedience, by Henry David Thoreau (1849), suggested government injustice be combated by peaceful, persistent disobedience of the law. Dr. Martin Luther King used the doctrine in the 1960s.

CIVIL LIBERTIES

Civil liberties are those granted to the individual citizen by law and which cannot be denied or abridged.

CONSCIENTIOUS OBJECTOR

A citizen who refuses to participate in a war when called by his country due to a moral or religious scruple is said to be a conscientious objector.

CONSCRIPTION

Conscription is the process of raising a military force by means of drafting the members of a designated segment of the population, usually young males.

CORRUPT BARGAIN

The 1824 election went to the House of Representatives. Henry Clay threw his votes to John Quincy Adams for the position of secretary of state. The defeated Andrew Jackson cried "corrupt bargain."

COUNTERCULTURE

In the 1960s, the term counterculture referred to that population segment that opposed the Vietnam war, engaged in communal living experiments, used illegal drugs freely, and had a devotion to rock and folk music.

CYBERSPACE

In his 1984 novel *Necromancer*, William Gibson coined the term cyberspace to describe a state of total human-computer interconnection. In contemporary vernacular, the term refers to the online world of the Internet.

DEISM

Deism, a popular 18th-century belief in a deity who created the world and did not interfere in its workings, was popular among the Founding Fathers. God was the "divine clockmaker."

DÉTENTE

The term *détente*, French for a lessening of tensions, was used to refer to improved relations with the Soviets after the 1968 election of Richard M. Nixon.

DOLE

During the 1930s Depression, before federal spending programs became necessary and acceptable, taking government aid was called "going on the dole." The negative connotation was of accepting charity rather than working.

DOVE

In political terms a "dove" opposes national involvement in a war or armed conflict.

ENLIGHTENMENT

The 18th-century Enlightenment emphasized the acquisition of useful knowledge. Its political ideas, especially the compact theory of government, deeply influenced America's founding fathers.

ESTABLISHMENT

In the 1960s, the older generation and sources of authority in opposition to the youthful counterculture were known as the establishment.

FASCISM

In the 1930s, fascist governments formed in Italy and Germany; these emphasized strong centralized control with no opposition or criticism allowed, and practiced aggressive nationalism.

FREE SOIL

After America's acquisition of the Mexican Cession (1848), the adherents of "free soil" called for the prohibition of slavery in those regions.

FREEDOM OF THE SEAS

Prior to the 1917 entry of the United States in World War II, President Woodrow Wilson advocated "freedom of the seas" in opposition to unrestricted German submarine warfare.

FUNDAMENTALISM

The term "fundamentalism" refers to an American Protestant movement stressing Biblical infallibility, anticipation of the Second Coming of Jesus Christ, and religious conversion by being "born again."

GREENBACK

During the Civil War, the Union government printed inflated currency not fully backed by precious metal to finance the war. The bills printed with green ink were known as greenbacks.

HARD MONEY

Hard money refers to currency backed at its full face value in precious metal.

HAWK

In political terms, a "hawk" supports national involvement in a war or armed conflict.

HISTORIOGRAPHY

Historiography is the study of the study of history. It examines specific historians and the schools of interpretation into which their work falls.

INDICTMENT

In legal terms, an indictment is a formal accusation of wrong doing, usually a felony, presented by a grand jury.

INFLATION

Inflation refers to substantial price increases caused by an expansion of the paper money supply without a corresponding increase in precious metals to support it, or by a proliferation of credit.

INITIATIVE

In political procedure, initiative allows a specified number of voters to propose legislation or a constitutional amendment and to compel a popular vote for its consideration.

INSULAR EXPANSION

In the 1890s, insular expansion referred to American acquisition of Pacific islands such as Hawaii to serve as coaling (fueling) stations for the naval fleet.

JINGO

"Jingo" is a 19th-century term for someone who exhibited dedicated, and at times fairly extreme, patriotism and national sentiment.

JUDICIAL REVIEW

Judicial review is the function of the United States Supreme Court, established in the 1803 *Marbury v. Madison* decision, to judge the constitutionality of laws and lower court decisions.

LAISSEZ-FAIRE

Laissez-faire is the economic theory that the government should involve itself as little as possible in the workings of the economy.

MANIFEST DESTINY

In 1845, John Louis O'Sullivan, editor of *United States Magazine and Democratic Review*, coined the phrase "manifest destiny" to describe the tremendous movement westward then occurring in America.

McCARTHYISM

McCarthyism refers to the four-year (1950–54) Communist witch hunt carried out by Senator Joseph McCarthy of Wisconsin. His zeal carried over into American society and caused a widespread Communist scare.

MERCANTILISM

Mercantilism views the world's wealth as finite. Nations work for a favorable balance of trade, exporting more than they import to keep wealth at home and thus to accrue more power.

NATIONALISM

Nationalism refers both to a patriotic belief in one's nation, but also in America, means to support the power of the central government over the rights of the states.

NEW DEMOCRACY

Early in the 19th century, the New Democracy was a frontier political movement that worked to gain wider citizen participation in government. Andrew Jackson was its chief symbol.

NULLIFICATION

Prior to the Civil War, the nullification theory held that if a state regarded a law passed by Congress as unconstitutional, it could refuse to obey that law within its borders.

ORTHODOXY

Orthodoxy holds any group to a standard of behavior or belief considered correct and proper. Most often it is used in reference to accepted religious doctrine.

PATRIOT

Patriots were those Americans who supported the Revolution against Great Britain.

PECULIAR INSTITUTION

The phrase "peculiar institution" was a 19th-century euphemism for the enslavement of African-Americans.

POPULAR SOVEREIGNTY

After the 1848 acquisition of the Mexican Cession, proponents of popular sovereignty wanted the residents of each territory to vote as to whether their future states would be free or slave.

PRAGMATISM

In 1907, Harvard psychologist William James praised those who efficiently tackled problems by concentrating on effective methods in his book *Pragmatism*. His ideas became the philosophy of the Progressive movement.

PREDESTINATION

Predestination was a Puritan doctrine drawn from the theologian John Calvin. Adherents believed a given population had been predestined to enter heaven, and that nothing could change that status.

PURITAN WORK ETHIC

The Puritan work ethic evolved from their belief in predestination. Assuming that the Lord would not suffer a sinner to prosper, the Puritans regarded economic success as proof of salvation.

RECALL

The recall provides for the removal of a public official from office by a vote of the people taken after the raising of a petition of a qualified number of voters.

REFERENDUM

In the referendum, legislative acts are put to a vote of the people for acceptance.

SECESSION

In 1860 and 1861, 11 states attempted to withdraw from the United States of America using the doctrine of secession.

SECTIONALISM

Sectionalism is excessive loyalty to one's state or region over a sense of national loyalty.

SEDITION

Sedition is the act of inciting discontent or rebellion against the government.

SOFT MONEY

Soft money refers to currency that is not backed at its full face value in precious metal.

SPECIE

Specie is gold, silver, and other coined precious metal, as distinguished from paper money.

SPOILS SYSTEM

When Andrew Jackson was elected in 1828 he was accused of using the "spoils system" to give his friends political jobs. Subsequent administrations, however, abused the power to a much greater extent.

STATES RIGHTS

Adherents of states rights believe that the states should exercise greater power over their affairs and be subject to less control by the federal government.

THEOCRACY

Theocracy is a form of government in which God or a deity is recognized as the supreme civil authority.

TORY

Tories were those Americans who supported the British during the American revolution.

VETO

Veto is the power vested in the President of the United States to negate a law passed by Congress.

XENOPHOBIA

Xenophobia is an excess fear of hatred or things foreign, and has been the cause of much anti-immigrant sentiment in the United States.

Bibliography

Bailyn, Bernard. *The Ideological Origins of the American Revolution* (1967)

Baritz, Loren. *The Culture of the Twenties* (1970)

Becker, Carl L. *The Declaration of Independence* (1922)

Bemis, Samuel F. *The Diplomacy of the American Revolution* (1935)

Billington, Ray Allen. *Westward Expansion* (1982)

Boller, Paul. *American Transcendentalism, 1830-1860* (1974)

Boorstin, Daniel J. *The Americans: The Colonial Experience* (1958)

Boorstin, Daniel J. *The Americans: The Nationalist Experience* (1965)

Catton, Bruce. *This Hallowed Ground* (1956)

Coffman, Edward M. *The War to End All Wars: The American Military Experience in World War I* (1986)

Dallek, Robert. *The American Style of Foreign Policy* (1983)

Divine, Robert A. *The Reluctant Belligerent* (2nd ed., 1979)

Driver, Harold E. *Indians of North America* (1969)

Fagan, Brian M. *The Great Journey* (1987)

Feis, Herbert. *The Atomic Bomb and the End of World War II* (1966)

Feis, Herbert. *From Trust to Terror: The Onset of the Cold War, 1945–1950* (1970)

Foner, Eric. *Reconstruction: America's Unfinished Revolution, 1863–1877* (1988)

Foote, Shelby. *The Civil War* (3 vols.,1958-1974)

Freehling, William. *The Road to Disunion* (1990)

Freidel, Frank. *Franklin D. Roosevelt* (4 vols., 1952-1973)

Handlin, Oscar. *The Uprooted* (1973)

Harrison, James P. *The Endless War: Fifty Years of Struggle in Vietnam* (1982)

Hartmann, Susan M. *The Home Front and Beyond* (1982)

Hicks, John D. *The Populist Revolt* (1931)

Hofstadter, Richard. *Social Darwinism in American Thought* (1955)

Kennan, George F. *American Diplomacy, 1900-1950* (1951)

Kennedy, David M. *Over Here: The First World War and American Society* (1980)

Leuchtenburg, William E. *The Perils of Prosperity, 1914-1932* (1958)

Leuchtenburg, William E. *In the Shadow of FDR* (rev. ed. 1985)

May, Henry F. *The Enlightenment in America* (1976)

McDonald, Forrest. *Novus Ordo Seclorum: The Intellectual Origins of the Constitution* (1985)

Miller, John C. *The Federalist Era, 1789-1800* (1960)

Miller, Perry. *The New England Mind.* (2 vols., 1939-1953)

Miller, Perry. *Errand Into the Wilderness* (1956)

Nevins, Allan. *The War for the Union* (4 vols., 1959-1971)

Nye, Russel B. *Society and Culture in America, 1830-1860* (1974)

Oates, Stephen B. *Let the Trumpet Sound: The Life of Martin Luther King, Jr. (1982)*

Sandburg, Carl. *Lincoln: The War Years* (4 vols., 1939)

Schlesinger, Arthur M., Jr. *The Age of Roosevelt* (3 vols., 1957-1960)

Starr, Paul. *The Social Transformation of American Medicine* (1982)

Tindall, George B. and David E. Shi. *America: A Narrative History* (1992)

Tytell, John. *Naked Angels: The Lives and Literature of the Beat Generation* (1978)

Webb, Walter Prescott. *The Great Plains* (1931)

Weigley, Russell F. *The American Way of War: A History of United States Military Strategy and Policy* (1973)

Woodward, C. Vann. *The Strange Career of Jim Crow* (1974)

EDITOR'S NOTE

This volume does not offer a comprehensive compendium of United States history. In fact, deciding what to include to achieve a reasonable survey of major events and characters proved to be an agonizing business. Many times I threw down my notes and books, but each time I had to remind myself that this work is meant for the use of a general audience, for the reader who requires a quick explanation or for the pleasure of the casual browser. Undoubtedly my colleagues will feel there are omissions, but just as I have always worked with my students to kindle curiosity, reasoning that that impulse will lead them to find out more about our nation's past on their own, so have I approached this project. Learning is a lifelong experience and a pleasure I wish to all who take this book in hand.

On a personal note, my particular thanks to Rilda Bess, Mary Lou Kelly, and Gail Granek for their help in proofreading and preparing key parts of the manuscript and to Ian Powling for his patience and guidance.

Rana K. Williamson, Ph.D.

Index